THE BURNING VEIL
A NOVEL OF ARABIA

BY

Jean Grant

*For Cheri,
with best regards
Jean Grant.*

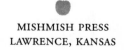

MISHMISH PRESS
LAWRENCE, KANSAS

Published by Mishmish Press
P.O. Box 442581, Lawrence, KS 66044
Book and cover design by Laura Rottinghaus
Printed by Lightning Source

This is a work of fiction. All of the characters, names, incidents, and organizations in this novel
are either the products of the author's imagination or are used fictitiously. No resemblance to any
persons living or dead is intended. There was a tragic fire in a girls' school in the kingdom, but
it was not in the Eastern Province where the novel is set.

Library of Congress Control Number 2009911559
Library of Congress Cataloguing-in-Publication Data

Grant, Jean.
The Burning Veil / Jean Grant.— 1st ed.

ISBN 978-0-9825074-0-7 (paperback)
ISBN 978-0-9825074-1-4 (cloth)
ISBN 978-0-9825074-2-1 (ebk)

Mishmish books may be ordered through booksellers or by contacting
Mishmish Press
Visit our website at www.mishmishpress.com

For Garth and Stephen
my dear sons

And to the memory

of the fourteen girls who perished

in Mecca, March 11, 2002

The Burning Veil

CHAPTER ONE

As SAUDI FLIGHT 113 ACCELERATED down the runway at New York's JFK, a man's voice floated over the intercom. His cry—half-singing, half-chanting—sounded like that of someone yearning for a lost lover. Sarah listened mesmerized.

"Please, could you tell me, what is that?" she asked the girl in yellow silk shantung pants who was seated beside her. "It's hypnotic."

"That? It's the prayer for travelers." The girl rested her fingertips on Sarah's wrist. "I'm going home. And you?"

Surprised by this warm touch from a stranger, Sarah felt already in a foreign world. She glanced down at the teenager's fingers, hennaed orange up to the second knuckle. "I'm going to work in Khobar. Ever heard of it?"

"Oh yes, the beautiful city of Khobar," the girl said, giggling. Funny. Ibrahim had never once described it that way. She would have asked about it, but the girl had already put on her earphones and seemed engrossed in her music. It would be rude to buttonhole her. Even when the flight attendant passed out thimble-sized cups of cardamom coffee, the girl kept on the earphones. Sarah pulled out her Arabic phrase book from her backpack, studied irregular verbs for an hour and then stood up to stretch her legs. Most passengers were napping, their heads lolling to one side or the other. At the rear of the plane, she noticed a brown curtain with a sign saying PRAYER ROOM. Curious, she sneaked a look inside and saw a man kneeling. It would be rude to intrude, so she went back to her seat. Halfway up the cabin, she saw a man with classic Arab features, handsome like Ibrahim. He was cuddling a toddler in pink pajamas and stroking her black ringlets. A gold bracelet glinted on the child's chubby arm. It seemed a good omen. She smiled at the child, then continued up the aisle, squeezed past the Saudi girl, and sank down in seat #12H by the window.

The girl took off her headphones. "I wish we'd hurry up and get there. These flights are too boring."

"Well, there's a lot of time to think," Sarah said.

"Think!" The girl giggled. "I don't like thinking."

Sarah was about to say the long journey felt like being in limbo, but the teenager would not know the meaning of the word. She was fiddling with the channel selector for the in-flight entertainment but stopped when she found a religious program; at least that is what Sarah assumed it was. Verses in exquisite calligraphy flickered across the screen, and the girl rocked back and forth, her lips moving as she read along. Would Ibrahim's family be religious like that? Sarah hoped not. She lifted the plastic shade, but outside the oval window, she saw no lights but only blackness, the dark Atlantic below. When she first met Ibrahim, he had commented on the courage of the Pilgrims crossing the Atlantic. It had been last fall when her brother Pete brought him home so he could experience an American Thanksgiving. Daddy stumbled over his name.

"It's Abraham in English, sir."

"I'll call you Abe then," Daddy said.

"As you like," Ibrahim said in a grave voice.

"No, Daddy, let's not," she said. "It's perfectly easy. Eee-bra-heem."

When she had studied Arabic for her foreign language at university, her classmates nicknamed their tutors—Yusuf and Mohammed—Joe and Mo. It riled them. Ibrahim did not look offended at the prospect of being called "Abe." She liked that about him, that he was not defensive.

"Pete says you speak Arabic," he said, turning to her.

"I used to be able to read a newspaper, very slowly."

He smiled, showing a tiny gap between his two front teeth. He had extraordinary eyelashes, the longest and thickest she had ever seen. She took his parka, the down lining still warm from his body heat, and hung it up on a hook in the hall closet. They talked about the weather. Snow was forecast, the first of the season, and he had never seen snow. What else? She could not remember. It was his voice that held her. She had never heard a voice quite like that, gentle, slow, and seductive. Pete, who was wearing his green-and-gold Packers sweatshirt, said Ibrahim was a Fulbright scholar doing graduate work. Perhaps embarrassed by the attention, he ran his fingers through his curly hair. Later, as Sarah lit the tapers at the dining table, she felt his eyes on her, but when she glanced his way, his eyes darted off. Hazel, they bulged slightly under those amazing lashes. She touched the collar of her lambswool sweater, wondering if it was too tight.

The Green Bay Packers were playing the Detroit Lions, and after supper they all went downstairs to the den to watch the game. Ibrahim was having a hard time understanding the rules. Apparently, in his country they played soccer, not football. Happily, the Packers won as usual, and when the game was over, he helped Pete bring in logs from the stack in the garage. Pete made a fire, and the three of them sat around awhile drinking hot chocolate, eating apple pie, and talking about the game. The telephone rang and Pete went off. The logs crackled as they burned, their edges brightly outlined. Sarah asked Ibrahim about his work, and he said he was a hydrologist.

"Not oil? I thought that's what the kingdom was all about."

"When I was in high school, I saw a crew drilling for water, but oil spurted up instead. In its crude state it is viscous ugly stuff, and I thought of how water was pure and clean. That is when I decided to study desalination. I feel I was put on earth for this," he said, touching his hand to his heart. "And you, Sarah? Did you always want to be a physician?"

"I was like any kid. I wanted to be a rock star. And if I couldn't be a rock star, then I wanted to be a waitress, bustling around, feeling in charge. Then my mother got breast cancer, and her doctor took an interest in me. Mom wanted me to be a nurse, but you need so much more compassion and patience for that. I insisted I was going to be very successful in medicine, and she couldn't argue with that. Medicine's been hard, but I love it. Still, I feel like I'm in a bit of a rut. I've been at the same hospital three years."

"My father's been at his forty years," Ibrahim said, smiling. "What's your field?"

"Emergency medicine."

He told her his father had trained as an orthopedist and that although he was too old to carry on an active practice, he still went into the hospital most days.

"That's nice." She toyed with an earring.

"Well, he founded the hospital so he takes pride in it. And it's a dignified retirement."

They sat listening to the fire sizzle and pop. Ibrahim asked why she had chosen ER work; she said she had planned to do dermatology because of her interest in rashes and discolorations, and then she considered family practice, but she thought she might get bored seeing the same patients repeatedly. She liked ER work because it was fast, exciting, and full of variety.

"Any drawbacks?"

"Sometimes they die. I don't like breaking bad news to the family."

"That's hard." Ibrahim put another log on the fire. Above the mantel hung a reproduction of Raphael's *Madonna and Child with Book*, and he remarked that the woman had his sister Layla's tender gaze. He did not seem to realize the painting's religious significance, which she took to mean he must be a Muslim, not a Christian. That was fine with her.

"So where exactly do you come from?" She went to the bookcase, took down the atlas, and their hands brushed lightly as she handed it to him.

"Show me," she said. He first looked in the index, then turned to the map of Saudi Arabia, and put his finger on a dot on the east coast. She stared at his hands, the supple skin such a warm color, the slender fingers with their short buffed nails.

"Here, this is my hometown, Qatif. My ancestors used to set out from here to hunt for pearls in the Arabian Gulf." As he handed her back the atlas, she noticed he did not wear a wedding band.

The following week, he invited her to meet him at the Goose Blind Cafe on the outskirts of Madison. He was waiting for her when she arrived. The place smelled of fries, and couples were dancing under the silvery disco ball that flashed over the dance floor. "Want to dance?" she asked.

"Unfortunately, I know only men's dances, dances with swords. But I will try." He stepped on her toes once or twice, but his hand felt warm in hers, and up close, he smelled of cinnamon. Afterward they chatted and sipped hot cider. She liked the attentive way he leaned in close to listen to her, but he seemed overly reserved and dignified. She wanted to make him laugh. It first happened on a sparkling day a month later when they had a date at the zoo. She wore a tangerine jacket with shiny brass buttons over her most flirty dress. The trees, glazed with ice, glittered in the sun, and a herd of zebras pranced on the ground, which was patchy with snow. She showed him the animals that were iconic of Wisconsin: some badgers, a family of otters, and a nursery of raccoons. Then he led her into a heated barracks where Arabian camels were kept. He whistled. One of them lumbered over, and he patted its tawny flanks.

"What big eyelashes it's got." Sarah laughed. "Sorry, I sound like Red Riding Hood."

He looked puzzled at the allusion. "Its eyelashes? Yes, the double row protects their eyes from the sun and sand."

"How Darwinian," she said, consciously refraining from remarking on his equally extraordinary eyelashes. She wondered what it would feel like to kiss him as they strolled along the path past the llamas, elephants, and buffalos. It was the first time he had ever seen a buffalo. He said he feared the camels might also become rare now that the Bedouins used pickup trucks for transport. They continued walking until they reached the apes. A couple of chimpanzees were swinging on tires, but most of them were busy picking fleas off each other's dark brown pelts. "There are scientists who think that helpfulness is genetically hard-wired in our ancestors," she said. "It's as if we're coded to be kind."

"I like to think so," he said.

"So do Muslims believe in evolution?"

"Yes and no. I do. My brother does not."

"My parents don't either. Someone asked Darwin, I think it was, or a friend of his, what his studies had taught him, and he said he had learned the Creator had an inordinate fondness for beetles." She squeezed Ibrahim's hand and glanced to see if he was offended. He frowned the way her parents had when she told them the anecdote, but then the corners of his mouth twisted upward in a glimmer of a smile. It made her feel that they were in harmony, and they began seeing each other every weekend. Saturdays they strolled up and down State Street, stopping for cappuccino in a coffee bar or for lentil soup at the Kabul Restaurant. They loafed in the Canterbury Booksellers and she would come away with a bestseller or two and he with an armful of Arabic-language newspapers, mostly *An Nahar* and *Al Ahram*. Sunday afternoons they would take in a free concert at the Elvehjem

Museum and afterward she would show him her favorite paintings. He knew nothing about art, but he strolled with her from gallery to gallery. He did not like abstracts, preferring the Old Masters. One Sunday she showed him her own work—portraits, nudes, and one landscape of a brook running through a forest. He seemed shocked by the nudes, and she made a quip about putting her study of *Gray's Anatomy* to good use. When spring came, they often went to the Saturday Market, where Ibrahim mingled with the farmers in bib overalls and the Hmong women selling bok choy, scallions, and dark leafy spinach. What they liked best was to go for drives in his white Mazda, always taking the back roads, with the plowed fields on either side, the Holsteins grazing near the red barns, larger than the clapboard houses with their peeling white paint.

When Pete asked what she saw in him, Sarah laughed nervously. "I couldn't even begin to tell you."

"So it's just Eros," Pete said. "A crush."

"More. Lots more."

"Well, what? You're not the type to need a guy to look after you."

They were in Milwaukee drinking beer in a dimly lit bar, under a poster showing a can of Schlitz and the catchphrase, "the beer that made Milwaukee famous." On the green wall opposite them another slogan stated, "With beer everything seems to go a little bit better."

Pete leaned forward. "I know what he likes about you." He glanced at her conspiratorially as he slathered brown mustard on his brat, stuffed in a hard semmel roll. He took a bite and wiped the grease from his mouth.

"So what does he say?"

"Fishing for compliments? Well, he says you're bright, alluring and free, whatever that means. Tell me. What's so special about him?"

"Oh, the whole package. Everything."

"That's not good enough."

"What can I say? See that sign?" She pointed to the beer advertisement on the wall. "It's like that. With Ib around, everything goes better. Sounds flippant, but it's the truth."

Pete took a swallow of beer from the brown Schlitz bottle. "He's old-fashioned."

"You know how curious he is. When I'm with him, I get to see everything as if it were for the first time too. Little things, like going through a car wash. When the water buffeted the car, he actually looked alarmed."

"He's never been to a carwash! What kind of dump does he come from?"

"Maybe he has a chauffeur." Sarah nibbled at a slice of dill pickle. She thought of Ib's nuanced way of thinking and his endearing quirks: the way he would place his palm on his chest, bow his head and close his eyes when he said thank you; the way he never looked at his watch or seemed to be in a hurry; the way he sent her glorious bouquets all the way from Hawaii.

"Know what I think?" Pete wiped the crumbs off the table with his paper napkin. "You're just tired of your own culture."

"Maybe a little. But that's not all there is to it."

"He puts you on a pedestal."

"So? What's the harm in that?"

"I like him too. A lot. But he won't stay on. He'll go when his visa is up."

"Come on, Pete. Give me a break. Let me enjoy it while it lasts." She drained her beer.

Pete gave her a funny smile and she could tell he assumed that she was sleeping with Ibrahim.

"You're very seductive," Ib would say when she snuggled against him. Then he would smile and step back. Perhaps he did not want to have an affair with an American, or being so pious, he believed intimacy was sinful outside marriage. Or maybe he was still in mourning for his wife Miriam, who had died two years earlier of a cerebral aneurysm. He confided in Sarah that Miriam's death had made him question God's goodness, but gradually he came to trust again in God's compassion.

"Passage of time," Sarah said gently.

What was clear was that he played for keeps. This both frightened and attracted her. Most of her colleagues were married, had live-in boyfriends, or drifted from one fellow to another. Only Roseanne, a Buddhist, believed in chastity outside of marriage. Sarah herself was unsure. Kevin, her first boyfriend, dumped her when she would not have sex. David Ritter, her ex-fiancé, ditched her when she became pregnant. They had lived together five years, and she pleaded to keep the baby, but David insisted on an abortion, adamant that he could not love what he called a child of sin. She had the procedure three years ago on a sleety January day. After that, she kept her distance from men.

A few days after Ibrahim told her about Miriam, Sarah said she did not want to keep any secrets from him and tried to explain about the abortion. She had expected he would understand. He did not. He dropped his face in his hands. "I can't believe you would do that."

"Please look at me," she pleaded, her hand pressing his knee. "I can't help what's past."

He moved back in the chair and planted his hands on his thighs, an implacable look on his face. "It was wrong."

"I was distraught, and it was a long time ago. It was a mistake."

"It was wrong. Wrong."

"Don't you sit in judgment on me," she shouted. "You can't in the least understand what it was like." She went flying out and slammed the door.

The next day, his apology made it worse. "It was not only about that. I thought, well, it sounds ridiculous," he stammered, "but I thought— well, I cannot help but be jealous."

With a flash of angry insight, she realized he wanted her to be a virgin. "Really, what do you expect? I'm twenty-nine!" She asked him not to call, and he did not. In a women's magazine from the stack in the staff room, she read that it took twenty-one days to break a habit, and she ticked the days off. The fourth week she was still waking up at night and obsessing about him. On the twenty-ninth day, there he was, wearing his t-shirt with the picture of a palm tree on it, waiting for her outside the ER at the end of her shift. He invited her for coffee and afterward they went to his apartment. "My gazelle," he murmured as they clung, fondling each other. He breathed into her ear. At once, she cringed and drew away.

"Darling, what's the matter?"

"Nothing." She did not dare say that David Ritter used to do that. Then she forgot all about David as Ibrahim sucked her fingers; when he hugged her, she felt his heart thudding through the thin cotton.

"Shall we go upstairs?" he murmured. Slowly they mounted the thickly carpeted steps. On the landing, he circled his arm around her waist and kissed her so deeply that her knees would have buckled under her if it were not for his arms tight around her. In the bedroom, he lit a candle and placed it on the chest of drawers. He undressed her—he had trouble with the fastening of her bra—and stripped to his boxers. She lay down on the bed, and he went to the chest of drawers and took out a muslin pouch. He untied the red-and-gold strings, sat beside her, and asked her to close her eyes. She felt something cool trickle in a straight line down from the hollow at the base of her throat, to her breastbone, navel, and pubis. Then the coolness moved up again, sprinkling her right nipple and her left.

"What—"

"Shh."

"It feels lovely. But what is it?" His gritty finger moved over her lips and the tip of her tongue. "Sand! It's sand!" She sat up, and the sand ran off her in a rust-red drift onto the white sheet. "Where did that come from?"

"Home. I brought it here as a memento." He looked sheepish, the moment of romance destroyed.

"And just now?" She bit her lips, wishing she had kept quiet.

"Well, I wanted to cover you with it, to make you mine."

"Hmm." She smiled, not sure what to think. Then she laughed. "It's kinky."

He shook his head. "Sand is clean. Like water."

"So your intent was honorable," she teased.

He tensed and his face darkened.

"Ibrahim, darling. What's the matter?" She put her arms around him and tugged him to her. "What is it?"

Fiercely, he pulled away. "You do not understand. After all, how could you? Americans do not think the way we do." He pulled on his t-shirt.

"I don't understand. Tell me. Please."

"It is a question of honor," he murmured in a voice so low she had to strain to hear him. "How low have I fallen that I bed a woman whom I esteem? Am I becoming that thing I hate—a man without honor?"

"Ib, for God's sake, come back. We love each other. That's what counts."

"No, not love. Honor," he said passionately. "I am a Muslim."

"I realize." Humiliated and angry, her body stifled with sexual long-ing, she gathered her clothes strewn on the floor and hurried into the bathroom, where she washed her face and put on her clothes.

"Forgive me," he said when she came out. "I didn't mean to insult you. I want to treat you with justice."

"With justice? That's odd," she said in an angry voice.

"And love. Especially love." He took both her hands in his. She pulled away, but he reached again for her hands. Implausibly, he found the words to make amends. Even though he did not propose, she under-stood that marriage was what he meant by loving her with justice. They continued to see each other, but they kissed rarely and then only on the cheek, or lightly and most cautiously, on the lips. At night, she had fantasies of lying in bed with him.

They had been flying ten hours. Sarah unlaced her sneakers, loosened the zipper on her jeans, and closed her eyes. She did not sleep. She switched her watch to Saudi time; it was mid-afternoon in Khobar. Already France and Italy were behind her. She felt cold and wound the navy blanket around her shoulders. Over the Mediterranean, the Saudi girl woke up and offered her Gummi bears. "Your husband. He lets you travel alone?"

"I'm single," Sarah said, choosing a red one from the sack.

"Never mind. Husband big baby." The girl giggled. "Your father, he lets you? Your brother too? They like?"

"Yes." Sarah forced a smile as she chewed the rubbery candy.

"Lucky you." The girl giggled again, drew a blanket over her face, and said she was going to sleep. Minutes later, she was making little snorts in her sleep.

Over Lebanon, the pilot dipped low and Sarah saw the mountains, not snow-capped now in late June, but beautiful anyway. She remembered Marlene, a Beiruti she had met in Madison who drank red wine, wore a red bikini, and danced hip-hop. If only Ibrahim were Lebanese. Marlene's cousin Samia had gone to Saudi Arabia and hated it. As the jet continued east and south over Syria and then Jordan, Sarah mulled over her mother's conviction that Muslims and Christians were like two different blood types and could never mix. Sarah had disagreed. She conceded she might be out of place for a while, but she would improve her Arabic and learn their customs; with Ibrahim to help her, it might be easy. Certainly, it would be an adventure. If it turned out to be a mistake, well, it would be her own. No one else's. She could come home, embarrassed but undamaged.

She picked up the in-flight magazine from the pouch in front of her seat and skimmed an article describing how in 1938, the oilmen, Saudis and Americans alike, toiled in the dust and burning sands. She closed the magazine and let it lie in her lap. Not long after they had met, Ibrahim told her how at sunset, in the early days of oil exploration, the Arabs would pray on carpets spread on the sand, while on the other side of camp, the Americans celebrated Happy Hour. Ib did not drink, but he was no fanatic about it, not like his brother. "All Shaheed knows is what they tell him in that school he attends, that *madrasa*," Ibrahim once snapped, his face darkening. "My brother has only one fault, but it's a grave one. He never thinks for himself; he just does what he's told. A good Nazi."

One balmy afternoon in late May, Ib arrived when she was making jam from strawberries they had bought at Saturday Market. The strawberries were bubbling and popping in the kettle on the stove, and he watched while she poured the jam into the sterilized jars and sealed them with wax. She made a pot of tea and toasted two pieces of bread that she spread with the hot jam. They had the tea outside in the backyard, fragrant with white and purple lilac. They sat on the cold stone bench, their arms touching. The sky was a clear blue, filled with puffy white clouds. The breeze was fresh, and he had on a white cashmere sweater. He told her about the job offer he had just received from the new desalination plant in the kingdom. He reached into his pocket, and took out a white velvet box. Inside lay a gold band with a pearl bordered by diamonds. "Please, will you come home with me? Marry me."

She had not been expecting the proposal and it flustered her. "It's too soon. We've known each other only five months."

"I love you," he said, a tremble in his voice. She could smell him, a mixture of nervous sweat and pine-scented after-shave.

"Then stay here with me. Let's live here. It'd be too hard for me over there."

"I must go back."

"I'm sorry." She opened his hand and pressed the ring in his palm.

His face darkened the way it did when he was angry or hurt, and he shoved the ring in the slit, snapped the box shut and hurried off, knocking the tea tray off the chair as he went. She ran out into the street after him.

Although they made up, neither would give in. She counted down the days they had left: sixteen, fifteen, fourteen... She slept fitfully and bit her nails. She snapped at the nurses.

"At least, no one can accuse you of marrying me to get a green card," she said as they walked the trail alongside the lake.

"So I could be a resident *alien*?"

"And then a citizen. Like everyone else."

"Of course, if I lived here, I would want that. But—"

"But what?"

"I checked into it. To get citizenship I would have to, and I quote, 'solemnly forswear and abjure all fidelity to my country.'"

"Oh, Ibrahim, you'd just sign the form. It's no big deal."

"It is an oath. Nothing is more serious."

She bit her lip—what a prig he could be. "Think of all the Cubans risking their lives just for a chance to live in the States!"

"Either a man is honorable or he is not. I cannot take that oath. I love my country, and fidelity is a matter of the heart."

She expected he would say something poetic and unreal about the pain of exile, but he did not. "So the wording is flawed," she conceded. "But it's been that way for years. In any case, no one will ever force you to be a citizen. You can be a resident alien forever. But seriously, you may want to…to…" she searched for a word he would like, "to *bestow* your allegiance. You like what the U.S. stands for. It's what you want for Arabia, isn't it? So why not enjoy it?" She could not fathom his compulsion to live there, especially when he said it was partly because his ancestors were buried there. She did not know, let alone care where her great-grandparents were buried. As for Arabia being the birthplace of the prophet Muhammad, that too seemed an incomprehensible attraction.

She did not want to lose him. Ten days before his departure she offered to get a visa and go meet his family. She had expected he would be ecstatic. "We don't have tourist visas," he said mournfully.

She laughed. "You've got to be kidding."

"No, just pilgrimage and business visas. Trust me. Let us get married right away. We will let ourselves go on the stream of the unknown together. At least, give it a try."

She promised to think about it.

The following weekend she drove to the Meccan River. Mist hovered over the surface, and she pushed a canoe into the river, got in, knelt forward, and paddled. It was slow going even though she put her all into it, each stroke smooth and strong. The river was narrow here, not much more than a stream, and bordered with chest-high grasses. She ducked to avoid an overhanging branch, startling a pair of green-headed ducks. After an hour of paddling, she rested the blade across the canoe and drifted, enjoying the clumps of pussy willows along the bank. Near here, she had once hooked a brook trout with red, yellow, and white spots on its iridescent skin. It was the most beautiful fish she had ever seen, but it got away. She trailed her hand in the water and thought how she did not want to lose Ibrahim.

She heard honking and looked up to see geese flying in V-formation north toward Canada. Last fall, she had seen geese heading south following their migratory path. Perhaps it was a sign that like them she could leave, confident of return. She dipped her paddle into the water again, with less effort now, as she glided past the familiar inlets and the bluish-green of rye grass. It would be wise to see Ib in his natural environment, to see how he and his family treated her before committing herself to him. It would be fascinating to see how medicine was practiced there. She had read that some Saudis refused to let male physicians treat their women, which meant she could save more lives. And she had taken so few chances in her life, sticking close to home as if she were as fragile as her mother's heirloom china. Her jaw set, she turned the canoe around. With the current against her now, she paddled harder. When she reached Madison, she drove straight to his apartment. She found him in the living room, where he was piling hydrology textbooks into a packing crate. She pulled him to her, kissed him deliriously, and said that she would sign on for a six-week locum.

She waited until after he had left to break the news to her family.

Pete sat hunched over his beer. "Are you sure about this? Have you checked out all the pros and cons?"

"Made a list? No. I'm going with my gut."

"Gotcha, you're in love. That hospital of his father's where you'll work, is it any good?"

"Like here, but smaller. I could make a difference. Help out. Know what I mean?"

Pete tugged off bits of the blue label on his Pabst. "What about Mom and Dad?"

"They'll come around."

"And his family? I bet they're not too happy."

Sarah smiled. "He says his father will like me for what he calls my emancipation of spirit."

"That sounds like Ibrahim." Pete promised to give her moral support when she told her parents after church. They were sitting at the dinner table, the smell of roast beef in the air. Mom had changed from her Sunday best into her jeans, but Daddy still had on his Harris tweed and striped yellow tie.

"Sarah, no!" Mom's mouth opened wide in shock.

"But it's what you've always wanted. Me married. Me happy with a family of my own."

"But not to a foreigner. Not like this."

"I start work July 1."

"You, the feminist? You'll hate it from day one," Daddy snapped.

"You have to make sacrifices to get what you want. Sorry if that sounds pompous."

"Why do you have to be such a rebel?" Her mother squinted her eyes.

"It's just for six weeks. What have I to lose?"

"Your Abe is a good man," Daddy said, "but not our kind. I can't bless this marriage and that's that."

"It's not as if I'm getting married tomorrow. I'm just going to check it out. See if I can stand it there. That's all. Why are you acting like this? You're not racists. When Thomas invited me to the senior prom, you let me go."

"That's different. Thomas may be black but he is a Christian."

"Say whatever you want, but Ib's got character," Pete said, sticking up for her. "He's a decent person."

"And what does his family think of your checking them out?" Daddy said in a surly tone.

"What they don't know, they won't object to." Sarah looked down at her hands.

"I raised you to be honest," Daddy said. "I'm ashamed of you."

Mom rose from the table, went to her desk, and came back with the family Bible tucked under her arm. "We need to pray about this. Let's pray for guidance."

"Mom, please. I can't." Sarah pushed her fork around the green puddle of spinach on her plate and her stomach churned. She sneaked a glance at her father; he had his head bowed and his eyes screwed shut. He prayed with long pauses. He asked that God would bless her and give her the strength and courage she needed to do the right thing. He prayed that God would heal her and comfort her with His love. He opened his pale blue eyes and fixed them on her. "As for me and my house, we will serve the Lord. The Lord is dealing with you, Sarah. You say you can't pray. But we'll say a little prayer for you every day."

Sarah clapped her hands to her ears. "Pray. Pray all you like, but I'm going." She rushed out of the dining room.

In the three weeks that it took to get her work visa, she read up on the kingdom, spending long hours in a sunny nook of Madison's public library. She was concerned about practicing medicine in a different culture. She had a senior position and was determined to live up to it. She expected mostly fevers, fractures, and heart attacks along with the usual pediatric parade. With the oil fields so close, there would be more burn victims, but a stint at Cook County's burn unit in Chicago had prepared her for that. What worried her was an article in a women's magazine saying that Arabs changed when they went home. That better not happen to Ibrahim. So far, it seemed okay. He called every night and reassured her that everything would be fine. However, when she gave him her arrival time at the airport, he said the hospital would send a representative to meet her.

"Why not you?" she asked, puzzled.

There was a pause. "Oh, there's something about it being against the rules," he said in a guarded voice.

"Rules? What kind of rules?" she cried.

"Really stupid rules."

It was unlike him to be blunt, and that worried her. "Go on. Tell me. I've got to know."

"Oh, stupid rules about mingling of the sexes."

"*Mingling*?" She laughed—it was such a peculiar word choice. She pushed him for information, but he sounded defensive, which was not at all like him.

Yesterday on the three-hour drive to Chicago's O'Hare airport, Daddy kept adjusting the rearview mirror, trying to catch her eye. "Honey, it's an infatuation. You've worked so hard to get where you are. Don't throw all that away to go live with a bunch of Muslims. It's not too late to change your mind. We can turn around and go home right now."

Her mother dabbed at her eyes with a tissue. "All he has to offer you is pain. There's nothing for you over there."

Mom always did exaggerate. Sarah, sitting in the back behind her mother, unfastened her seat belt and leaned forward to massage her mother's taut shoulders. In a quiet voice, she told her parents she would miss them. She promised to be back in six weeks if things didn't work out and told them what they could more easily understand: with her new salary she could pay off her student loans, all one hundred and ninety-five thousand dollars.

Sarah must have fallen asleep, for she was awakened when her seatmate fumbled to retrieve her carry-on bag under the seat in front of her. "Home, we'll be there soon. Beautiful Khobar." Beaming, the girl headed toward the lavatory. As the plane began its descent, Sarah gazed out the window at the rolling banks of cloud cover. After a while, the plane swung low over an expanse of salmon-colored sand, flat as a pancake. Gradually, the color shifted to orange, then yellow. Black rectangles appeared below—Bedouin tents. In the expanse of sand, she spotted a grove of palm trees. Perhaps it was a mirage, Sarah was thinking when a woman in a voluminous black cloak sat down next to her.

"I'm sorry, the seat is taken." Sarah could not see the eyes behind the dark veil. She felt ill at ease, almost as if she were talking to a mummy.

The woman placed her hand on Sarah's. "Mine, it's mine."

Instantly Sarah recognized the orange fingertips. "Oh, I'm sorry."

"Never mind," the girl giggled.

Other women dressed in slinky pants and jaunty dresses sauntered down the aisle and entered the lavatory. They exited identical, cloaked in somber black and puffed up to twice their natural size. Yes, she really had come to a foreign land. Feeling mounting trepidation, Sarah went to change. In the cramped lavatory, she smoothed out the wrinkles in her new silk pants. Ibrahim had suggested she dress conservatively, and these were loose yet elegant, with a narrow satin strip down the sides. She rubbed moisturizer on her face and neck, applied her make-up and spritzed on a floral scent. Ibrahim had reminded her of the importance of covering her hair—just like St. Paul advised, she told her mother—so she threw a turquoise scarf over it. Back in her seat, she saw the ailerons lowered, and the 747 came in low over the tarmac, touched down, shuddered, and rumbled along the runway before lurching to a stop. The passengers clapped, and jostling each other, hauled their bags down from the overhead compartments. They crowded the aisle, the women cocooned in black and the men in long white robes looking like priests.

Inside the airport terminal, at immigration, she waited in the line for foreigners. When it was her turn, an officer in an olive uniform with gold epaulettes flipped through her passport, found the page with her visa, and keyed its number in his computer. He studied her photo, comparing it with the face in front of him: sapphire eyes, freckled cheeks, and shoulder-length auburn curls tucked under the scarf. He asked the purpose of her stay and when she told him she was a physician coming to work in the Suleiman Hospital, he stamped her passport and waved her through. She collected her luggage and headed to customs where men were jostling one another. Eventually a line was opened just for women. While she waited, she studied the entry stamp in her passport and saw it was dated according to the Islamic Hijri calendar: back home, it might be June 28, 2001, but here it was second month of spring in the year 1422. Finally, it was her turn. She hoisted her red backpack and the two blue suitcases onto the inspection table. She unlocked and opened her suitcases for an officer who dumped a heap of her clothes onto the counter and proceeded to grope around her slacks, blouses, and lingerie. He unzipped her cosmetics bag and spilled out sunscreen, lipstick, and mascara. He searched her handbag, riffling the pages of her sketchbook.

"What are you looking for?" she asked through gritted teeth.

He scowled. "Nothing."

"What?"

"Bad pictures."

"I don't have any."

"Whisky?"

"No."

"No parties in Saudi Arabia." He slapped pink labels on her bags.

"Forbidden. Understand?"

She gave him a chilly smile. Seeing a sign in English that pointed toward the arrivals hall, she followed it, her stiletto heels clicking on the marble floor. In the vast arrivals hall, pots of yellow chrysanthemums edged a marble fountain. She set down her backpack and reached out her fingers to let the cool water trickle through them. In the flat light from the banks of fluorescent tubing, women in black cloaks crouched against the wall like boulders. Through their veils, they could see her but she could not see them, which made her feel ill at ease for it put them at an advantage. When a white-robed man approached them, they rose altogether in one uncompromising mass of black. Their banshee-like cry made the hair on the back of her neck prickle. In her years in the ER, she had heard groans and screams, but nothing bloodcurdling like this howl, primeval yet controlled. Unnerved, she scanned the hall for the hospital representative who was to meet her. A tall man at the rear of the cavernous hall was striding toward her. Flung over his white robe was a beige cloak trimmed with gold braid. She stared blankly a moment or two, and then her heart beat fast. Ibrahim. There he was.

"Sarah, at last." He stood inches from her, his hand outstretched.

It was the first time she had seen him in his national costume. A white headdress framed his forehead and fell straight to his jaw line, and with his curly hair covered, his mustache seemed fuller, his eyes enormous.

"You came after all," she cried. Her knees felt shaky, and she leaned toward him.

"Not here," he said. She knew his every intonation and could tell how nervous he was as he repeated in a choked voice, "Please, not here." He gripped her hand, shaking it, shaking it, shaking it. "The *mutawwa'in* are everywhere."

"Who? Where?" She jerked back her hand and looked around her.

"The religious police. They would wonder who you are and ask to see our marriage license. Let us hope we will soon be able to oblige them." He smiled. The tension broken, he asked in a normal voice about the flight and her father and brother.

"Fine. Fine. And Mom's fine, too." It was their private joke, how he never mentioned other women.

Again, the eerie cry poured forth, the women's voices rising and falling. "What's that?" she asked, feeling alarmed.

"We call it the *zaghareet*. For us, words are not enough. That is when women do the *zaghareet*. It frees them, helps them express their joy or grief."

"Both?"

"Yes. Today it is for joy." He grinned. "If I were a woman I too would throw back my head and flap my tongue to welcome you."

They stood smiling at each other until she heard a tapping behind her and she spun around to see a scrawny man with a bushy beard advancing on them, banging his stick on the floor. Ibrahim stiffened as the stranger thrust himself between them and shouted in guttural, harsh Arabic, the words too fast for her to understand. Ibrahim, his face set like stone, did not interrupt until the brute finished. "Dr. Moss is a guest in our country," he said.

"Her hair. Make her cover." The *mutawwa* banged his cane on the floor.

Instantly she raised her scarf over her hair. It must have slipped down when she had taken off her backpack.

"A guest," Ibrahim repeated, his hands clenched at his sides. "And you, where are your manners?"

"A guest, so you say." The *mutawwa* took a step back and merged into the crowd.

"I hate those men. Usually they stay away from the airport. I'm so sorry."

"It doesn't matter. No harm done," she said, embarrassed at how panic-stricken she had felt.

They continued to chat in a desultory way but it felt stilted, and after a few minutes, she said that the hospital representative would be wondering where she was. "He's over there." Ibrahim gestured in the direction of a balding man seated behind a desk with the sign SULEIMAN HOSPITAL. Sarah tightened the knot of her head scarf and headed off.

"Dr. Moss, I presume?" The representative greeted her pleasantly and asked for her passport. She took it from her bag but held it to her chest. "Your passport. Please," he repeated.

"But—" She hesitated.

"Just a formality. Not to worry."

"All right then." She handed it over.

He flipped through it. "Everything appears to be in order." He tucked it in his attaché case and hailed a porter.

Outside it was boiling. The heat rose from the sidewalk up her ankles, baking them. Rivulets of sweat seeped behind her knees, and she gasped for breath in the heat. She closed her eyes against the glare and then opened them and rummaged in her bag for her RayBans. Opposite the terminal, a parking garage disgorged taxis, limousines, and pick-up trucks. When the hospital van drew up to the curb, she started to slide open the door, but the handle was burning hot, and she jerked back. "Madam, allow me," the driver said. She did not get in right away, but scanned the crowd of men loitering outside the terminal. The hospital representative got in the front passenger seat. "We can go now," the driver said.

"Please, just a minute." But she did not see Ibrahim anywhere, so she climbed in. She leaned back into the plush upholstery and gazed past the blue dice dangling from the rear-view mirror. They passed a mosque and a smaller terminal with a bevy of stretch limousines parked outside it—the royal pavilion, a sign said. At a cloverleaf junction, a highway divided the desert into two figure eights, and four lanes of cars moved in each direction. The median was planted with palm trees and adorned with sculptures, not the usual rulers and warriors, but surreal replicas of a coffee pot, an incense brazier, even a bicycle. The driver switched on the radio, and a woman's melancholy song filled the van. Outside, under a milky sky, the desert stretched, barren like a lunar landscape, vacant except for the silvery pipeline that flashed in the sunshine. The driver turned onto the Dhahran to Khobar highway, passing bleak trailer camps signposted with names like Bangladesh Bungalows, Jaipur Residences, and Lahore Rooms. She felt lucky not to be living in any of these forlorn compounds. In twenty minutes, they reached the marker announcing KHOBAR: POPULATION: 357,072. They passed a wrecked car hoisted next to a sign which read, "Dear driver, remember your loved ones." Now skyscrapers lined the road; one of them, sheeted with copper, reflected the orange-pink of dusk, and another had a wall mural of oryx, gazelles, and camels. Billboards advertised Burger King, Kentucky Fried Chicken, and lots of Arab names, all of which passed in a blur. As they waited at a traffic light, she gazed out the dark-tinted window. A shop sign **MIXED NUTS** flashed on and off in red neon above pyramids of what must be cashews, pistachios, and almonds.

"Ah, if only I could bite into them. Alas, God gives nuts to those with no teeth," the driver grumbled. "Oh, if only I'd known how old I'd live."

"Well, what then?" the hospital representative said.

"I'd have taken better care of my teeth." The driver laughed, the light turned green and they sped off. Soon they were in a residential neighborhood with satellite dishes and silvery water tanks on the roofs of villas sequestered behind high walls. They passed several hotels, and at the Marriott, they turned onto the Corniche, the boulevard that ran along the seaside. Here youngsters played soccer, and men strolled hand-in-hand while a Ferris wheel revolved, its spokes lit up in red and purple lights.

It was dark by the time they arrived at the western compound where the apartment building for the hospital's female staff was located. The driver opened the door for her, and when he smiled, she saw what he had meant about his teeth—the gums were a healthy pink but he had only three teeth. He carried her luggage into the lobby, handed her a key and left. She took the elevator to the top floor and let herself into #602. Her apartment smelled of fresh paint, and white curtains flut-

tered in the breeze of the air conditioning, which someone had thought-
fully turned on for her arrival. On the coffee table was a gift basket
from the hospital, decorated with red ribbons and filled with cherries,
a pineapple, and three types of pears. She bit into one. The juice ran
down her thumb, and she licked it off. In the living room, sale stick-
ers were still on the yellow leather armchairs, the recliner, and the flat
screen television. She picked up the remote and flipped through the
channels—several Arabic ones plus BBC and CNN. A flier on the coffee table listed the week's activities—bingo, craft workshops, massage
therapy, and video night. She was surprised at how western it seemed;
she might as well be in Madison. On the kitchen counter, she found a
bowl of cashews and a welcoming note from a colleague named Annie.
Beside the sink was a sign: "Sweet water drinking only. Brackish water
all the rest." She turned on the faucet on the right and took a sip. "Ugh,"
she said aloud and poured the salty water down the drain.

The bedroom felt monastic with white walls, a desk, dresser, and
single bed. She unpacked and hung up her clothes in the closet, where
a veil and black cloak were hanging. She tried them on, looked at herself
in the mirror, and grimaced. She certainly did not want Ibrahim seeing
her looking like that. She remembered how her art history professor
once said that almost every culture made masks—funeral masks and
masks to scare demons and enemies—and how Jackie Kennedy veiled
in black at JFK's funeral. A mourning veil was understandable, but
otherwise, one should look people straight in the eye. These ugly veils
seemed—quite simply—impolite. She thrust the veil and cloak back in
the closet.

The telephone rang; it was Ibrahim. He apologized again for the scene with the *mutawwa* at the airport.

"Thank God you stood up to him. What a creep."

"They're not all like that. What do you think of Khobar?"

"Like a surreal Houston. I expected to see gas flares."

"Not any more. But when I was small, we saw them, bright coral flames, roaring as they leaped up into the sky. They terrified my sister and me. We would run to my mother, and she would spread her cloak wide and we would hide under it."

"And you felt safe under there?"

"Absolutely. Layla too. She would stop trembling."

"How about your brother?"

"Well, sometimes Mother would shoo Shaheed away."

"That wasn't very nice of her."

"I suppose not. He is her stepson from my father's first marriage. I doubt he was ever truly afraid. Layla is still deathly afraid of fire."

"Speaking of fear, the *zaghareet* is spine-tingling. I'd like to be able to do it.

"My sister can teach you. You will like her. Everyone does. She wants to invite you for a swim."

"Okay, darling. Right now, I better get some sleep." After she hung up, she walked out on the balcony and leaned against the turquoise railing. The air had a salty tang, and a crescent moon shone on the inky ripples of the water below. She had expected desert and desolation, not this stunning sea view. As she nibbled on cashews and pistachios, she tried to picture Ibrahim and Layla hiding under their mother's abaya.

It seemed odd that he was afraid of fire. Still, Sarah felt touched that
he would confide in her. She liked that about him—he was not macho.
He talked about his mother a great deal, and in the States, he used
to telephone her every weekend. His mother was good-hearted, he
said, stubborn and bossy perhaps, but she would rush to the defense of
her family.

A mother protector, Sarah thought gloomily as she returned to the air-
conditioned cool. In the bedroom, she found a Qur'an in the drawer in
the bedside table. She leafed through the thin pages until she fell into a
fitful sleep, and in a dream red neon signs flashed: MIXED NUTS, MIXED
NUTS, MIXED NUTS.

CHAPTER 2

ALL SARAH KNEW ABOUT IB'S SISTER was that she was passionate about fashion. Wondering what Layla might wear at home, Sarah went to her closet and took out several outfits. She tried on a linen pants suit. One look in the mirror and she peeled it off. Too tight, she decided as she tossed it on the bed. She put on a blue dress and thought it might be perfect, but it had short sleeves. Two changes later, she settled on a silk emerald blouse and a straight ankle-length ivory skirt. Confident that she was dressed just right, she waited for the Filipino driver she would be sharing with Layla.

At four o'clock on the dot, Johnny arrived. He had slicked-back hair, a gold front tooth, and he was wearing a t-shirt with the slogan, "I love the USA."

"Very sweet Mrs. Layla is," Johnny said as he helped Sarah into a white Lincoln. "The children too. You'll see." The traffic was fierce, with cars weaving in and out of the lanes without signaling. A limousine cut in front of them, and he joked that Saudis used to kick their camels but now hit the gas pedal. They passed a car with a bumper sticker that read: SAUDI ARABIA, LOVE IT OR LEAVE IT. "We love it, but fast as we can, we leave it," he joked.

"Well, I plan to love it, pure and simple."

"Ah, Dr. Sarah, you have just arrived," he said sagely. "You're in the honeymoon period." He and his wife Eliza had lived in the kingdom for three years. In Manila, Eliza used to be a teacher but now she worked as a nanny, helping take care of Layla's children. His own children were in Manila with Eliza's mother. Once he had saved enough, he planned to return to Manila to open a restaurant, a family affair, with paintings on the walls and flowers from the garden on the tables. Eliza would still teach school but she would also wait tables on the weekends and he would be the chef.

They entered the university grounds where Layla lived with her husband. The buildings were of contemporary design with clean lines and serried arches. Jets of water sparkled in the sunshine outside the library, a remarkable octagonal structure with blue stained-glass windows. There was a Research Institute and a mosque with flying buttresses, delicate as a house of cards. At the crest of a hill, a slim fluted column overlooked the campus. This water tower was beautiful, nothing like the one at home, a metal box propped high in the sky and relegated to the edge of town like an unavoidable evil. They cruised down a hill bordered by a chain-link fence facing Aramco, the American oil compound. Two speed bumps later, Johnny turned down a side street and parked in front of a privet hedge. They had arrived.

Sarah unlatched the gate and strolled down the short path that led under a pergola of pink oleander to the bungalow. She slipped off her sandals and added them to the pile on the porch. Eliza, a short woman wearing a blue-check housedress, opened the front door and led her into the living room, which was cool and fragrant. There were Persian carpets underfoot, sky blue drapes at the windows, and the one painting, a calligraphy in gold leaf, caught the sparkle of the crystal chandelier. A silver-framed photo of a heavyset woman sat on the coffee table next to a bouquet of lilies. The woman had a gap between her front teeth, furry eyebrows and high cheekbones, and she wore a tight dress with black and gold stripes. She looked like a tigress. Sarah recognized her as Ibrahim's mother for he had kept a copy of the identical photo on his desk in Madison. As Sarah settled herself on the beige sofa, a Persian cat bounded from a French provincial armchair onto her lap. Delicately it sniffed her face and allowed her to stroke its silken silvery fur.

Minutes later, a barefoot woman in a pair of classic white jeans, a cherry-colored blouse and a half-dozen bracelets in every shade of pink and orange bustled in. Her eyes sparkled under lashes as blunt and stiff as a doll's. On each earlobe she wore two pearls unlike any Sarah had ever seen for they were oblong and shone with a lunar luster. Her heart-shaped face had a rosy glow and shone with excitement. She had Ib's smile, the same tiny gap between her front teeth.

"'Ello, 'ello, 'ello, welcome to Arabia," she said in a silvery voice as she kissed Sarah's right cheek, her left and then her right cheek again. "I'm sorry to make you wait but I had to finish my prayers. Ibrahim has told me so much about you and your family. Oh, you are beauteous. What a lovely outfit, so fashionable, like a Vogue model. A doctor, too. Emergency room, he says." She cocked her head to one side. "And what sort of people go into that?"

"Impatient ones like me," Sarah said lightly.

"Every mother wants her son to be a doctor." Layla patted her on the hand and smiled, showing dimples in her cheeks.

"And her daughter?" Sarah stroked the cat purring on her lap.

Layla giggled and sat down very close to Sarah. "Oh no, we are too feudal." Just then, the children ran in, two boys in Scout uniforms and a little girl with pink ribbons in her hair and wearing a frilly white dress. "Here are Fawzi and Farouk, and Lulu my darling."

The twins shook her hand, but Lulu shyly put her arm over her eyes and then darted to the sofa where she sat kicking her feet. Sarah gave them gifts—Mickey Mouse sunglasses for the boys and a Barbie for Lulu—and they squealed and raced around until Layla shooed them outside.

"A cigarette? No?" Layla tapped a Winston and lit it. "It's those boys. They fight and get on my nerves, so I turn to my little addiction. It's a bad habit, very bad. I can't help it. My mother doesn't know. Please keep my little secret."

Smiling, Sarah promised she would. She asked about the family, and Layla said that both her grandfather and great-grandfather had been captains of pearling vessels, and that for generations the family had hunted pearls in the warm waters of the Gulf until the late 1930s when the Japanese flooded the market with cultured pearls.

"It sounds like a romantic life."

"Not for the crew, poor souls." Layla described how the divers would pinch their noses shut with wooden clips, fasten stones to their feet, and jump overboard. On the seabed, they scooped the flat shells into baskets hung around their necks, and when they could not stand it any longer, they yanked on the ropes around their waists and were hauled up. After sunset prayers, under the captain's watchful eye, they slit the shells to extract the pearls. Layla touched the pearls at her ears. "These come from my great-grandfather. Mother gave them to me when I named Lulu. Lulu means 'pearl.' Mother, you see, is passionate about pearls. When she feels sad or lonely, she plays with them and sings the old songs. She keeps telling me the lesson of the pearl, harping on how suffering can lead to good. Mother says it's what every girl needs to know. Imagine, the rubbing of sand against a shell, irritating it, that pain is what makes a rosy pearl. Isn't that a wonder!" Layla laughed and stubbed her cigarette in the marble ashtray. She went to the bookcase, came back with a photograph album and opened it to a black-and-white portrait of a dignified-looking man standing at the helm of a dhow. "That's Grandfather. He taught Mother the songs of the pearlers. Handsome, wasn't he?"

"Mama, Mama," came a scream from the courtyard.

"Oh, those naughty boys." Layla ran out to the courtyard and Sarah followed.

Fawzi was lying on the grass in his white thobe and Farouk was thumping and kicking him. Both boys were barefoot, but Farouk might as well have been wearing jackboots. Layla wrenched him off, yelled at him, and sent him to his room.

The women went back to the salon. Now, I'll show you the rest of us." Layla turned the pages of the album slowly, stopping only when Sarah expressed interest as she did when she saw the photo of a newborn being bathed in a pink tub, set on a weathered table beneath a palm tree. Rose petals—yellow with pink-tipped ends— floated on the bathwater and one lay on the baby's pudgy thigh. The baby wore an amulet of blue beads on her bare chest, and a beautiful girl in a red dress splotched with water stains cradled the tiny wet head. "That's Mother giving me my first bath," Layla said.

"Ibrahim resembles her," Sarah said. "Same springy hair and extraordinary eyelashes."

"I suppose." After dozens of photos of the twins—as toddlers in their first thobes, making sand castles, playing with Legos and doing all the things boys do—there were a few of Lulu sucking a pacifier and taking her first baby steps. Finally, there was a photo of Ibrahim. He had his arm around a woman with haunting green eyes. "That's Miriam," Layla said. "So sad, her life snuffed out."

"Yes, he told me. Do you have other pictures of him?"

"Oh, sure," Layla flipped a few pages forward. "See. That's him at the American University of Beirut. He studied there, you know. Once, when he came home at semester break, Mother sheared his hair, shouting that he could never get into paradise looking like a girl. Now let me show you my wedding pictures. See, here's my husband. Cute, isn't he? Older but cute. Ah, once, Ahmed loved me so much." She pulled off her wedding band and showed Sarah the two swans etched inside. "Swans mate for life, only once. No polygamy for them. How he loved me on our wedding day. Now he's never here, always off in Riyadh. Politicking, he calls it." She sighed dramatically. "And here's Tisam," she said, turning the page to a picture of a slender girl in white with a red rose pinned in her dark hair. "She's my husband's sister. Her real name is Ibtisam, but we call her Tisam. She's a photographer. And here's my brother Shaheed. The Sheriff, I call him. Tisam snapped his picture when he wasn't looking. He says photos are immoral, graven images."

Sarah took a closer look. Shaheed was a bearded, unsmiling man with insolent eyes. Like all Saudi men, he wore the white robe called a thobe, but his was so short his skinny legs stuck out of it; a bandoleer criss-crossed his chest; and in his belt was a dagger. He looked like a pirate.

"He makes us sick with worry." Layla lit a cigarette.

"Really? Why? What does he do?"

"What doesn't he do?" Layla rolled her eyes. "He's a bad seed. When he was young, he got addicted to alcohol. His faith cured him, so he said, but really, it just made him worse. He went off to Afghanistan to fight the Communists and came home a real *mujahideen*. A hero, to some. Then he started switching girls who let a bit of hair show and boys who hung around the malls during prayer time. Once, he blew up a truck filled with liquor. Still you mustn't blame him too much. You see, his degree in Islamic studies is useless, so he works for the Ministry."

"The Ministry? What's that?"

"The Ministry for the Encouragement of Virtue and the Suppression of Vice. You know, the *mutawwa'in*."

"I've heard of them." Sarah squirmed as she remembered her unpleas-ant encounter with the *mutawwa* at the airport.

"Shaheed and his wife are crazy in love. Even though he's so pious, at times he skips prayers to make love. On pilgrimage, he insisted Susu wear the face veil, which is not proper to wear there. And for why? So she wouldn't tempt strange men. You see how jealous he is, how much in love." Layla giggled and rested her fingers on Sarah's wrist. "Why,

Sarah, your eyes are sparkly. You must be in love too."

"Oh no." Sarah flushed.

Layla closed the album. "Why aren't you married, such a pretty girl?"

Sarah pushed back a wisp of hair. "Oh, my work."

"Really? Are you an orphan?" Layla looked at her with intense curiosity.

"No."

"Won't your parents find you someone?"

Sarah thought sourly of the type of man they would pick and said she liked to make her own choices.

"A modern woman. Still, your relatives should help. Don't you have a cousin? When Ahmed was looking for a wife, my auntie suggested me."

Sarah raised her eyebrows. "His mother chose?"

"But he wanted to see me before he asked for my hand. It would have been humiliating for my family if he rejected me, so one day when I was visiting, Auntie hid him behind a screen so he could peek at me. I didn't know he was there. Two days later, he asked for my hand."

"But he's your cousin."

Layla flicked the ash off her cigarette. "I hadn't seen him since I was a child, so for me he was just a man. Anyway, a cousin is better than a stranger."

"And you were how old?"

"Sixteen. It was time. Several of my students are that age. I worry for them. If they can't concentrate on their studies, they should marry. It's safer."

"Mmm," Sarah said, trying not to be judgmental. "Didn't you want to choose for yourself?"

"A few girls are doing that, but not in our family. In India, they have arranged marriages too. Most of the planet does." Layla spread her arms wide. "Can a billion couples be wrong?"

"But how could you trust Ahmed was the best if you hadn't met other men?"

"Thank God, I was lucky. But why should I be nervous? I knew my family would pick someone good, like my brothers." She stubbed out her cigarette.

"But which one? Shaheed or Ibrahim? They're so different."

Layla looked baffled. "They're both good Muslims. Since you ask, Ahmed is like Ibrahim. If anything, he's even more liberal." She picked up the silver bell on an end table and rang it. "We don't choose our brothers, do we? Yet, we love them. As we say, love comes after marriage."

Eliza brought in the tray with a pitcher and sugar-frosted glasses and then left to check on the children. Sarah stroked the cat purring in her lap as she watched Layla pour the lemonade. How trusting Layla was to let others decide the course of her life. She could not be like that. Nor did she want to.

"I can't bear to think of you all alone," Layla said as she passed the glass to Sarah. "I want you to take Shadow to keep you company. She's a good cat, and you can take her everywhere. She likes to go in the car. Now, no arguments. And because you're so nice, I'll tell you another little secret." She leaned forward and spoke in a low voice. "My husband and Shaheed don't get along. It makes things hard. Ahmed's not a good father although he could be the best of them if he chose. Off he

flies to Riyadh and abandons me with the children. Thank God for Shaheed. He spends a lot of time with them. He complains I leave them too
much with Eliza because she's Christian and not Muslim. The Sheriff,
he is *so* strict." Layla sighed dramatically.

"Is your mother like that too?" Sarah took a sip of the lemonade. It
was too sweet.

"Not so bad although she tells my father to fire anyone who drinks
whisky, and she won't let me wear jeans. As you see, I disobey, but not
when she's around."

Sarah stared at the photograph. "She sounds fierce."

"Mother? Oh no." Layla smiled indulgently as if ferociousness were
part of her mother's charm, as if with such a protector, they were safe
from all harm.

Sarah set down her glass. In a deliberately casual voice, she asked,
"What does Ibrahim say about me?"

"Oh, so much. About how your mother baked him an apple pie. That
irritated Shaheed. I must warn you, he doesn't like Ibrahim to hang
around Americans."

"But what does he say about me?"

"That you were kind to him." Layla took a swallow of lemonade,
made a face, and added a spoonful of sugar. "It's too bad you can't visit
with him here. Oh, it's so silly. We don't have what you call platonic
friendship. Oh dear, you will think we're backward. If people saw you
and Ibrahim alone together, they'd call you bad names. Silly, isn't it?"

When it was time for ladies hours at the pool, Layla grabbed an abaya
from the hall closet, tossed it on, and wrapped a black head scarf around

her hair. As they walked, she gripped the abaya with her elbows to keep its flaps from blowing open. Every now and then, she would cock her head, turn to Sarah, and put her hand on her wrist. "Not too hot?" she would ask in her friendly way.

However, Layla might not be so pleasant if she knew the truth about herself and Ibrahim. Sarah felt a little guilty at being devious, but even if Layla approved, it was perfectly clear she couldn't keep a secret. She would tattle on them to her mother, and no good would come of that. As they approached the recreation center, a red-faced jogger sprinted by in a sweat-stained undershirt and shorts. "Look at him," Layla said in disgust. "Just look at him, dressed like that! That's revolting. If Shaheed saw that, he'd have the man flogged."

"You're kidding."

Layla giggled. "I never kid about the Sheriff."

When Sarah came out of the changing room, she felt relieved she had opted for her black swimsuit rather than her yellow bikini. All the women, both Arabs and Westerners, were in one-piece suits. Layla called to her from a blue-and-white striped lounge chair near the toddlers' pool. She was completely covered; under her black tank suit, she wore opaque black tights and a long-sleeved black t-shirt. It looked like she had on a wetsuit—an odd outfit for a woman crazy about fashion.

"See them?" Layla pointed up at the workers hammering shingles on the roof of the recreation center. "Know what they're doing? Ogling our legs." She wrapped her arms around her knees and grinned. "I've tricked them. They won't see mine."

"What's wrong with legs?" Sarah dragged her chair into the shade. She refrained from pointing out that the tights emphasized the shapeliness of Layla's plump legs and narrow ankles.

"Men get tempted." She giggled. "Better cover up or the *mutawwa'in* will get you. They will switch you." She crushed her cigarette on the pavement, swung her legs over the chair, and pulled Sarah to her feet. "Let's do cannonballs." At the edge of the chlorine-smelling pool, they jumped in, making two massive splashes that splattered the kids playing *Marco Polo*. After a few laps, the women climbed out. "What I'd like," Layla said as she toweled herself dry, "is for you to come camping with us."

"Camping? Here? In the desert? With no lakes, no forests, no shade?"

Layla looked offended. "Oh, still it's nice. Usually when it's hot like this, we go to the beach, but not this time. It's nothing special, just family, but we relax and catch up on the gossip. The men hunt. Maybe they'll get a bird." She laughed as if it were most unlikely.

Sarah pulled a tube of sunblock from her backpack and smoothed it on her thin arms. Layla offered to put it on her back where Sarah could not reach. Her feathery pats felt wonderful.

"So you'll come?" Layla twisted the cap back on.

"If I'm not working."

"Now you sound like Ibrahim."

"He'll be there, won't he?"

"Like you—if he's not working. He's unhappy, you know. He says we shouldn't tear down old buildings to build malls, and then the next moment he says he misses the States. He exaggerates, don't you think? He can have his pizzas, Big Macs, and Twinkies here—anything really, but still he's restless. All he does is work. He never gets away. I'm going to insist he come, but getting away for a weekend isn't enough. Now that he's home, he needs to marry."

"Marry?" Sarah repeated the word.

"Of course. It's been two years since Miriam died."

"What does he say?" Sarah tamped down her anxiety.

"That we shouldn't pressure him. That God will bless him with a wife when it is the right time. It's too irritating."

"And just who would he marry?"

Layla shrugged. "Some cousin or other. Mother wants grandchildren."

"She's already got them—yours and Shaheed's too."

"Silly girl. That's not enough." Layla flicked the beach towel at her. "Grandchildren by Ibrahim."

Sarah felt a hot spurt of anger. "Oh? And what does he have to say about it?"

"He tells Mother not to bother, but she has her eye on someone."

Sarah imagined this mother could work on her son. "So who is this girl?" she asked.

"Tisam, the girl dancing in the picture."

"Oh, the brave photographer." Sarah sprang from her chair, strode to the pool's edge and dived in. She kicked underwater half the length of the pool, then surfaced, gulping for air, and thrashed toward the far end. Panting, she hung on to the ledge. She felt furious. Ibrahim should have told her about his mother's playing matchmaker, and he should have made it clear that they could not meet.

CHAPTER 3

JULY I, HER FIRST DAY AT WORK, wearing a white coat, badge and pager, Sarah was signing forms in the personnel office when a curvaceous, smiling woman strode up to her. "Hi, I'm Annie Ameen from the ICU. I get to show you the ropes." She looked Sarah up and down. "Thank God they didn't send another man."

Sarah smiled back, glad to see another westerner, and surprised at how blatantly Dr. Ameen violated the dress code. Gold hoops glinted behind her straw-colored hair, and her eyelids were heavy with green eye shadow. As she steered Sarah down the glistening corridors, she chattered about the best doctors on call and the director of nursing's mania for forms.

"And the procedures for making referrals, Dr. Ameen?"

"Annie. Call me Annie." She took Sarah first to the ER, where she introduced her to the attending physicians, residents, RNs, and the clerk-translator. In the distance, a woman cried, "Help, somebody help me. I need help," the usual background noise of an emergency department. Everything seemed familiar: the books in the library, the digital equipment in radiology, the muffled tones of the loudspeaker, and the

patients hooked up to machines. Then Annie took her off to meet Chief
of Staff John Hunter, a thin-lipped man with wire-rimmed glasses and
a clipped British accent with a reputation for being a stickler for the
rules. "You'll like the head honcho better," "He likes to be called Mr.
Suleiman, instead of Dr. Suleiman. He's humble. Ancient, too, and
Saudi, but nice."

Sarah felt very glad to hear that.

Omar Suleiman, Ib's father, was a kindly-looking man with soft jowls.
He pushed on the crook of his ivory-headed cane to help himself up,
and as he took her hand, Sarah thought he might kiss it like a French
courtier. "Ah, my dear, such an energetic handshake." He eased himself
back into his chair, "If I may say so, you are our dream come true." He
continued in the same mellifluous voice as Ib. "My dear, there was a
time when Islamic medicine led the way. Yes, Muslims were the first
to do cataract surgery, to use anesthesia, to cauterize wounds and to
discover the cause of epidemics. In the tenth century, our doctors were
already setting bones. Then it all disappeared. When I was a boy, we
had no doctors. Our people had to travel to Bombay for treatment.
Many died at sea, my brother among them. Then oil was discovered
and…" He broke off, as if it were unseemly to speak about money.
"And I established this hospital with one doctor and two nurses. Now we
have a team of sixty physicians with specialties in cardiology, vascular
surgery, nephrology, and all the rest. Please forgive an old man's pride."
He hobbled to the bookcase. Emphysema, Sarah guessed, still in the
early stages. She asked about women on staff; there were a number of
them, but few stayed the course. "God willing, now that you've come to

be their mentor, more will persevere." He rubbed his arms. "It's a little chilly. Please open the window, my dear."

She cracked it open, and hot air pressed in. "Ah, that's better. Easier to breathe. I hate feeling closed in—it's my Bedouin past."

"We all need to be free." The words jumped out of her mouth, startling her.

Mr. Suleiman peered at her from behind his bifocals. "And we have something else in common, do we not? My son. I will be forever grateful for the hospitality your family showed him."

Sarah rubbed the back of her neck and remembered with discomfort how Daddy had called her treacherous for taking this job without letting Ib's family know her true motive.

"Now my dear, I need your advice." Mr. Suleiman poked his cane into a heap of gowns stacked on a credenza. "These won't do."

"They're standard issue," she said mildly.

"But undignified." He clapped his hands. "Hamid, bring the new stock."

The orderly left and returned with an armload of clothes. Mr. Suleiman took a pair of blue pajamas from him. "Aren't these better than johnnies that don't cover your nakedness?"

"Perhaps." Sarah smiled.

Next, Mr. Suleiman held up a flowered nightgown. "See? It buttons down the front; that's convenient for nursing mothers."

Curiouser and curiouser, she thought. She asked if he was planning to change the nurses' uniforms, and he said that the scrubs dispelled suspicion. "Our men distrust women who know too much about the body. For many, it is of the utmost concern. Ah, my dear, there are Muslims and Muslims, different sorts in this one kingdom."

At lunch, Sarah joined the line in the cafeteria, a sunny room with circular tables and many potted plants. Arabs sat with Arabs, Western-ers with Westerners, and third world nationals with their compatriots. In the physicians' dining room, Annie called her over. Sarah joined her, setting down her tray on the table facing the mural of a jungle scene, wonderfully wild with lush green foliage and tropical flowers—anthurium, birds of paradise, and red ginger. Sarah poked the yellow rice mixed with chunks of mutton and tomato.

"At least it's not camel meat. Just a joke," Annie said. "So what did you make of Mr. Suleiman? A bit sappy, eh? Your residents will be starry-eyed too. Talk to them, and they'll say they want to save the country. That's baloney! Those girls just want to get away from home where there's nothing to do but mope and wipe babies' bums." She forked a hunk of steaming mutton and blew on it.

"The hospital seems first rate."

"It's okay, but nothing like the one in Riyadh. Always the best for the royals. King *numero uno* had zillions of wives, only four at a time, to be sure, and those girls let him see every inch of their bods—except their faces. Becoming nervous? Good. You should be."

Sarah felt like asking what it was like being married to an Arab, but she did not want Annie to think she was nosy. Instead, she asked why she had come to work here rather than staying in the States.

Annie shifted in her seat. "Hey, I'm Canadian."

"I'm sorry, I just assumed—"

"It's okay. Happens all the time." Annie broke the crust of her crème brulée with her spoon and tasted it. "Delicious."

"Well, why not live in Canada?"

"Oh, Ramzy—that's my husband. He's Egyptian. An archeologist. Apparently, there are tells around. A tell, in case you don't know, is an archeological site, and until the dig, it's just an old trash mound. Long ago people built in clay, which crumbles. When it came time to rebuild, they would level off the debris and put up new buildings on top. Ramzy dreams of finding a city buried near here. Get this: its doors were made of gold and inlaid with ivory." Annie laughed at the improbability of it.

"So you came because of his career."

"Mine, too. And well, why not?" she said lightly. "How about you?"

Even though she liked Annie, Sarah did not trust her enough to give more than her standard reply. "Oh, seeing new things, the tax-free salary—"

"Take the money and run." Annie adjusted an earring. "Nothing the matter with that. Help the Saudis build their roads, fix their plumbing, and diaper their babies. All in a good cause. So how are things?"

"So far so good, but the language is harder than I expected. My teachers were Lebanese and Saudi Arabic sounds different."

"Get tutoring. Get Munira. She's the best. And you'll catch on. People give stock answers. Ask a woman how many kids she has, and she'll say, 'Ten, praise God.' You'll socialize with expats, anyway. You know, as in expatriate. Almost everybody speaks English. Still, I try to speak Arabic. In the market the other day, I mispronounced the word for navel orange.

So there I was at the fruit stall asking for a kilo of prostitutes."

Sarah burst out laughing.

"Still, you better watch out. You've heard of Eve Teasers, right? They're crazy about redheads. Just remember, if it's fun, it's forbidden. *Mamnua.* Very *mamnua.* So which are you here for, the two-week or six-week locum?"

"Six."

"Someday, just someday, I wish someone would come and stay a good long time. A really long time."

"What's it like for you, being here?"

"At first, it's sheer hell, but then you get over it. My husband tells me you need to live in a place a very long time before making a judgment. Just remember the expat motto, 'Don't rock the boat.'" She winked, showing green eye shadow, and sashayed out of the dining room.

Sarah's first case that afternoon was a threatened miscarriage. The girl, only fifteen, had already lost a half-liter of blood. Sarah dragged the stool to the examining table where the girl lay, black hair fanned over the pillow. She should have come in sooner.

"It took a while to track down her guardian," the nurse said.

"Guardian?" Sarah said blankly.

"Her father or husband, the male relative. The one who signs the operative consent form."

Sarah took the girl's pulse, had her slide down to the edge of the table, and put her feet in the stirrups. The girl's cervix was soft, the uterus enlarged. "Strong. My baby will be strong," the girl kept repeating. The ultrasound was wheeled over, and Sarah placed the transducer on the girl's abdomen. The fetus appeared to be in the fourteenth week. She ordered IV fluids and two units of packed red blood cells and called obstetrics and gynecology to alert them that a patient was on the way. The afternoon continued with the usual cuts, burns, and feverish, wriggling babies. During her break, she signed up for Arabic tutoring. Back in the ER, she treated a toddler who had sucked the candy coating off his mother's Elavil, a youngster with an allergic reaction to peanuts, and an elderly man with a broken femur. She was finishing her report on him when an ambulance siren blared, and she hurried to the nursing station.

"A young woman," said the nurse monitoring the ambulance radio. "A drowning, or near drowning." The wall clock read 4:46 when the ambulance careened into the arrival pad. The medics wheeled in a stretcher with the woman, who was unconscious, her cheeks sunken and pale, no heartbeat, no breath. Drenched with water, a black cloak clung to her. Tense with anticipation, Sarah felt the adrenalin rush as she always did in a life-and-death situation. She started CPR, shocking the patient with the defibrillator. "Hurry!" she shouted. "Epinephrine! Get me epinephrine." She kept on, fighting to resuscitate the woman, looking up from time to time to glance at the monitor. The blue line stayed flat. After twenty minutes, she was aware of the residents exchanging disapproving glances over their masks. Forty-five minutes later, there was nothing to do but to pronounce her. For the last time Sarah pressed the stethoscope to the cold chest, and heard no sound. She pressed the side of the unwrinkled neck, and felt no pulse. The black eyes remained fixed and dilated. Sarah glanced up at the clock.

"Okay, that's it." She peeled off her gloves. As she trudged off to do the paperwork, she noticed the woman's name had already been erased from the triage board. Sarah filled out the death certificate and hurried to the staff room to find her young residents in case they needed her. Vividly she remembered her first death, the Latino teenager, his white t-shirt sopping with blood out of the bullet hole in his chest. "Losing one patient is not the end of the world," the attending physician had told her, but it had not seemed that way to her.

Now she cornered Annie in the hall. "Have you seen Dr. Nadia and Dr. Aziza?"

"No. Want to know the scuttlebutt? Your patient had cousins swimming nearby. Guys. They didn't lift so much as a finger to save her. Pretty shabby, eh?"

"Listen, I've got to go." Sarah, who half-expected to bump into one of her residents crouched behind a laundry cart mumbling how she just could not take it, considered what might be helpful for her to hear—perhaps that it was always terrible and it was normal to feel awful, but that the resident had done good work. "Just hang in," she would say. "It'll get easier." Ten minutes later, she found them drinking tea in the staff room. "It was a hard one, that death," she said, looking intently at each in turn. "Are you all right? Do you want to talk about it?"

"To Allah we belong and to him we return," Dr. Aziza said in a calm voice.

"It is very sad," Dr. Nadia added in a voice devoid of emotion. "God give us strength."

Sarah left the staff room feeling thwarted. She had been burning to help, but they did not need her.

When she arrived home, Shadow rubbed against her ankles and she bent down to stroke the silken fur. In the kitchen, she shook some dry cat food into a bowl, and then went to the living room, where she put on a CD and flopped on the yellow couch. But even with Enya crooning and Shadow purring curled up in the crook of her knees, Sarah could not stop thinking about the drowned woman. She pictured her wading in the shallows, black cloak wrapped around her, then the misstep, and her floundering, flailing her arms, screaming for help.

The telephone rang. It was Ib asking how her first day had gone; she did not want to burden him, so she told him only about how much she liked his father.

"And you will like Mother too. Let me take you home this weekend to meet her."

"Can't we wait? The camping trip is coming up soon."

"You sound nervous."

"I realize she's not a serial killer, but…"

"You worry too much. It will be pleasant. You and Layla can visit the women's baths, and afterward we will go to Mother's."

"But it's you I want to see. It's hard being here and not getting to see you." She curled and uncurled the telephone cord.

"You do not sound like yourself. Something is the matter."

"I lost a patient today."

"I'm sorry. Very sorry," Ib said, sounding as if he meant it.

Perhaps because he did not pry, she told him about it. "Those cousins of hers could have rescued her, but they didn't even try."

His voice became guarded. "Sarah, they were afraid."

"That's crazy. Afraid of what?"

"Consequences. It would be improper for them to approach her, let alone touch her."

"But they're her cousins for God's sake. They could have thrown a rope. Done something."

"Those poor guys did not know *what* to do." He tried to explain how boys were taught to fear women's power over men, but the more he said, the less sense it made. Then he said how Arabia and America were two different worlds and each took getting used to. When he first arrived in the States, he too felt out of place.

"But do I want to get acculturated to a system that's objectively wrong?"

"But it will evolve. We just have to help it along a little." He took his string of prayer beads from his side pocket and rubbed the amber as if that were action enough. He was so passive and fatalistic. Her young residents too had accepted the unnecessary death. The professional calm of the experienced physician was desirable, but their response was altogether different and she did not like it.

CHAPTER 4

SPARKS OF STATIC ELECTRICITY CRACKLED as Sarah brushed her hair. She patted sunscreen on her nose and cheeks, and then went to the window to wait for Ibrahim. When she saw him arrive, she grabbed her sunglasses and rushed out the door. She jabbed the elevator button, waited a minute, and then gave up, raced down the stairs, through the lobby and out into the heat of the parking lot. He was wearing blue jeans and a baseball cap. "Where's the thobe?" she grinned. "What happened to the Lawrence of Arabia look?"

He opened the passenger door of his white Audi. "Think I can pass for an expat?"

"Hope so. Where's Layla?"

"At home. Lulu has fever and an earache."

Glad there would be no chaperone, Sarah settled into the leather seat. They drove through the compound past the co-op, the swimming pool, and the recreation center up to the security gate, the sole entrance in the fifteen-foot wall around the Western Compound. The wall was intended to keep children from wandering off into the desert, but Annie said it was also to keep Saudis from seeing wicked foreign women. Once on the Corniche they passed the many foreign compounds, the houses set behind walls, with water tanks visible, one per rooftop. Fifty million gallons of water were piped into Khobar every day, and the desalination plant where Ib worked would soon be supplying much of it.

"It's going to be quite something when we get to the start-up stage," he said proudly. "Then I'll know that all the little bits have gone together in the right order." He continued down Prince Sultan Street and parked outside a drab four-story structure whose cement wall seemed about to crumble. "That's where Layla works. Girls School 13."

"Just a number? No name?"

"Sorry. That's only for private schools."

"I'm surprised she'd work in a place like that."

"There are some good private schools. Ahmed and I keep after her to get a job in one of them, but she will not hear of it. She is loyal to her students."

Sarah looked at the rusty gate set in a seven-foot high wrought iron fence with spear-tipped finials. Even the top floor windows had bars. "She should leave or change schools. It looks like a prison."

"We keep trying to convince her." They set off again. Beyond the city limits they drove in a monotony of buff-colored sand with only the pipeline, rusted oil barrels, and a few derelict trucks to break the emptiness. What came next was worse: the salt flats, She had imagined caravans curving around dunes, falcons winging overhead, and the sands puffing and swirling. She doubted now that the oasis would be as she had hoped, a tiny lake with a fringe of palm trees. Qatif had been a trading center since the third millennium B.C., a link between the civilizations of Mesopotamia and the Indus Valley. Before the advent of Islam, Zoroastrians, Jews, and Christians lived there. And before them, the inhabitants followed the cult of Ishtar, the goddess of love and war. Archeologists thought a sculpture of her seated on a golden lion was hidden nearby. "Apparently Ishtar had a fondness for men," he said.

"Like me for you," Sarah said lightly. "Maybe Annie's husband will get to excavate there."

"I doubt it. A few years ago, British archeologists tried to get permission to dig, but the women of the oasis objected."

"An odd thing to protest."

"Not at all. It is *their* place."

"So who won?"

"The women. The archeologists grumbled about our ways, but there was nothing for them to do but to pack up and fly off."

"To more tolerant realms?" She rested her hand on his knee. "And the women?"

"Still there. Mother goes all the time."

All at once, the scenery switched to green, cultivated land with palm trees and irrigation ditches lining either side of the highway. Sheep and goats grazed in green pastures. A white donkey with orange henna markings trotted alongside them; it was pulling a wooden cart loaded with hundreds of plastic water bottles. Soon the highway was replaced by straight streets bordered with five-story buildings, and then by residential compounds. Ib parked in front of one of them. It looked exactly like the others except for the gigantic tree, whose huge dark leaves sprawled across the compound wall. They had arrived.

"Will your father be here?" Sarah asked.

"Probably not. He's mostly at the hospital, but Shaheed and his family will. They live upstairs."

Sarah stared at the front door, painted a faded turquoise with a diamond pattern carved on the astragals. "I don't feel up to it. Not yet." She bit her thumbnail. "She won't want me, not for a daughter-in-law."

He considered this. "Of course, she would prefer I marry within the tribe. How could she not love you? I think our chances are good."

"She's not political, is she?"

"Mother?" Ib laughed. "No. All she cares about is family. Really, she is an admirable woman."

"Oh, of course, she must be, but I just don't feel up to it."

"You have to meet her, sooner or later. She knows you're here."

"But not *why* I'm here. I don't like duplicity. What I'd like is to go to the tell."

"O.K. You might bump into Mother. She goes there all the time. It's not far."

He drove a couple of blocks and parked in the shade. Before they got out, he reached into the glove compartment and pulled out a mass of black silk. "You'll feel more comfortable wearing an abaya. People here are not used to foreigners. Take this. It's one of Layla's." He draped the silken cloak over her shoulders.

"Just don't tell me I look beautiful in it," she grumbled.

"Actually, you do—quite alluring. Now this." He smiled and handed her a veil for her face, and she fingered the gauze, light as dandelion fluff. She decided to make a concession, just this once. She spread the fabric between her fingertips and lifted it; the black silk, which smelled faintly of tobacco, floated above her. As it alighted on her brow, shadows replaced the glare. It was like wearing enormous sunglasses, but something about it distressed her, and she took it off, folded it into a square, and pressed it into Ib's hand. "I'll cover my hair, but not my face."

"Okay." He put the veil back in the glove compartment. "You are dressed modestly, and that is all that is required."

As they strolled down the lane, she pressed her elbows against her sides, the way Layla had showed her, and the cloak stayed put. They turned down an alley where men were lined up outside a bakery, and through the window she saw the baker kneading dough, a blue gingham apron tied around his huge belly.

"The tell is that way, not far." Ib pointed to a dirt path by a stack of palm frond kindling beside the bakery. "I will buy picnic food and meet you back at the car in an hour."

"You're not coming?"

He grinned. "You want those crazy women to stone me?"

"Oh, that's right. It's a woman's place. I forgot." She laughed, glanced around to make sure no one was watching them, and pecked him on the cheek.

The sand was gritty between her toes but within a few minutes, it became moist, beaten earth. It felt cooler too. Beyond the mud walls lay plots of okra, alfalfa and rye in a radiant patchwork of green. Ring-necked parakeets screeched overhead, flashing yellow-green across the

sky. Doves moaned from the groves of peach and apricot and quince.
A few hundred yards down the path, she found herself in a clearing.
Directly in front of her rose the tell—a steep truncated pyramid. Nestled at its base was a basin of emerald water, dappled by sunlight, where
bosomy women in white slips were scrubbing themselves with loofahs
while others frolicked in the shallows. When they noticed Sarah, one
of them waved at her. "*Yalla*, come," she called, her hair swirling behind her.

Sarah took off the abaya and set it at the edge of the pool. She hitched
her pink skirt to her thighs and dangled her feet in the cool water as
more women swam toward her.

"*Amrikiya?*" yelled a woman treading water.

"Yes," Sarah shouted back.

"Come, *Amrikiya*, come."

She stripped to her bra and panties and slipped waist-deep into the
pool, balancing herself on a rocky ledge. She did not like them staring
at her, so she pushed off. Deep from its underground source, warm water pulsed around her like a healing whirlpool. She squinted her eyes to
shut out all but the outline of the tell. It towered above her, centuries of
rubbish and treasure hidden beneath the dark slopes.

"*Amrikiya!*" the woman yelled again. Water glistened on her shoulders
and a gold pendant nestled between her breasts.

Sarah glided toward her and followed her through a crevice in the jag-
ged stone to a pool beyond. Here the water was cooler. She duck-dived
and opened her eyes to a massive wall of cut stone. So, the legend was
true; a city once existed here. She kicked to propel herself deeper until

she neared the wall's topmost crenellation. Then, short of breath, she pushed to the surface and gulped for air. The woman swam over and patted her arm, beckoning Sarah to follow as she headed for shore. A few feet from the bank, where the water was chest high, the woman stooped and cupped water in her hands. She drank it and motioned Sarah to do the same.

Sarah shook her head. She worried about germs, bilharzia especially.

The woman laughed. "Water clean. Better than tap water."

Sarah hesitated. Against her better judgment, she cupped her hand in the water and raised it to her mouth.

"You like?"

"Yes." It tasted sweet, not the least bit brackish. The water bubbled around her as if she were in a giant Jacuzzi.

"Follow me," the woman said. Sarah would have preferred to stay in the pool, but she followed, clambering up onto the bank. The woman patted a spot on the ground beside her, and Sarah joined her. A lizard scurried past, looking like a miniature dinosaur. At the far edge of another pool, women were laundering thobes, undershirts, and school uniforms and then spreading them to dry on the bushes. Sarah glanced at the woman seated next to her who was combing her hair, primping it with hennaed-orange fingertips, and down at her own pale hands and trimmed doctor's nails. She was imagining what they would look like dyed with henna when the woman reached over and touched Sarah's hair. "Red!" she exclaimed as she rubbed a strand between her fingers. She patted herself between her legs. "Same-same here?"

"Stop hounding me," Sarah whispered fiercely in English and turned away, embarrassed. The woman giggled and pinched Sarah's thin arm. "Americans are too thin. You must eat. How many children?"

Sarah wanted to spit out, "seven just like everyone else," but in a small voice she said, "none."

The woman clucked her tongue in sympathy. "Husband?" She twisted her wedding band.

Sarah shook her head.

"Never mind." The woman laughed. "But why no marry?"

Sarah frowned. There it was again, that irritating question.

"Is something the matter with you?"

"No."

"Then marry." The woman flicked her wet hair behind her and wriggled into her long brown dress; she cradled her arms a foot in front of her belly and said, giggling. "Marry and have many babies." From a string bag, she pulled a hard-boiled egg, cracked it on her knee, and peeled it, letting bits of shell fall onto the ground. She popped out the yolk and placed it in the palm of Sarah's hand. "Be strong. Eat."

"Thank you." Sarah forced herself to chew the soft yolk, which was so dry and tasteless she wanted to spit it out. "This is a pretty place," she said politely.

"The Adari pool is more beautiful by far. We also call it, 'Pool of the Virgin.'"

Sarah squirmed. If any word here was loaded, it was "virgin," but she forced herself to sit still, a forced smile plastered on her face.

"*Kaan ma kaan*...it was, it was not," the woman began in the slow voice of the storyteller. "Long ago, a prince on a white stallion was journeying in the desert. From far off, he saw a girl standing alone. He galloped up until he was so close he could see the flutter of her eyelashes, and at once, he fell in love with her. He said he couldn't marry her unless she was a virgin. The girl averred she was, but he insisted on a test. He told her to stick her little toe in this sand, and if she were truly virgin, water would spring up. The girl did as he said, and water bubbled up." The woman ran her fingers through her hair. "Such an excellent story."

"Yes, very nice," Sarah said. The women gathered up their laundry and started to leave. At the fork in the path, they looked back and waved goodbye. At last alone, she reached down to dabble her fingers in the water. What would these women think of the anecdote about the statue of 'Honest Abe' in Madison—that Lincoln would rise up from his bronze chair if a virgin passed by—a phenomenon so unlikely that he would be sitting there forever? She lifted her hand, and the droplets shone in the light and fell soundlessly back in the water. It was beautiful here, but Ib was waiting. As she threw on the cloak and headed back toward town, she decided that one day she would return to paint the scene.

He carried the picnic basket as they walked through the fields, the shrill cry of cicadas filling the air. They passed a scarecrow—two crossed sticks with a tattered thobe thrown over them—and a hundred yards further they came to a shack with a pitched roof. Inside, diamonds of light wavered on the sand where the sun pierced the latticed slats. At the far end, tawny cattle were lowing and one was licking her calf's ear. Ib spread a white cloth on the sand and set out the food: black olives, roasted chicken, a round of goat cheese, and sliced tomatoes sprinkled with parsley. He passed her a paper plate and asked if she had seen his mother.

"I don't think so." She reached for a Pepsi.

"Shall we visit her after we finish eating?"

"Oh, please, not today, not when I've finally got you to myself."

He squared his shoulders and said stiffly, "Sarah, you do need to meet her. I'm beginning to worry about it."

"Well, I like Layla and your father, so I'm sure it'll be just fine." She gnawed on a garlicky chicken leg and reached for the dates.

"Are you missing home?" he asked.

She had not considered the idea, but she supposed she was, especially her mother. "I wonder how the early oilmen managed without e-mail."

"But you're surviving?"

"Yes. Work is good. It sounds pretentious, but I like being a role model for my residents. And I like Annie."

"I am glad." He slashed a pomegranate with his penknife and dug out the ruby seeds. "Here, try them."

She made a face. "They're too tart. I'd rather have dates." She ate three, one right after the other, each soft, sweet and chewy.

He chuckled. "A true woman of the desert."

"How about you? Don't you miss the States?"

"The States? Oh, sure. The four-way stops... oh, and the cheerleaders with red pompoms. And let us not forget the squirrels."

Laughing, she rumpled his hair.

"And you?"

"Lots." She drew her knees up under her chin. She pictured the chickadees in the fragrant pine woods; skinny-dipping in the cold lake on dark summer nights; eating salty popcorn at the movies; walking hand-in-hand with him down State Street in Madison.

"You look sad."

"Maybe I am, a little. Still, it's peaceful here. It's as if we're a million miles from anywhere."

He took her hand, traced light circles on her palm, and then licked the sticky date off each finger. He brushed the hair from her forehead and ran his hand over her temples and cheeks. He kissed her eyelids and the curve of her ear, and she felt his tongue spiraling. Then he drew one finger over her lips and they kissed deeply. He stroked her throat, and she put his hand on her breast and he kissed it. He undid her blouse buttons and was pushing back her bra to suck her nipples when out of nowhere burst a shout. "*Quf*!"

He stiffened, and jammed his hand over her mouth. "Shh." She pulled away, gathering the cloak around her. "What is it?" she whispered, nauseous with mingled desire and fear.

He crept to the door and pulled the flap aside. She saw the flock huddled in a tatty-fleeced cluster and the shepherd shaking his staff as he clambered after an errant sheep.

"We're lucky he didn't see us." She buttoned her blouse, her throat so dry she croaked out the words.

"It had nothing to do with us." His eyes glittered, and he was breathing fast.

"We better be careful. I don't want to get, you know, stoned," she stammered.

"I got carried away. Forgive me." He picked up a pebble and clenched his fist so hard around it that his knuckles formed white knobs. "Allah, have mercy," he cried and hurled the stone.

It clinked somewhere off in the distance. She thrust her hands into the abaya's narrow sleeve openings. Last winter in Madison when they had watched children making snow angels, he had said angels were made of light energy and were watching, writing down their deeds. He had tapped his right shoulder, and a flurry of snowflakes flew off. "This angel here records my good deeds, and this one"—he tapped his left shoulder—"my bad deeds. We're accountable." Another time when he had heard about a serial rapist sentenced to four years in prison, he had been incensed. "Think of those girls," he had said. "Ruined! Four years is not justice! Then the predator will be back on the streets. He should be executed."

Now she studied his profile. "Did you ever take part in a stoning?"

"What? No, it would make me quite sick."

"What about your brother?"

Ib shrugged. "Shaheed believes it is his duty, everyone's duty. Otherwise, it is not a deterrent. I do not agree, but I understand him."

"Well, I don't. You're always making excuses for him. I was just thinking..." her voice trailed off. "I was just thinking about...well, I find it difficult to accept your devotion to Islam."

He colored. "What are you saying? That my faith is a pretense?" Indignant, he raised his voice. "I may not say *Insha'Allah* every two minutes the way my brother does, but I am sincere."

"I'm sorry," she said quietly. "I didn't mean to insult you. I'm trying to understand you."

"People like my brother are the ones you need to understand. Things are changing so fast. Now it is all computers, cell phones, and satellite TV. Not everyone adapts. His fundamentalism gives Shaheed a sense of certainty and being a *mutawwa* gives him respectability. He has put in a lot of time to become one. He is dedicated. But he never thinks before he acts; he just reacts. He is too easily swayed by his boss and those who believe things were best long ago when the Prophet lived. I try not to argue. After all, the issue is deeper than logic so we have to be patient."

"Patient?" she laughed. "You know me. It's not my nature."

"Just remember, you need not have anything to do with Shaheed. Ever."

"I sure hope not."

Ib crossed his arms. "What is that supposed to mean?"

"Just that I don't think I'd like him."

"Soon you will decide, for us or against us. After all, that is why you are here. To see if I am what you Americans call an 'acceptable risk.'"

She took in his hostile tone. "You know I don't talk like that," she said softly.

"But you think like that. Look, I realize you need to be able to tell your family, 'I have seen it over there. I can take it.' And if you cannot, you will go home and say, 'Oh no, I could never live *there*.' How do you think it makes me feel to know that you are judging us every minute?"

"But you asked me to come. And I am trying." She paused, searching for a non-offensive way to phrase her concern. "But everything—your religion and culture—is so *hard*."

"But you are flexible and courageous. Please hurry and decide. Meet my mother, please."

She smiled and squeezed his hand. "But not today. Next weekend at the camping trip."

CHAPTER 5

IT WAS LATE AFTERNOON when they reached the campsite. Lulu and the twins tumbled out of the SUV and raced toward the white tents, spread in an east-west formation on the horizon. Ibrahim's father, as the patriarch, was the first to greet Sarah. It seemed strange to see old Mr. Suleiman out of the hospital setting, but he was cordial and asked her to call him Omar. Ibrahim's grandmother, wizened and stooped with age, with a V-shaped tattoo of blue-gray dots on her forehead, stood on tiptoe to kiss Sarah's cheek. Shaheed's wife Susu, her cheeks pocked with teenage acne, came up, an infant in her arms. Sarah held out a finger, and the baby grasped it. "Such a strong grip," she said.

"Yes, Saladin will be like his father." Then, noticing that Ib was approaching, Susu slipped off.

"Well, this is it. You look so tense," he said. "Are you ready?"

Sweat slid down Sarah's arm pits. It was just the heat, she told herself as she brushed the collar of her mouse-gray dress. High-necked, long-sleeved, and ankle-length, it looked like a nun's habit, but it was what Ib had suggested she wear to meet his mother. He held the tent flap open, and she went in. It took a moment for her eyes to adjust to the darkness. At the rear of the tent sat a husky woman, adorned like a barbarian queen. Silver coins dangled from a black head scarf onto her high cheekbones, and when she raised her hand for Ib to kiss, gold bangles jangled on her wrist. She had a dowager's hump, and under the cloak she wore a dress of metallic gold. Sarah had the oddest sensation that his mother expected her to kneel at her huge feet and kiss the turquoise ring on her horny big toe.

"Mother, I have the honor of presenting Sarah, the sister of my friend, Peter," Ib said in Arabic.

Malika's eyes darted from Ib to Sarah and back to her son again. "Oh, so you're here," she said coldly.

Sarah flinched at the snub.

"Mother!" Ib said, shock in his voice.

"Dr. Sarah is a physician at our hospital," his father said, a troubled look on his face.

"Call me Um Ibrahim," Ib's mother commanded.

So. She Who Must Be Obeyed had spoken.

"It means 'mother of Ibrahim,'" Ib explained as if Sarah did not know that. "It is our custom for a woman to be named after her first son."

"It is my honor to meet you." Sarah gave her a bright false smile.

Cataracts clouded Malika's rust-brown eyes, her waist was thick and her black hair was shot through with gray.

"Welcome. Sit." Malika gestured toward a bolster covered in green paisley.

"So now we have a doctor in the tent," Ib said wryly, to defuse the tension.

His father gave a belly laugh and covered his mouth. "Please forgive me. I laugh all the time and show my bad yellow teeth."

"What has brought you to Arabia?" Malika asked.

"Oh, to work, and well, just to see it." Sarah forced a smile.

"It must be pleasant to travel just because you want to see something."

Sarah squirmed. Accustomed to the deference of patients and staff, it had been a long time since anyone had made her feel insignificant. The name Malika meant "queen," which seemed ominous.

"Now—tea." Malika's muscles shifted under her cloak as she poured it into Sarah's gold-rimmed glass.

"No sugar please. I don't—"

"The more the sugar the greater the welcome," Malika pronounced, and plop, plop, plop, in went three sugar cubes. In the next quarter hour, she refilled the glass four times. Nostrils flared, she kept glancing from Sarah to Ib, who was doodling with his finger in the sand. It was as if his mother suspected something and was trying to sniff it out, and Sarah tucked her head to avoid the scrutiny. Layla came in and asked if Sarah would like to go see the camels.

"I'd like to ride one," Sarah said.

"Not now," Malika said. "Now it's too hot. And to ride a camel is tiring for a woman.

Sarah looked at the pretty brown and pink striped dress that Layla was wearing. It was cinched at the waist with a narrow belt, which must be uncomfortable in the hundred-degree heat. Sarah didn't directly contradict Malika, but she described the British travelers of the nineteenth century—women like Jane Digby and Lady Hester Stanhope—and how they had crossed Arabia in riding jackets of green satin, riding sidesaddle on camels. If those women could do it, then she wanted to try too.

"Don't," Layla said. "Mother is right. You're not used to the heat, but those jackets of green satin, how beautiful they must have been. I'd love one. Come now, let me show you our falcons. You'll like that."

"A fine idea," Malika said. "You go now."

Sarah grumpily followed Layla out. Falcons did not interest her. She thought of the camel caravans of the past, the ungainly beasts bearing packs stuffed with incense, ivory, perfume, and precious stones.

"I suppose I should have asked Mother to come too. She fancies herself a falconress." Layla put a few quail eggs and a leather cuff in a basket, and they walked to the end of the campsite where two falcons were tethered on posts covered with remnants of carpet. Each bird wore a leather hood, neatly peaked in a feather. Layla stretched out her arm and Sarah strapped the cuff onto her wrist for protection against the bird's claws. "Bright Eyes, you first. That's what Mother calls him. Handsome, isn't he, with his dappled breast and narrow pointed wings. He's a Barbary falcon. It's Shaheed's." Once unhooded, the bird shuddered, gave a raucous cry, and clenched its talons. It hopped onto Layla's wrist and pecked at the leather cuff until she fed it the eggs. Feeling slightly disgusted, Sarah turned and saw a man plodding through the sand.

"Look ever there. Someone's coming," she said.

"It's Shaheed back from Mecca. I'd like to introduce you, but I better not." Layla hooded Bright Eyes and set him back on his post.

"Why not? I meet men all the time in the hospital."

"Well, that's different."

"What was he doing in Mecca?"

"Some sort of *mutawwa* training. I wish he'd find a proper job. Those men can be monsters. Well, I'm introducing you whether he likes it or not. Stand still a second." She tucked in a strand that had slipped out from under Sarah's head scarf. "You don't want the Sheriff to see your curls."

When he was within hailing distance, Layla called out, "Shaheed! Over here!"

He had a lamb slung over his shoulders, his pointed face was half-hidden by his black beard, and he looked just like his picture in Layla's album. He wore his robe shin-length. Hard-liners wore it that way, Annie had once told her, because it was the fashion in Muhammad's day.

"Shaheed, this is Sarah, the sister of Peter, Ibrahim's friend," Layla said.

Sarah forced a smile and stretched out her hand, but Shaheed put both of his behind his back and stared fixedly at a spot a few inches to the right of her face. Feeling insulted, she let her hand fall. He stalked off, muttering something about needing to help Ibrahim with the barbecue.

"He doesn't mean to be rude," Layla said. "I should have told you that his gang don't shake hands with women. He's not used to seeing women unveiled—except for our family. But you needn't have anything to do with him, so don't worry about him."

"You must be a special family to be so divided and yet get along." Sarah felt irritated, but she kept her voice neutral.

"Sometimes it's war." Layla laughed.

"Your father is so easygoing and modern yet your mother is traditional. It seems a little odd the two of them got married."

"Anyway, who talks politics in bed? Ah Sarah, you must marry, but find a man who's not in love with politics."

"But politics is good. It's how we can make things better."

Layla laughed. "You sound like Ahmed. Oh, politics, politics. Everywhere politics."

That night there was a party in the women's tent. The women were dressed in silks and sequins, and Sarah wished she had brought along something more elegant. Her rival Tisam was there, in a shimmering dress of pongee silk, an arm flung affectionately around Malika's shoulders. A maid came in with a beaker of rosewater and went from one woman to another pouring a thin stream of rosewater into their open palms. A CD of dance music was playing, and Tisam was the first to get up. She stamped her bare feet on the striped carpet, her anklets jingling, and shooting flashes of light. Her hair cascaded down her back, and she twisted a red scarf back and forth across her slim hips. The women started to clap in time with the music, and Tisam kept dancing until she swung the red scarf and it floated across the air to Sarah.

"Dance, Sarah, dance," the women chanted. At first, she did not want to, but she got up and the women cheered her on, saying how amazing it was she could dance like them. She was feeling hot and happy, when much later Layla took her by the hand and led her to the long table where platters of food were set on the gold and white embroidered tablecloth. On a bed of saffron rice, sprinkled with almonds, pistachios and raisins, lay a lamb, an apple between its pointy teeth. She divined it was the lamb she had seen a few hours earlier on Shaheed's shoulders.

"Eat! You eat," Malika plucked a hunk of lamb and put it on Sarah's plate.

"Please, sit with me." Tisam patted a place next to her on the green paisley bolster. She was curious about Wisconsin and listened with inordinate interest while Sarah told her about the pleasures of Madison. Meanwhile the other women argued about the new identity cards. "Show my face to a strange man? Never," Malika said. "And that includes a photographer. My name is on my husband's passport. That's good enough."

"Darling Auntie, you deserve your own card," Tisam said, jumping in. "And I myself will take your picture."

Layla touched the pink chiffon ruffles with picot edging that formed the collar of her dress. "This is what I'd like to wear for my ID card. Still it's just a piece of plastic and won't make any difference."

"Of course, it will," Tisam said. "Absolutely, it will."

"Rubbish! What difference can a card make? None, I tell you," said a woman in a gold caftan.

"Oh, Fakriya, of course, it will," Tisam said. "It's a baby step, but we will go step by step, and soon we shall be free. Little by little, step by step, that's the way." She called for one of the maids to bring Perrier and apple juice. "Saudi champagne," she cheered as she filled their glasses. "For you, too, Auntie Malika. Sisters and friends, sisters, all of us. Raise your glasses. A toast to identity cards. You, too, Fakriya." Tisam clinked her glass and spread wide her arms and ululated, and all the women threw back their heads, opened wide their mouths, and yowled, flapping their tongues. It was the eerie cry Sarah had heard at the airport, but when she opened her mouth, trying to go along, she could not. After dessert—*baklava* and *petits fours*—a maid brought in an incense burner, and the women passed it from one to the other, wafting the fumes through their hair and under their glittering dresses. Tisam handed the brass-studded burner to Sarah. "It's frankincense—the deodorant of the desert. Try it."

As she had seen the others do, Sarah wafted the incense through her hair and then spread the skirt of her gray dress wide and felt the aromatic fumes, hot against her thighs.

"It won't burn," Layla said, laughing. "Ladies, ladies…listen. Our Sarah is a doctor. Sarah, tell everybody about your work."

"And do you like sick people?" Tisam asked.

No one had ever asked her that. Sarah reflected a moment and said, "I like curing them."

"Don't you think the hospital is backward—just a little?"

"Oh Tisam, what a terrible thing to say," Layla said.

"No, it's excellent, but it could be even better." Sarah told them about the teen who had miscarried her first day at work and said the baby might have been saved if the girl had come in earlier on her own instead of having to wait for her guardian.

"No, no Sarah. It's not like that. Not at all," Layla said, patting her hand. "How awful it would be for that poor girl if she had to come in all alone, to get terrible news all alone. Every girl wants a man from her family, to be there for her, to help break any bad news."

"But if she'd arrived earlier, there might have been no bad news."

"That can't happen very often, and she can have other babies. Don't worry about her. The person to worry about is you. How do you cope with all the deaths?"

"Sometimes we joke, rather grim jokes. It keeps us detached. And we—that's all of us, doctors, nurses, techs—we have *esprit de corps*."

"And when someone dies?"

"We're trained to be detached, and we pull most people through. Most days we just treat cut fingers, sore throats and headaches. Little things."

"But when people die, what's it like?"

"Sometimes I worry half the night that I've screwed up."

Layla threw up her hands. "But it's not your fault."

"Sometimes just being a minute or two quicker makes all the difference. Anyway, the doctor is always potentially at fault."

"That girl who miscarried? Perhaps it was her fate."

"Of course," Malika said, joining the conversation. "The physician is not responsible. Allah decides. Allah provides the cure. The doctor and the medicines are just his instruments."

"Oh, Auntie, the doctors are good," Tisam interjected. "I wish you would let them cure your blindness." She smiled up at Malika and stroked her iron-gray hair.

"Nonsense. In paradise I will see perfectly."

Someone turned up the volume and more women stood up to dance. They spread their bright skirts, made bird-like movements with their hands, swung their hair from side to side, and barely moved their feet as their bellies rippled beneath the frothy dresses. Meanwhile the women left at the table were gossiping. "See her?" Tisam pointed to one of the women dancing. "She beats the nanny because her husband sleeps with her. I bet that doesn't happen in the States."

"We don't have nannies, at least not many. But I've treated lots of battered women, especially after big games when husbands take out their anger on their wives for their team's loss."

"Every now and then our men beat us, but really they are the ones who are afraid. They're terrified we'll run off to Lebanon to get an abortion." At that word, Sarah flinched, remembering her own guilty secret. Tisam hastened to explain. "Too many babies, you see."

"Impossible," Malika growled. "A child is a gift from Allah."

"Oh, Auntie, we have too many of these gifts."

"Don't jabber, my girl. Let me tell you, in some places, women do something to learn if they're carrying a girl—"

"Those are sonograms, Auntie."

"Never mind, it doesn't matter the name. When they find it's a girl, they abort her. That is evil. At the Day of Judgment, the baby girl buried alive will be asked for what crime she was killed."

"Auntie, Auntie." Tisam patted her on the arm. "I don't want abortion, just birth control."

Malika ranted on about how birth control led to promiscuity until Layla got up and put her arms around them both. "Don't fight. Please don't fight. Let other women practice birth control. For myself, I want lots of babies. Yes, Mother, lots." She reached her hands up and played with her earrings. "At least one more—four pearls at my ears, four dear babies in my heart."

"Four?" Sarah said.

"And the next one should be a girl. Lulu needs a sister." In one of her lightning shifts of topic, Layla placed her hand on Sarah's arm. "Do you know Tisam reads three newspapers a day? Amazing!"

Sarah smiled politely at yet another of her rival's accomplishments.

"They're interesting," Tisam said. "Today I read how a father whose son was killed agreed to accept blood money. Everyone cheered, and it was as joyful as a wedding until the mother shouted, 'If there is no punishment for crimes, there is no peace.' So her husband, poor man, had to call back the executioner."

"Aiyeee," Layla cried. "And then?"

Tisam sliced the air with a swift downward chop with her hand.

"Oh, she should forgive him." Layla was trembling, her face deathly pale. "If her husband could forgive the murderer, she should too. She must."

"Don't get upset, my daughter. It is the Law of Moses. Those who kill are killed in turn."

"And if she had forgiven him?" Sarah asked.

"Well, then he'd be free, of course." Malika looked at her as if she were an idiot, but it seemed to Sarah that she had asked a perfectly reasonable question. Murderers should not get off scot-free because the victims' families forgave them, whatever that meant.

"Layla's right," Tisam put in. "Forgiveness is best, but still we must fight evil."

"Do you know how Tisam does that?" Layla tittered. "With comics."

"Political cartoons," Tisam corrected.

"Oh, they're bold," Layla said. "Go get them to show Sarah."

Tisam left and came back with an oversized black case. She pulled out several strips of *Aisha the Warrior*. Sarah studied them, secretly pleased her rival was not particularly talented at drawing. One strip showed women washing dishes with their degrees above the sink, M.A., B.S., Ph.D. M.D., while Aisha rode a hot air balloon trailing the message, "Celebrate Saudi inferiority."

"This is my favorite." Layla picked up one that depicted a woman standing beside a Mercedes, a Cadillac, and a Rolls Royce. The caption was, "I own them. Let me drive them."

"If we make fun of the system, people will see how ridiculous it is," Tisam said.

"But aren't you afraid?" Sarah looked up at her.

"Of course, but I won't let that stop me," Tisam said passionately, "*Abadan*. Never. My friends say my work is disrespectful. Oh, they are so timid."

"And you are far too bold," Layla scolded. "Politics, politics, always politics. I get so tired of it. Let's not talk politics tonight. Let's dress Sarah like a princess."

There seemed no polite way to get out of it, so she said that would be nice. As Layla ran off to get the dress, the others went back to dancing, leaving Tisam and Sarah alone.

"Sarah, may I trouble you? It's a delicate matter." Tisam glanced over her shoulder as if to check no one was eavesdropping. "Well, this is it, then." She lowered her voice. "Might you have a Bible that I could borrow?"

"A Bible?" Sarah was taken aback. "I'm sorry. I don't."

"Oh, I assumed you were a —"

Sarah suggested she try the bookstore in the mall.

"There's no point. Nobody has them. Please don't tell anyone I asked. You see, I think so often of evil, and I remember how Jesus, peace be upon him, once saved the life of an adulteress. Why did he save her miserable life?" Tisam's eyes flashed. "The commandment is to stone her. Of course, I may not get to paradise either as I'm quite bad." She looked down at her hands, folded in her lap.

"Oh no, that's not so." Sarah would have liked to continue the conversation, but Layla was back with a gown, and the women crowded around. Sarah took off her mouse-gray outfit and stepped into the diaphanous dress, which was purple, heavily embroidered with gold thread, and studded with sequins. As Layla fussed over her, applying eyeliner, mascara, and rouge and exclaiming how milky her skin was, how thick and red her hair, Sarah felt with some humiliation as if she were a doll to be dressed and undressed. Then she felt Malika's eyes on her, watching her as if she were a slave on the block, every bit of her up for inspection. "Such short hair just like a boy." Malika grabbed a strand of hair with her ring-encrusted fingers and tugged it. Sarah winced and pushed away the probing hand. Malika leaned over to her neighbor, whispered in her ear, and the woman guffawed. Had Malika really said Sarah had a boy's behind? She was about to bolt when the grandmother bellowed at Malika to mind her manners.

"Yes, Um Omar." Malika bowed her head.

"Auntie Malika, everyone can see that Sarah is slender," Tisam said sharply. "Like Susu, but slenderer."

"Yes, slender as a reed," the others chimed in, and Sarah felt much better.

"And beautiful, too, now I've made up her eyes." Layla dabbed perfume behind Sarah's earlobes. "Do you like this? It's grapefruit, the fragrance of this season."

"Fashion, fashion," Malika grumbled. "All this girl of mine cares for is fashion. New dresses. New perfumes. New shoes. It's always the same. Brand-new this and brand-new that."

"Hair so beautiful, the color of saffron, so lucky your husband will be," Layla said, paying no attention to her mother. She put a mirror in Sarah's hand. "See what a beauty you are."

How quickly her own moods changed, Sarah thought as she looked at herself, dressed in iridescent purple and gold with red lips and kohl-rimmed eyes. She felt surprised and oddly proud at looking so sexy.

"Ah, such a beauty. And free," Tisam whispered in her ear.

When Malika lumbered over toward her, Sarah jumped up and skittered off to put Lulu to bed. At first the child whined, but Sarah tucked her in the cot and sang her a Brahms lullaby. She lit a few candles and the tent filled with the glimmer and smell of wax as Lulu lay stroking the satin edging of her blankie. As Sarah undressed, she thought she would like Ib to see her dressed in this finery, but he was off with the men of the family. A while later, the grandmother came in and said her prayers. Something about her loud whisperings sounded familiar, and Sarah groped about in her mind for what it could be.

The crone blew out the candles and climbed into bed. "Sarah," she whispered loudly. "Is it true what Layla told me, that in your country, you send children no bigger than Lulu to sleep in a room all alone?"

Sarah pulled the sheet up to her chin. What could she say? That, of course, it was true and nobody thought anything of it.

"They say Americans let even babies sleep all alone. And you, my dear, why is it that you've wandered so far from home? How must your parents feel?"

"I have a good job. I like to travel. They are happy for me."

"Praise Allah." The grandmother yawned noisily, and soon her breaths came in little rasps. Lulu was still asleep, curled up with her thumb in her mouth. Sarah stroked her frizzy ringlets and then slipped out of the tent.

The sky was blazing with stars big as mothballs, and the sickle moon shone so brightly she could make out the camels couched for the night between the water trucks. She picked her steps, creeping behind the line of tents, careful not to trip over a guy rope. A small camel tottered toward her on spindly legs, and she patted its soft fur. She sat there a while, wondering if Ib would appear as he had said he might. Never before had she seen so many stars. The one time that came close was one night on Deep Lake in her canoe far from the shore. Now as she spotted the Big Dipper, she wished she could tell the constellations apart and know them all by name. It came to her then what was familiar about the grandmother's prayer: it was the sound of love in her booming, the same as in Mom's tone of voice when she prayed.

Ib stepped out of the shadow and sat beside her on the cool sand. "How did it go?" he asked.

"Tisam and Layla were nice, and your grandmother likes me. She yelled at your mother."

"She is deaf."

Sarah explained about his mother's nasty remark. "You have an aunt in Riyadh, don't you? Maybe your grandmother would be happier living with her."

"With us, the mother lives with her eldest son."

Sarah dug her toes in the sand, making a little rut. "Truthfully, do you like living here? Don't you find it just a little bit boring? No movies, no concerts, no dances."

"You are thinking that a camel ride might be fun. A little adventure." He squeezed her hand. "I will see what I can do."

"About your mother. I don't know what to call her. Nothing sounds right."

"Why not Um Ibrahim? It is an easy way of being respectful."

"Mother of Ibrahim? That makes it sound like you're her property."

"It works both ways," Ib said smiling. "It is good both ways."

"So you say. I don't know."

As they ambled back to the tents, he held her hand. With the starlight, there was no need, but she was glad of it.

"See, there is Venus," he said, pointing a finger at the sky. "Your name for the goddess Ishtar."

"The one who had a fondness for men?"

"Like you for me. Remember?"

She felt pleased that he had not forgotten their only date here. He showed her Mercury, and Mars, then Cassiopeia, Sirius, and the Pleiades. With his finger, he drew an imaginary line from one star to the next, tracing the constellations dot-to-dot. They did not touch, but in his romantic way he called her his companion star and told her how ours was the smallest one of seven universes folded within the palm of God's hand, and how it would take humans billions of years to count the stars, but God created and controlled them all. The heavens showed the abundance and excess that was the glory of God.

She edged away from him. "You're so spiritual. Maybe I'm not right for you. Maybe Tisam—"

He pulled her to him, his arms tight around her. "She is just a cousin to me. Nothing else. Nothing. In any case, she would not have me."

"Why not?"

"Frankly Sarah, I do not care."

CHAPTER 6

THE NEXT MORNING WHEN SARAH AWAKENED, she was alone. She peered through the tent flap and saw Malika squatting by the campfire pounding coffee beans in a mortar. Clang. Clang. Clang. On a chest in a corner of the tent was a basin with lukewarm water, and Sarah washed, pulled on her jeans, tossed an abaya over her shoulders, and stepped out. Instead of the eternal flat blue sky, a cloud floated above, fleecy white above the rippled sands; it was a perfect day for a jaunt in the desert.

"Another of the Lord's glorious days," the grandmother boomed. She patted a space beside her on the carpet where plates of bread, olives, jam, and hard white cheese were set. Opposite them, Layla was brushing Lulu's tousled hair. Once she had smoothed out the mass of tangles, she made a part, separating the hair into two bunches, each of which she would braid into three plaits. "See over there?" she said, turning to Sarah. "Shaheed's boss." She motioned toward the strangers sitting cross-legged around the far campfire.

"Which one is his boss?"

"The handsome one, Kabeer. Shaheed would follow him into a blazing furnace." Layla continued braiding.

Kabeer was patting a honey-colored saluki dog. When he stood up, Sarah saw he was slim, about six feet, and fair-skinned with symmetrical features. The instant he saw her, he turned his back on her.

"All because of him, my husband left the camp. Just an hour ago. Or maybe Ahmed was just looking for an excuse to get away."

"That's too bad. I was hoping he'd come camel riding."

"Ahmed? Camel riding?" Layla doubled over laughing. "Never. He's a city boy."

Sarah glanced over to the men. She could not make out what they were arguing about, but she could imagine. With Kabeer there, Shaheed would say that she was a woman and must stay with the women, and that would be that. She would be stuck brushing off sticky flies and personal questions from Malika. She jumped up. "I'm going to talk to them."

Layla tugged her back. "Better not. It'll just make things worse. Would you do me a favor?" She lowered her voice. "I'm dying for a cigarette. It's been fourteen hours since I had my last one. Keep an eye on Lulu for me, would you?"

"Sure." It was pleasant piling up the sand and sifting it through her fingers. She would have liked to make a sand castle with Lulu but the sand was too dry to shape. Instead, Sarah drew a grid for tic-tac-toe in the sand, and they played that for a while. Then they amused themselves by making hearts of all shapes and sizes in the sand until Layla came back. She had good news: Ib had persuaded his father to let Sarah come by insisting that she was a guest too, every bit as much as Kabeer.

"So. Hospitality rules," Sarah said, miffed that they had felt obliged to have her.

"Don't put it like that. I'm coming along so you won't feel lonely with all those men. Want to borrow a face veil? You're already sunburned. It'll give you a little privacy too."

"Oh, no, I'll be fine."

"It might be a good idea. It's windy."

"Oh, I'll be fine." It was far too complicated to explain how it was a point of honor with her not to cover her face. She would wear the head scarf and the abaya, but as for covering her face, well, that was different. There she drew the line.

"As you like." Layla puckered her brow. "Mother is already singing those sad songs she likes. I'll go cheer her up. She doesn't like it when we all go off and leave her."

Malika sulking? A hot mean spurt of pleasure zipped through Sarah.

Her camel was chocolate brown with matted fur, a full hump, and a droopy lower lip. Ib tossed a red blanket over the saddle. "Isn't she a beauty!" he yelled.

Sarah eyed the slobber running from the camel's mouth. The camel hissed, bared her yellow teeth, and Sarah jumped to avoid the spittle. "I'll call her Spitter."

"A good name," Ib said, laughing. He pulled at the black-and-white harness and persuaded Spitter to crouch, kneeling first on its forelegs and then swinging backwards to rest on its hind legs. With Ib's help, she managed to swing one leg over the padded saddlebags and to seat herself forward on the saddle, her legs spread so wide that she felt as if she were doing the splits.

"Giddy-up. Giddy-up," she cried. The camel did not budge.

The twins rode up alongside. "Thwack her," they yelled in unison.

She did, and at once Spitter lurched backward, then so far forward onto its knees that she almost toppled off. Ib handed her one end of the rope he had looped through one of Spitter's nostrils. "Are you sure you want to do this?"

"I've been horseback riding since I was five. It can't be that different. Let's go. Giddy-up, giddy-up."

"Here we say, houtch, houtch, houtch." He mounted his camel, scrambling up its neck, and kneeled on the saddle, balancing on the soles of his feet. Leaning forward, he cried, "Houtch, houtch, houtch, nyin, nyin nyin, houtch, houtch," and he was off.

She mimicked his call, "Houtch, houtch, houtch…"

"Shout like you mean it," Ib yelled, turning back.

She tried again, but Spitter did not stir until Ib circled back to call "houtch, houtch" into its ear. The saluki hounds loped alongside as she, Ib and Layla plodded three abreast along the rocky, sand-covered ridges. It was unlike riding a horse, more of a swaying motion, like being at sea, and after a while, Sarah relaxed. "There now, easy does it," she crooned as she tilted back and forth in the saddle, the shadow of the Spitter looming on the sand to the west. They rode past clumps of thorn bush and sage, and at the crest of a dune, she spotted a fox, its ears raised. She could not imagine what a fox was doing in the desert, but no one paid it any attention, and it slunk off.

The wind picked up and Layla doubled the veil over her face. They were traveling faster, and Sarah's back and legs ached, and particles of sand stung her face like red-hot needles. However, none of that mattered. What mattered was following Ib's red-and-white headdress whipping in the breeze as they advanced along the sands.

"Sure you're okay?" He drew up so close that his camel brushed against hers. "If you like, we can go back, the three of us. It's okay with Layla."

"Oh, no, I'm fine," she lied. She glanced at her watch. They had been riding over an hour without a break. "Maybe, do you think we could go just a little slower?"

He quit his Houtch-nyin call, and the camels slowed to a steady plodding. As they fell further behind the tribesmen, Layla told her how when Ib was young, he once made the pilgrimage to Mecca partway by camel. He and Shaheed had flown to Riyadh and then traveled westward for twenty-one days along the routes used in antiquity by the spice merchants.

"Three weeks of this," Sarah said to him. "How could you stand it?"

"He was on pilgrimage," Layla said. "It's supposed to be hard."

"I was doing it to prove myself—vanity really—but Shaheed did it out of pure spiritual desire. Even so, I felt part of something vital. My grandfather had just died, and the pilgrimage consoled me."

"Holy people say the pilgrimage enables us to forgive," Layla put in.

"Sounds more like a macho test," Sarah said.

"If you say so." Ib laughed a deep belly laugh. "And that year the pilgrimage fell in spring, which made it pleasant." He glanced up toward the blazing sun. "Sure is a scorcher today."

Eventually they caught up with the men, who were seated in a circle and chatting while they waited. Nearby the falcons ruffled their feathers as they perched on posts buried in the sand. As Sarah dismounted, her legs wobbled, and her blouse, drenched in sweat, stuck to her. She had forgotten her Raybans and the glare had given her a headache. She took off her sandals and placed them beside Layla's pink Jimmy Choos, far from the heap of stout leather thongs.

Ib left her and Layla and went to join the men on the far side of the carpet. A few minutes later, he came back looking grim.

"What was all that about?" Sarah asked.

"Kabeer is fuming because you are not veiled."

"Oh, I'll just do it," Sarah snapped. She felt exhausted and faint, and thirsty.

"There is no need. I told him that you kept your hair covered, which is all that is required of American women."

"Sarah, dear, you're white as a sheet." Layla touched her cheek. "Your skin feels clammy."

"I'm fine," Sarah lied. Her face was burning and she wished she had worn a veil, this once, but it was too late. Ib had already put himself out, and if she changed her mind now, it would make him look silly.

The sun was directly overhead, and Kabeer led the noon prayers; Shaheed, Ib, and the tribesmen gathered in a line behind him while the twins and Layla stood behind them. Sarah sat apart some distance away, alone on the mat, feeling alien and unattractive, her lips cracked by the sun, sand in every pore, and her mouth dry. She felt half-dead with thirst; the cooler with bottled water and cans of Pepsi was just a few feet away, but to reach it, she would have to cross in front of the men at prayer. That would be unforgivable, so she staggered a hundred yards back to the spot where the camels were hobbled, only to find her water bottle was not in Spitter's saddlebag. She trudged back, but met the others who had finished their prayers and were ready to leave. The water cooler was nowhere in sight. She hoped that they were returning to the camp, but the men had sighted prey. They headed up a dune. "Houtch, houtch, houtch, nyin nyin nyin, houtch, houtch, houtch." She held on for dear life, sweat running down her sides.

"Bustard to the west," Shaheed yelled. "Straight ahead, halfway up." He unhooded Bright Eyes, untied it from its jesses, and raised his wrist; it caught the scent and was off. The salukis, long ears flapping, raced ahead as the falcon soared, circled wide, then spiraled inward, and plummeted.

"*Yalla.* It's down." Shaheed cried.

When the men came back, Shaheed plucked the dead bustard from his camel bag and showed it off, spreading its wings. The tribesmen massaged their toes and argued interminably about the price of falcons. Kabeer caressed his, a gray saker falcon with a white speckled breast. "Last winter I kept mine in the garage. That saved me buying a new one. Sixty thousand riyals, the price of a pickup truck."

"A pity," Ib said. "I would set the bird free. Otherwise, it is just a pet. I wish to admire that which I love." He looked directly at Sarah as if he intended this as a compliment to her.

"Please, somebody, may I have water?" she called in a weak voice. The throbbing in her head was excruciating.

Shaheed, who was next to the cooler, took out a bottle of Perrier, and

walked all the way over to Layla, who was sitting a few feet beyond
Sarah, so his sister could hand it to her.

"What do you think I am? A leper?" Sarah hissed at him. She drained
the fizzy liquid. She could not stand the sight of him; she could not take
it an instant longer; she would head back on her own. She rolled to her
side and tried to push herself up; the sand burned her palms, and she
sank back onto the rug. Again, she tried to stand, but her knees buckled.
"Ib, help me. Please help," she called. Again, she tried to get up, but she
slumped all the way over.

She thought she heard Kabeer shriek, "An infidel and a woman! You
dishonor yourself by touching her."

As if from a great distance, Ib roared, "Shaheed, for the love of God,
hand Sarah up to me."

There was a cry, "*Allah akbar*," and she felt herself hoisted up into
his arms. She smelled his scent of cinnamon and felt his arms tighten
around her. He held a bottle to her lips, but the water dribbled down
her chin. He wet an edge of his headdress to moisten her lips. Then she
must have fainted for all was a blur until they reached the line of tents,
and he was carrying her, limp in his arms, into the women's tent.

"Ibrahim! In God's name, son, what are you doing?" a heavy voice
snarled. "You mustn't touch her. Put her down. At once."

"Allah, have mercy," a low soft voice said, and Sarah felt a hand soft
as kid leather on her brow and the smell of milk. Dear Susu. Then came
the murmur of women reciting the ninety-nine names of God. "God
the beneficent, God the merciful, God the compassionate, God the
generous…"

"She may smell the garden of paradise by dawn," a woman's voice boomed. It was followed by the howl of the zaghareet.

"No, no keening. No keening," cried the same heavy voice that had reprimanded Ib.

Sarah felt herself wrapped in a cold, wet sheet and settled in the rear of the van. A gnarled hand tucked a cushion under her head and drew the dark velvet curtains. Then all was dark.

CHAPTER 7

AN INDIAN NURSE FROM THE SULEIMAN HOSPITAL was sent to stay with Sarah at home during her two-day convalescence. Asha tucked her in the cool sheets and wiped her brow with a lemon-scented cloth while murmuring soothing words in Bengali. If only all medicine were such simple healing, nothing to do but wait for the body to recover in its own time. She gazed onto the Gulf waters where there was always something to see: in the middle sea, the oil tankers; and on shore, fishermen casting nets and children skipping stones. Today, Sarah was feeling stronger. She got up, dressed in her jeans and a striped sailor top, and was engrossed in a jigsaw puzzle of the Wisconsin Dells when shortly after three p.m. the doorbell rang. She had been expecting Annie, but it was Layla who swept in. She handed her cloak and veil to Asha, plunked herself down on the sofa opposite Sarah in the living room, opened her madras bag, and took out her embroidery. Without a word, she poked the needle in and out of the square of damask. Layla was fashionable as usual, wearing a turquoise Marimekko t-shirt and harem pants, but what made her different today was her silence.

"About fainting and causing all that trouble, I feel so foolish," Sarah said. "Imagine a doctor getting heatstroke. I should have realized —"

Layla pulled the blue yarn tight; she pursed her lips; she scowled down at the cross-stitch.

"Something's the matter."

"For the love of God, why didn't you tell me?" Layla exploded, her eyes flashing beneath her thick eyelashes. "About you and Ibrahim? I suspected, but now I know. Mother told me how he looked when he carried you in. So I confronted him and he told me. Everything."

Sarah bit her lip. Her stomach churned, and she averted her eyes. She fixed her gaze on the needle poking in and out of the cloth, flashing with every stitch. "Let me explain," she pleaded.

"I've been honest with you. How can we be friends if I can't trust you to be open with me?"

"I'm sorry." Sarah flushed. "I should have told you. I think about him all the time."

"Think! You think too much." Layla stabbed her needle in the cloth. "The devil plays with people like that."

"I'm so sorry."

"That's easy for you to say." Layla snapped open her silver case and pulled out a cigarette. "Mother saved you, did you know? Grandmother was bellowing that you were as good as dead. She was keening—did you know that?— when Mother shut her up and got Ibrahim to take you to hospital." Layla clamped the cigarette between her lips.

"Your *mother* did that?" Sarah felt appalled at the huge debt she now owed Malika. If only someone else had saved her. Anybody but Malika.

"Yes. Mother's furious. She suspected all along, but I told her no. Well,

I was wrong, wasn't I? You made me look like a fool." Layla struck a match and lit the cigarette. "But Mother has been on to you from the start. Not once did you trick her. Not once…" she hesitated, as if trying to find the idiom, "not once did you pull the wool over her eyes."

"I'm sorry but— "

"You come here, accept our hospitality, and you abuse it. We come to care for you and then we find out you…you knew." She jabbed her cigarette at Sarah. "You knew my mother was looking for a bride for him. You should have told us straight away you wanted him for yourself. It would have saved a lot of trouble."

"I'm sorry. Terribly sorry."

"Deceiver!"

Feeling ashamed, Sarah put her hand to her face.

"You should have trusted me," Layla snapped.

"I wanted to tell you, truly I did, but I didn't know you well enough, and then, well, when I did, well, then, it was too late. Please, let's go back to the way things were before."

Layla exhaled sharply, blowing out smoke; she looked Sarah in the eye.

"I can't tell you how sorry I am. Please, forgive me. Please, won't you have a cup of tea? I've got all kinds, green tea, jasmine, Darj—."

"Jasmine? Did you say jasmine?" Layla said in a gentler voice.

"Yes, and there's marzipan too."

"Marzipan!"

Layla's face softened, and the tightness in Sarah's throat eased as she asked for advice on what to do.

Layla jerked her head up from the embroidery. "It's simple. Marry him."

"Back home my friends said we should see a marriage counselor."

"But why?"

"To see about our chances of success."

Layla burst out laughing.

Sarah flushed. "I don't see what's so funny."

"Why do you need someone like that when you have family?" She put her hand on Sarah's and looked into her eyes. "You should marry him right away. Stop all this silly worrying."

"It's a big decision."

"Do you know what Mother says? That you're judging us, as if the U.S. is so much better—"

"I just don't want to make a mistake. I need to think about it."

"There you go again: think, think, think." Layla raised her voice. "What kind of love is so calculating? Really, you're not in love at all."

Sarah felt worn out—it seemed futile to explain—still she owed it to Layla. "Please try—"

"Oh, my darling, what have I said?" Layla wiped away the tear on Sarah's cheek. "Here I am barging in when you're still weak. Of course, you love him. The fact you followed him here proves it." She puffed up a cushion and propped it behind Sarah. "And I do want you for my sister. No one else. It's simple. Marry him. Mother will have to accept it."

"How about Shaheed?"

"Forget Shaheed. He doesn't matter."

"I'm not Muslim."

"That doesn't matter. For someone of your religion, you're a good person.

Someone of your religion— that was another subterfuge to clear up. "I think—"

"There you go again. You think too much," Layla said crossly. "Where would you be today if Shaheed had stopped to think before he lifted you up so Ibrahim could carry you to safety?"

"Shaheed did that? Wow!"

"And with his boss screaming he'd burn in hell for it too. Poor Shaheed. He's so insecure. When Kabeer is there, he follows him. When Ibrahim is there, he follows him. He must have been on the rack, having them both yelling at him."

"I must thank him."

"Oh no, better not. Anyway, let's not talk about him."

Asha brought in the tea tray. An art anthology was lying on the coffee table, and Sarah set it on the couch to make room for the tray. She poured a cup of tea for Layla and offered her the plate of marzipan. Layla took one shaped like an apricot. "Mmm. About Mother— she finds you hard to understand too. She says you smile too much—"

"I'm just trying to look cheerful."

"That's what I told her. She complains about the silliest things."

After she finished her tea, Layla picked up the book on the couch beside her; she leafed through it, pausing every now and then at an illustration. She showed Sarah a painting of a woman in a red dress bathing a newborn. "Ah, such sweet babies you and Ibrahim will make." She touched her pearl earring.

Sarah laughed self-consciously.

Layla turned the page. "Aiyee," she squealed. "Who's this poor woman?"

"Lucretia." Sarah told her the legend of the Roman heroine and how she had taken her own life by stabbing herself after being raped.

"Death before dishonor," Layla nodded sagely. "But did it do any good?"

"Sure. It made the Romans so angry that they drove out the occupiers."

"A martyr, that's what she was. Tisam would like this picture." Layla nibbled on marzipan and idly turned the pages until she came to Michelangelo's *David.* "Oooh. Look at him. Naked! How did you get this through customs? You should hide this book. Hide it right away." She shut it, put it back on the table, and giggled. "Don't let the Sheriff see it."

Two cups of tea later, her mood turned somber. At the mirror, she adjusted the folds of black over her face. "About you and Ibrahim—if you have to think, and maybe you do, think about this: you mustn't give any excuse for people to talk. Mother wouldn't like that."

After Layla left, Sarah re-opened the book to the reproduction of *David.* With his air of innocence and lean torso, he resembled Ib more than her David, who was portly, thin-lipped and dressed in black. He was a theology student, and she had met him the fall of her senior year in high school. Three times a week they went for coffee and every Sunday they strolled hand in hand to church. In the springtime, it became serious. "Hooray. Hooray. The first of May, outdoor sex begins today," he whispered in her ear as he pulled off his black sweater. As they lay under the fragrant pine boughs, he vowed that they were husband and wife in the eyes of God. But that October when she began to show, he dumped her. He was not ready to marry, and she tarnished his Christian image. She would never forget, entering alone into the abortion clinic, the old man who had spat at her, "Bitch. Baby butcher!" A few years later, she heard through her parents that he had become the youth pastor of their church, what he had always wanted. Her parents voted against his installation, but they did not tell the congregation why. "What good would it do?" Mom had said. "It would make people think badly of you."

Sarah turned the pages, stopping at her favorites—the Vermeers, El Grecos and Gauguins. When she came upon Grünewald's Crucifixion, she shut the book; she could not endure witnessing pain without trying to alleviate it. She went out to the balcony and let the velvety heat of the July evening envelop her. She thought of her friends back home, single by choice, who lived full lives. She was lucky not to be saddled with David, but she wanted a family, and that slanted her view of marriage. But could she live happily ever after *here*, in this alien land? There were all sorts of marriages: marriages of convenience, marriages where a spouse was alcoholic, abusive or suffered from sexual anomalies, or worst of all, a selfish heart. Cultural differences were a small challenge compared to those. The telephone rang. It was the hospital asking whether she would return to work in the morning. She could hardly wait. In the ER, she trusted her intuition. There was never time to "think, think, think," as Layla would put it. Why couldn't she be decisive in her love life too? She dug in her pocket and found a coin. Heads, she would stay, tails, she would leave. She clenched the *halala* tight, flipped and caught it, then slapped it on the back of her other hand. Tails! She put the coin back. That was no way to decide.

About eight o'clock that evening, Annie came to visit. "You almost
fried your brains. Oops, I've left a mark." She fished in her magenta bag
for a tissue and wiped off the lipstick smudge on Sarah's cheek. They
talked for a while and then Annie wanted to help with the puzzle of the
Dells, sorting the pieces by color: blue sky, gray rock, and green foliage.

Sarah touched her sleeve. "Remember when I said I took the position
here for the benefits?"

"Mmm." Annie clicked a piece of sky into place.

"That's not the real reason. I didn't know you well enough to—"

Annie clapped her hands. "*Amor. Amor.* I knew it. So, what's his
name?"

"Ibrahim Suleiman."

"The boss's son. Ramzy told me about him. He's the guy who's bringing water plants to those villages in the north."

Sarah smiled. "Yes, that's him."

"Are those from him?" Annie pointed to the white roses on the credenza.

Sarah curled a strand of hair behind her ear. "Have any advice about
marrying a Saudi?"

"I don't know much about it."

"You must. You married one."

"Ramzy's Egyptian. It's different. With a Saudi, it's a tough call. At the
end of the day, well, I don't know. His friends may tell him he's lucky to
have a wife he can talk to, but they'll be thinking, God help him, poor
fellow." Shadow rubbed her head against Sarah's ankle and she picked
the cat up and patted the silvery fur. "Most guys here want blind cats."

"Blind cats? What's that?"

"Haven't you heard that expression? It's pure Saudi. A pet that's help-less—that's what your average guy wants."

"Ib's not like that."

Annie shrugged her shoulders. "So what's the problem?"

"I've got to make up my mind about getting married. My contract is almost up. Just another couple of weeks. But his mother—"

"Hey, watch out. The moms? You need to get along, or it'll end up in a tear-stained split. Typical expat romance."

"He's a grown man. I don't see why she has such a hold on him."

"Better suck up to her. Or else, she'll laugh at you, then she'll fear you and finally she'll hate you and she'll get back at you any way she can. Don't give me that look. It happens. You heard about Joanie, the dieti-tian? It happened to her. She couldn't take it, so they have mad passion-ate flings when Faisal goes to see her in the States, but he took a second wife to please the tribe."

"Not nice."

"Yeah." Annie crossed her tanned arms. "Going to the party at the consulate next week?"

"I would if Ib were going, but he's not. He says he needs to patch things up with his mother. Are you?"

"Ramzy isn't keen. It'll be Saudis on one side and hardened expats on the other. Still you should go. Meet a cute expat. Take your mind off Ib. There might be someone your type."

"And what's that?"

"Oh, you know. The reading type, intellectual and romantic."

"Sounds like Ib." Laughing, Sarah walked her to the door.

"Yeah, but Cinderella, it's time to give him competition, time to put on your dancing slippers."

CHAPTER 8

ON THE NIGHT OF THE PARTY, Sarah was combing out Shadow as she listened to Louis Armstrong singing *Come to the Cabaret* on Radio Bahrain. She had felt at loose ends all that evening. Combing the cat's back, sides, and neck was easy, but the purrs turned to snarls when she turned the cat over and dragged the metal comb through the thick fur on her stomach. Sarah tossed the handful of silken fluff in the wastebasket and went into the kitchen. Shadow followed and rubbed against her ankle as she poured milk into a bowl and set it down. The pink tongue darted in and out until Shadow lapped the last drops and then, sitting on her haunches, pawed a droplet off a whisker. The telephone rang. It was Layla calling about the consulate party.

"Ahmed's trying to sweet-talk me into going," she said. Apparently, he wanted to chat up a prospective business partner, but she was worried she would have no one to talk to, and that men would accost her and ruin her reputation. "Please, darling Sarah, come and save me from wicked men."

Delighted to have an excuse to go, Sarah showered, dabbed on perfume, and selected a cocktail dress. It was a long time since she had dressed up, and as she put on her chandelier earrings—she really wanted pearls like Layla's— and slipped the jeweled evening sandals on her tanned feet, she felt excited. When her ride arrived, she hurried outside, two inches taller, glistening in satiny sapphire, and ready to let go a bit.

Cars were backed up on the road to the consulate waiting for inspection. When they reached the sentry box, a Marine shone his flashlight into each of their faces and then checked Ahmed and Johnny's identity cards, while another Marine inspected the chassis of the car. After they passed inspection, Johnny was waved on to zigzag his way around the concrete blocks to the entrance of the consulate.

"See that?" Sarah said when they saw the floodlit Stars and Stripes that dominated the complex. "Life, liberty and the pursuit of happiness, that's what it stands for." Suddenly, she felt abashed. She did not want Layla and Ahmed to think she was preaching at them.

"Exactly what we need here," Ahmed said. He seemed to be one of those easygoing men who can talk with anybody about anything, but then Sarah remembered how he had left the campsite to avoid Shaheed and Kabeer. Now, as they walked toward the consulate, he reminisced about his days studying petroleum economics at Stanford. He seemed every bit as liberal as Layla had said. He had just returned from Riyadh where he had tried to convince some cabinet ministers to adopt a platform empowering women in the next Five Year Plan.

"Darling, I wish you'd empower me by staying home more," Layla teased, and he laughed good-naturedly.

He was intensely curious about American family life. He asked if American parents and their adult children shared similar political views.

When Sarah said that her parents were Republicans while she was a Democrat, he chatted about John F. Kennedy and the first moon landing. "Ask not what your country can do for you. Ask what you can do for your country," he quoted. They made conversation about which was the best place to take the children for the holiday celebrating the end of the fast of Ramadan, which was coming up soon. Layla and Ahmed were trying to decide between Orlando, the Grand Canyon, and Hawaii. By the time they stood at the bronze front door, Sarah felt she both knew and liked Layla's husband.

In the entrance hall, the commercial attaché's children, both dressed in hula attire, grass skirts and skimpy tops, said "Aloha," and offered them fresh flower leis. Sarah and Layla selected creamy ones, so as not to clash with their dresses, and Ahmed picked a purple dendrobium. They each stooped so the little girls could place the leis around their necks. Another little girl held a basket of loose orchids for the women— to go behind the right ear for single women and the left ear for those who were married. Sarah pinned hers behind her right ear.

"Next time behind the left ear, God willing." Layla smiled at her, and Sarah felt she had been forgiven for her deception.

"I should have worn my Aloha shirt," Ahmed said as they stepped into the reception room where the band was playing *Hawaiian Wedding Song*. A massive bouquet of red ginger, anthuriums, and birds of paradise decorated the drinks table, which featured Hawaiian punch, both spiked and virgin. There were three or four men for each woman, just the way Sarah liked it.

Layla said something and nudged her.

"What did you say?" Sarah shouted over the buzz.

"Ahmed's gone off."

"But we've just arrived." Sarah glanced around the room. "Where?"

"Oh, I knew this would happen. Oh, I shouldn't have come." She wrung her hands.

"It'll be okay. Pretend you're vacationing in Maui or on the Big Island. Here, have a macadamia nut."

"But my girlfriends haven't—" Layla twisted her wedding ring.

"Don't worry, we're going to have a great time."

Layla frowned and whispered angrily. "Those men. They're staring at us."

"At you, because you're gorgeous." In her shimmering gold dress with its diaphanous sleeves and nipped-in waist, Layla looked like a monarch butterfly in a collection of moths.

"They've very bad manners," Layla said.

"They don't mean anything by it. And your friends will be here soon. Just be patient."

"No, they won't."

"Of course they will. Why wouldn't they?"

"I'll tell you why," she said morosely. "People will talk."

"Of course they won't. Why should they? Ahmed's here."

"But where? Off drinking and politicking in a back room. Oh, I hate mixed parties."

Sarah thought Layla might feel better if she ate, so she steered her toward the buffet table. It was covered with real sand, seashells, and co-conut-scented candles that were burning in hollowed-out coconut shells.

The long table was laden with platters of seafood, pineapple chicken, and sweet potatoes. There was even a bowl of poi, smooth and creamy. A card on the table said NO PORK. Sarah felt disappointed because she had hoped to try Kalua Pig, roasted in an underground pit. Layla, on the contrary, cheered up and filled her plate. She had never before sampled poi, and said it tasted like sweet glue. By the time they had finished eating, however, her friends still had not appeared. There was no denying that she was being stared at. Reluctantly, Sarah suggested they go hang out in the ladies' room until Layla's friends arrived. It seemed the least she could do for Layla, who looked miserable.

"No, you stay," Layla said. "You're having fun."

After Layla left, a consular official, thirtyish with a shock of blonde hair and a boyish grin, approached Sarah.

"Hi, what can I get you? We've got it all—punch, champagne, whisky, gin, vodka, and rum."

"I thought all that was illegal." She smiled up at him. A nametag on his shirt said Greg.

"In theory, yes, but we have a diplomatic dispensation. Washington thinks liquor helps. Now, what—"

"A glass of champagne, please."

When Greg returned with her drink, she asked about the guests, and he said they had the usual executives along with a few arty types from the university.

"No Saudi women? My girlfriend is feeling out of her element."

"I'm sorry about that. You know how things are." Greg looked around the room. "See that fellow who just came in? That's Prince Misfer. He's

quite a…uh…friendly fellow, but he'll be a useful contact for somebody." Greg looked at her glass, which was half-empty. "What about the
bubbly? Is it okay?"

Sarah took another sip. "Altogether delicious."

Prince Misfer was staring at her. He was short and his thobe stretched
tight across his paunch. When she saw him making his way toward her,
she excused herself and went to chat with a colleague, Vera Donleavy. It
turned out that Vera's husband worked at the university, and they lived
a block away from Layla and Ahmed. Sarah was on her way to find
Layla and introduce them when another colleague waved her over. Jim
had the gift of the blarney, and soon she was laughing as loudly as the
others and enjoying herself. Jim knew everyone. He introduced her to a
visiting Islamic scholar from Japan, a road safety engineer from Sweden,
and finally, to a young architect, Billy Devine. Dressed in a buff suit
with a blue shirt that matched his eyes, he looked debonair, every inch
the architect, from his striped bow tie to his well-polished shoes. When
she finished her drink, he went to the bar and came back with another
glass of champagne for her. "Sorry, what was that you said?"

"I was asking where you're from," she shouted, to make herself heard
over the din.

"Atlanta. I'm a…"

"What's that? I'm sorry. I didn't catch what you said."

"Where I'm from. I'm a Georgia peanut."

Sarah grinned. She gestured to the bowl of macadamia nuts on the
table and suggested he try one. He laughed and took a handful. He
had come to design a series of municipal water towers. Over the din, he

talked about making the water towers the hubs of communal activity the way village wells used to be. He had a quiet voice, almost as soft and mellow as Ib's, and several times, she had to ask him to repeat himself. As the party became noisier, she suggested they go outside. She opened the French doors and he followed her onto the courtyard, where they settled themselves in white Adirondack chairs. The night air was heady with the scent of frangipani, and Billy was easy to talk with. It turned out that they shared an interest in art and design. She mentioned the campus water tower she had seen when she had gone to visit Layla, and he said his company had designed it. He had grown up in the kingdom, for his father had come from West Texas to work in the oil industry in the mid-1960s. He called himself an "Aramco brat," for he had lived on the compound in Dhahran until he was sent off to prep school in the States. He reminisced about hunting for scorpions and rock crystals, playing Little League baseball, and windsurfing on Half Moon Bay. When she asked if his parents still lived in Dhahran, a look of sadness crossed his face. They had both passed away the previous year.

"One thing they taught me, though, is to seize the day. *Carpe diem,* my mom always said. That's one thing I like about the Saudis. They don't obsess with guilt over the past. They're generous. Slow to anger. Never petty."

She smiled. "But phlegmatic."

"Better than that. They're accepting. They don't rage against the dark. It saves energy."

"You can be too accepting. I like people to have hope and make things better."

Billy smiled. "A few of them manage that, too."

Sarah nodded, thinking of Ib.

Billy knew Arab history and spoke knowledgeably about colonialism and Franz Fanon. The kingdom was exciting for him professionally because the Saudis welcomed innovative design in their civic buildings. He mentioned a couple of the new skyscrapers, and she admitted that she was scared of heights.

"So was the architect of the World Trade Center. He wanted to design one-story buildings overlooking drifts of flowers. And look what he ended up with—the Twin Towers." As they talked, Billy kept smiling at her and looking into her eyes. It was flattering, but it made her feel self-conscious; she did not want Layla to come and find her alone with him.

The rasping of a man clearing his throat broke the silence. A muezzin belonging to what Billy called "the ugly school" was preparing to give the call to prayer. She clapped her hands against her ears and suggested they go in. She felt Billy's hand on the small of her back as they stepped into the reception room, where guests were standing around nursing their drinks. After a while, the music started up again, and a few older couples danced sedately.

"Shall we?" Billy was a fine dancer, and he held her close, much closer than Ib would have. She thought of him a little guiltily, remembered her promise to introduce Layla to Vera, and excused herself. She was almost at the ladies' room when she felt someone plucking at her dress.

"Hey! Where you from? What you doing here? You married or you work here?" Prince Misfer's warm, whisky breath seeped over her. He played with the emerald cufflinks on the cuffs of his thobe. "What you say to a drive? You wouldn't believe how fast my Lamborghini can go."

"What about the speed limit?"

He rolled his eyes. "No problem. So, a cop waves me over. He asks for my license. I pull it out, and he sees my name. 'So sorry, your highness,' he'll say. You see, we do what we want. It is our country." He went to put his arm around Sarah's shoulder, but she moved a step back.

"Yes, it is *your* country," she said coldly. She excused herself and weaved her way through the crowded room looking for Layla. A man with a Texas drawl stopped her and called her "sweetheart." Clearly, he was drunk. She turned away and asked the woman standing beside him if she had seen any Saudis.

"No, not yet," the man replied. "The 'sheets' will still be kneeling with their bums in the air."

"John, honey, stop it," the woman said.

"Hey, if they spent less time praying and more time learning the meaning of that little four-letter word 'w-o-r-k,' we'd all be better off."

"John, you stop it right now!"

"Don't look, but one of their women just came in," John said, slurring his words. "See, just behind that little Paki waiter. At last we'll get to see an MBO in the flesh." He peered at Sarah over his Jack Daniels.

"MBO?"

"'A Moving Black Object,' alias, a Saudi female." John snickered. "See, there's one." He gestured toward Layla who was standing alone at the entrance to the room.

"How dare you be so rude!" Sarah spun on her heel and hurried toward Layla.

"Darling Sarah, where have you been? I've been looking everywhere for you." Nervously she twisted the ring on her finger. "Just like I told you; they haven't come."

"Who hasn't?"

"My friends. They promised, but they haven't."

Sarah persuaded her to stay on a little while, and twenty minutes later, the Saudis started drifting in, all men. Just as Annie had predicted, they clustered in small groups on the opposite side of the room from the expatriates. Billy Devine was the only one to cross over the invisible line to join them. Sarah suggested that they find Ahmed to introduce him to Billy.

"No, that would be awful. Ahmed is already tight. He's a disgrace. I want to go home."

"Oh, so soon?" Sarah glanced at her bracelet watch. "It's not even ten."

"Please," Layla said with a pout.

Sarah felt disappointed. Apart from lecherous Prince Misfer and the awful Texan, she had been having fun and would have liked Bill Devine to ask her to dance again. However, Layla already was on her cellphone to Johnny.

"That Ahmed," Layla fumed when they were ensconced in the Lincoln. "He insists I come, positively insists, and then off he goes and forgets all about me. My friends will find out, and there'll be talk. If I had known I'd be the only Saudi girl, I wouldn't have come. She put her soft hand on Sarah's. "Still, I hope you had a good time."

Sarah touched her lei. "Actually, yes. It was like being in Hawaii." She joked about Prince Misfer, calling him Prince Abominable.

Layla nervously twisted and untwisted a corner of the black abaya that she had flung over her beautiful dress. "I hate it that he ogled me. Ahmed would be furious. He wants me to be the free western woman, but he's frightened of scandal too."

After Johnny dropped off Layla, they headed toward the western compound. Sarah thought about Ib and what kind of pressure his mother had exerted on him. She imagined Ib listening to her, looking grave and sad, his fingertips pressed together. Tisam would be there, and Malika would argue that it was Allah's will that he marry one of his own kind. It occurred to her that she still had not found Tisam the Bible she had promised her. She had heard that most Filipinos were Christian, and she leaned forward and asked Johnny if he was.

"A Catholic." Johnny undid the top button of his Polo shirt, pulled out a gold cross, and then tucked it back in.

"Might you have a Bible I could lend a friend?"

"Dr. Sarah! Don't you know? They can throw you in prison for that."

"Okay, never mind." Tisam was probably in Qatif now, her arms around Malika's knees, hanging on to her every word, the perfect daughter-in-law candidate. She would flash her smile and Ib, on the sofa opposite, would be dazzled. Of course, he had denied any interest in her, but with Malika hounding him, it was possible, easily possible.

On Pepsi Cola Road, Johnny stopped for a traffic light, and Sarah saw the shop she had first noticed coming in from the airport. Even at this late hour, it was open wide. In the window were the pyramids of pistachios, cashews, and peanuts, and above them the sign MIXED NUTS.

Billy Devine called himself a Georgia peanut. She liked and respected him; he was cute, smart; furthermore, he was "her kind" as Daddy
would say. The light turned and Johnny sped ahead. She craned her
neck and looked back to see the letters flashing on and off in an ennead
of devilish red: M-I-X-E-D N-U-T-S.

CHAPTER 9

It was her day off, and Sarah was fiddling with the Wisconsin Dells puzzle, now mostly finished. She had been to the Dells once with David Ritter so he could try out the go-carts. Afterward she persuaded him to take the scenic cruise up the river, by the sandstone bluffs. They hiked a quarter mile through pine forests to see one of the local attractions, a German shepherd that leaped across a dry ravine. The puzzle portrayed this scene. As she slotted in the tiny piece for the dog's ear, Sarah felt that she too was trying to jump across a perilous chasm. A few days ago outside the hospital cafeteria, she had met Ib's father for the first time since her heatstroke on the camping trip. Hobbling on his cane, he greeted her pleasantly, inquiring about her health and saying in his usual dignified way, "God preserve you as a treasure to your father." But the wary look in his eyes made her realize that he now knew the true reason she had taken the job at his hospital—as a way to get into the kingdom to check out the Suleimans as potential in-laws. That was unfortunate. When his family did not know, Ib could pretend not to be offended by her motive, but now he must feel ashamed. Most likely, that was why he had not called, and it had nothing to do with the alluring Tisam.

To clear her mind she went out for a jog around the perimeter of the compound. After a half-mile, she had had enough; even at nine a.m., it was sweltering. She slowed to a walk when she passed the playground where the mothers, all younger than her, sat on benches around the sandbox watching their toddlers at play. She smiled and waved at them, but nobody smiled back. They thought she was odd. Maybe they were jealous of her because she had a job, a salary, and an independent life. She did not belong with them any more than she had with the expats at the party—all except Billy Devine. He had called yesterday when she was out. She supposed he wanted to date her.

The day stretched in front of her. In Madison on her days off, she would paint, read a good book, or go to the zoo. The zoo was out of the question as it was not Women's Day, so she thought she would return to Qatif. It was Johnny's free day too, so she decided to try out the local bus. She put on her most conservative clothes, an ankle-length skirt and long-sleeved blouse, and tucked every strand of hair under a head scarf.

When the minibus arrived, she climbed into the back section, which was reserved for women. It was empty. The conductor was in front, but there was a fare box in back, and she dropped in her fare. At the stop in front of the MIXED NUTS store, another woman joined her; she neglected to pay. A few miles later, some man, probably her husband, thumped on the plastic separation between the two sections, and she got off, letting in a searing gust of wind. The bus started up, and Sarah watched the dreary trailer camps on the outskirts of town give way to miles of stony desert, then more miles of glinting salt flats, and a shabby village or two. All of a sudden, she was in the oasis with its large shady trees bordering the wide boulevards. She got off at the stop for the market and found her way to the bakery, recognizing it by the palm frond kindling stacked against the wall. She took the dirt path that led to the baths.

It was quiet in the late morning, with no moans of doves or chirps of parakeets. Beyond the low mud wall, vegetables were growing in rows on the sandy soil. In the distance, a boy shimmied up the trunk of a palm tree and disappeared in the fronds at its crown. Farther ahead at a clump of pink oleander, the path narrowed and then opened into a clearing.

In front of her rose the tell, its dark bare slopes casting a shadow on the surface of the green water below. She sat down on the sparse grass on the bank and raised her hand to shield her eyes from the sun. She felt glad to be alone, immune from prying questions: *What you doing here? Why you come? How many children you? Why you no married?* She thought about the tell, storehouse of the debris of centuries. What mysteries did it hold? She imagined a high priest, with Shaheed's impertinent eyes, a scimitar grasped in both hands, standing over a woman who lay bound on a roughhewn altar. She shook her head. That was a ridiculous fancy. This was a blessed place. Perhaps devotees of Ishtar once danced here, swirling bright scarves or singing songs of the ancestors. She took off her sandals, ambled down to the water's edge, and dipped her foot in the cool water. She hesitated, and then she stripped to her bra and panties and slipped in, feeling the water pulse against her bare thighs from its source deep in the earth. She felt a rapturous aliveness, the feeling she should have had that day in May when Ib had begged her to let

herself go with him on the stream of the unknown. Her feelings for him
were even stronger now, but she could count on the fingers of one hand
the number of times she had seen him. Annie once suggested a tryst
at Safeway—meeting him between the cabbages and the cucumbers—
but that was foolish and risky what with the *mutawwa'in* patrolling the
aisles, tapping their sticks against the slick linoleum.

   She had judged Ib to be the contemplative type while she saw herself as a woman of action. Caught up in the whirl of her work, she
knew what to do and did it, almost reflexively. But in her personal life,
she lacked courage. She ruminated, hesitated, and stalled. That shilly-
shallying had proved foolish. If she had come here as Ib's bride, his
mother would have had no choice but to accept her. She swam harder
now, doing a fast crawl until she felt exhausted and headed back. With
the water now hip-deep about her, she waded toward the shore. As she
clambered up on the bank, she trod on something. "Ow," she cried
and rubbed her heel. She had stepped on a sharp curl of eggshell. She
picked it up and remembered how the Saudi woman had offered her a
marble-sized yolk to eat. Sarah might well have refused it, but that had
not deterred the woman. She had been generous, open, and bold. So
were most Arabs; Billy Devine was right about that. They did not com-
plain, unlike the Western expats who moaned about the dust, the racket
of construction, and the crazy primitive ways. She too had been on the
lookout for ugliness. She put her hand to her face, ashamed as she considered her life. She had allowed herself to love Ib, but lacked courage
enough to risk marrying him. It was as if she felt entitled to a guarantee
of success over a lifetime. That was impossible. In any case, was not the

present moment what mattered? When she was with Ib, she felt tingly alive. "*Carpe diem*," she whispered to herself. *Carpe diem.*

When she returned to her apartment, there were three messages on her answering machine, two from Layla and one from Billy Devine. As for Billy, he could call again. She called Layla's home number, but no one answered. A moment later, her phone rang.

"Oh, Sarah, I'm at the hospital," Layla's voice was edged with terror. "It's Fawzi. His arm…There was blood everywhere and bone sticking through the skin. He heard it snap."

"Have they operated yet?"

"No. We're waiting…"

"Ask for Dr. Boulos. He's the best."

"He won't help me."

"Why not?"

"Not without Ahmed's permission."

"Where's Ahmed?"

"Out of town—he makes me so angry, his stupid politics."

"Your father?"

"He's visiting cousins."

Sarah was getting exasperated. "Ibrahim?"

"I can't find him. He's not in the office."

"Well, what about Shaheed?"

"He refused."

"What! He refused?"

"He said that we must accept God's will, whatever it might be." Layla rushed on. "So I brought Fawzi in by myself. The ambulance drove like crazy over the speed bumps, and Fawzi screamed and screamed. It was awful. When we got here, I asked for you. Where were you? We've been waiting a long time."

"I'll be there in a flash, and if Dr. Boulos won't operate, I will."

Twenty minutes later, she charged down the corridor to the ER. She checked the roster and saw that Mona was the triage nurse on duty. Mona was a stickler for the rules. "I'll deal with Dr. Hunter," Sarah told her. "You get the child ready. Now!"

"As you wish, Dr. Moss," Mona said, her forehead creased with worry lines.

Once the x-rays were taken and Fawzi was anesthetized. Sarah inserted the metal pins into the bone to bind the broken ends and applied a cast from wrist to elbow. After the procedure, he was wheeled off in a gurney to the recovery room, and Sarah went to see the chief of staff. She wanted John Hunter to learn about it from her first, but someone must have already told him because he made her wait, and she suspected it was deliberate, his way of showing where she stood in the hierarchy. She drummed her fingers on her knee and remembered how two weeks ago, a girl had been brought in with earache. The father could not be found, both the child and mother were screaming, and the attending doctor asked Hunter for the okay to treat the child with only the mother's permission. Hunter refused, the jerk.

Twenty minutes later, Dr. Hunter opened his door and pointed to a seat. As Sarah sat down, he picked up a ruler from his desk and ran his fingers along it. "It is our duty to follow the rules as they are stated."

She jutted out her chin. "You've heard of the Hippocratic oath? The mother sought my help in healing her son. I was duty-bound to accept."

"Now, Sarah, please. Let's discuss this reasonably. We're both professionals, both committed to our work." His voice softened and he set down the ruler. "Dr. Boulos was scheduled to treat the child as soon as we got permission. We didn't anticipate it would take so long to reach the woman's guardian. The staff did their best to contact every man in her family."

"Her father is Dr. Suleiman." Sarah said accusingly. "An orthopedist, for God's sake."

"Apparently he's out of town."

"You know him. He'd never object."

"Legally we'd be on shaky grounds. We could not afford ourselves the luxury of second-guessing his decision." Hunter took off his wire-rimmed spectacles and set them on the desk. "Please try to see it from my point of view. What if the woman's husband were later to object?"

"What parent could object to setting a child's broken arm?"

Dr. Hunter leaned forward, his elbows on the mahogany desk. "Dr. Moss, quite a few of them object to inoculations on religious grounds," he said in a frigid voice. "Do not presume to predict their wishes."

She got up from her chair. "But how can I stay on in a position where I cannot operate freely?"

"Now, now, I didn't mean to upset you. I would never question your integrity." He blathered on about every job having boundaries and learning to operate within them. Finally, he said that as long as it didn't happen again, he would turn a blind eye. As she left, Sarah made an effort not to slam his door; she stormed down the corridor to the staff locker room. Sitting on the bench by the steel blue lockers, she closed her eyes and did deep breathing exercises. *In and out. In and out. In and out.* The air conditioner hummed, its breeze cool on her neck.

Annie came in and put her arm around Sarah. "I heard. You must be furious."

"He's a stupid bureaucrat. A martinet."

"It's how he gets his kicks. What an asshole. Don't think about him. He doesn't know diddly-squat."

Feeling much better, Sarah went to the recovery room, where she was informed that Fawzi had already been taken to the pediatrics ward. Sarah went to see him. He lay on the bed, the right sleeve of his blue-and-white striped pajamas cut short to accommodate his casted arm, which was propped on a pillow at his side. Four women, their black cloaks touching, were reciting suras at the far end of the square, high-ceilinged room. Sarah lowered the bed's metal sides and placed her hand on Fawzi's brow. It felt clammy, and his eyelids were purple. "It's all right. You'll feel better soon," she murmured. She felt a touch on her arm and turned.

Malika gripped her hands. Stunned, Sarah looked down at the chunky coral rings and felt herself being kissed on both cheeks. Could it be? Malika smiling at her? Malika embracing her?

Layla and Susu hugged her in turn. Layla had finally reached Ahmed a few minutes ago and reported that he was planning to fly in tomorrow from Riyadh.

"I'm on duty tonight. If you like, I will drop in to check on Fawzi,"

Sarah offered.

After the women left, she went to the cafeteria to grab a hamburger, and when she came back, Fawzi was sleeping. She worked steadily in the ER the next few hours until the end of her shift when she returned to the pediatrics ward.

"Ib," she said. "I wasn't expecting you." She closed the door, and suddenly they were in each other's arms. After a while, she stepped back. "I've good news. Your mother smiled at me. Actually kissed me. Do you think there's a chance it'll last?"

"God willing," he said gravely.

"Maybe I can win her over—perhaps not right away, but I'll be patient, and if things sour, I'll conceal my feelings."

He shook his head. "That won't work. Be yourself. Nobody but yourself."

They sat side by side in the blue leatherette armchairs in case a nurse or orderly should walk in. She had not spoken to him since his visit home. As she had predicted, Malika had pushed Tisam on him. He had made his mother promise to try to get along with Sarah.

"So that's why she smiled at me—to please you. It had nothing to do with Fawzi."

"And now it's your turn to reach out to her."

About three a.m., Fawzi woke up and complained of headache. He vomited and looked unwell, his eyes flat and his face pasty. Thinking that he might have suffered a concussion from the fall, Sarah medicated him and every two hours woke him up to check on his heart rate and blood pressure. Ibrahim went to the cafeteria and came back with coffee and a sack of apples. Fawzi was sleeping, and as she bit into the crisp white flesh, she told Ib about her trip to the tell. She glanced at his slim olive hand and imagined a gold band on his ring finger. A second later, and she would have said she wanted to marry him. But he said the tell was his mother's favorite place, and the moment passed.

CHAPTER 10

By morning, Fawzi's fever and headache were gone, but he remained lethargic. Luckily, her shift was busy—a heart attack, drug over-
dose, and the usual feverish kids—or she would have fallen asleep on
her feet. At two o'clock, she dashed to the elevator, jabbed the button
and waited impatiently, shifting her weight from one foot to the other
until it arrived. She took it up to the pediatrics ward, rushed down the
corridor to Fawzi's room, skidding to a stop at the open door. Ib was
there, but so were the others, Layla and Ahmed chatting in a corner,
and Malika sitting on Fawzi's bed stroking his good arm.

"Sarah, here you are." Ib hurried up to her, his hand outstretched, his
eyes on hers. Ahmed had just arrived, and he thanked her, and said that
few would have had the courage to operate without a guardian's consent.

Feeling embarrassed, Sarah shook off the compliment. Malika rolled
her eyes, which made Ib frown. "Mother! Sarah is here," he said, rebuke
in his tone. As if she knew she had gone too far, Malika heaved herself
up from the bed, grabbed a box of candy from the bedside table, unwrapped the cellophane with her pudgy hand, pushed the box at Sarah,
and commanded, "Eat." So today, there would be no embrace, no grate-

ful smile. She took a piece of the nougat and unwrapped the rice paper covering it. The candy was chewy, sickly sweet and stuck between her teeth, but she forced a bright smile as she thanked Malika.

Malika gave a smirk and returned to her spot beside Fawzi.

Caught again, Sarah thought resentfully—smiling too hard. She should try to make small talk—asking about Malika's health, or about whether baby Saladin was letting Susu sleep through the night. Still, why should she always be the one to make all the effort? She grabbed a chair and started a game of checkers with Fawzi, which left Malika with nothing to do but watch the antics of the Sesame Street puppets on television. Meanwhile the men went on about how technology was changing politics. The royals could no longer exile dissidents with the expectation that they would never be heard from again, not with the Internet. Ib favored working for change within the system rather than alienating those princes who were in a position to bring it about.

"Look at our rulers, all old men. Now is the time to strike." Ahmed jabbed his index finger in the air.

"No point in courting danger," Ib said.

"Of course, there may be martyrs, but martyrs never die in vain," Ahmed said.

"You sound like Shaheed."

"Ahmed. Ibrahim. Stop it. No more politics," Layla scolded, lightly slapping Ahmed on the wrist. "Sarah is the only one paying attention to Fawzi."

"Such a good mother she will make one day," Ahmed said, smiling with a knowing look at Ib. Malika scowled and said it was time for her afternoon nap. Before Ib left to drive her home, he told Fawzi he would come back that evening. He turned to Sarah, said he hoped she was on duty, and Malika glared despite her promise to try to get along.

Glad that he was not letting his mother steamroller over him, Sarah continued the game of checkers. Fawzi was a good player for his age, and the first game ended in a draw. She let him win the second, then found him a Batman comic book from the pile at the foot of his bed, and went to sit by Layla who was quizzing Ahmed about Riyadh. He was saying that he had seen several unveiled women in the street. "Now, that's progress," he said.

"But a girl should unveil only if she herself wishes to—not just to please her husband," Layla said. "Oh yes, that's most important. After all, we're not schoolgirls any longer. And those ugly brown skirts my students wear, they're hideous. If we must have a uniform, at least let it be stylish."

They continued to argue, and Ahmed became testy. "Enough. I'm sick of all your complaining. Work at the international school. They don't have stupid rules."

"Abandon my students? Sawson, Reem, Nur and the others? Never."

"The building is a shambles."

"But my students are very fine."

"Listen, the fall term is beginning soon. Don't wait until it's too late. The international school has everything you like. Think about applying. Do it now."

"Leave my students? Never. I would miss them too too much. And in the fall, we will read Jane Austen. Oh, they will love her."

Ahmed turned to Sarah. "You've seen the place. Don't you agree?"

"Ahmed, my darling. No more," Layla said. "I'd miss my girls."

It was obvious that they had had this argument before. Sarah, wanting to say something conciliatory, suggested a change might be good: the hours would be better, and Layla had her family to think of.

"My little family," Layla said, laughing. "This morning Farouk yelled he hated Lulu because she did not let him play with her Barbie. He gives us such trouble, that boy. And still, I want another child, fool that I am." She fluttered her eyelashes at Ahmed and touched an earring, sending the pearls swinging. "Ah, babies, they smell so sweet. Do you know when I love them best? When they're sleeping. I stroke their hair, and sometimes they smile. Oh, how I'd love another one."

Sarah watched the pearls shift back and forth on Layla's neck. Layla was too sentimental, but she herself was missing out on life, and it was passing her by. She had her mind ninety-nine percent made up to marry Ib, but she was not positive. Just yesterday after she'd set Fawzi's arm, Malika had smiled at her, but already—so soon—they seemed enemies again. Still, what should she make of that smile? When she asked Layla about it, she looked blank. "When? Mother smiles all the time."

"For me it was just that once."

Layla reached for another cigarette. "*Insha'allah*. God willing, Mother will accept you. Oh, you will make such pretty babies." She bobbed her head up and down, which set the pearls at her ears dancing.

When Sarah got home, the telephone was ringing. It was Billy Devine. He asked if he could see her again, and she tried to let him down gently as she told him there was someone else. "Lucky fellow," Billy said gallantly.

When she returned to the pediatrics ward that evening, she heard peals of childish laughter coming from Fawzi's room. For a moment, she could not believe her eyes. Ib was pumping orange juice from the glass on the dinner tray into a syringe. He handed it to Fawzi who was crouched beside the open window, his casted arm in a sling. "One, two, three shoot!" Ib ordered, and a jet of liquid squirted out onto the cars in the parking lot below.

"We were just having a little fun," Ib said.

"That's enough of that." Playfully she shook her finger at him; she felt pleased. A prig would never do that. She gave Fawzi her present—a Superman comic book and Magic Markers.

"Super. Now everybody can write on my cast," he said. "Everyone except Farouk."

She smiled at that. "But he's your brother."

"I hate him. He called me 'Fatso.' He pushed me down the stairs."

"He's still your brother. And now it's your bedtime?"

"I don't want to sleep," he whined. "Do I *have* to?"

"Yes, but first I'll tell you a story my mother taught me. It's about a man who killed ninety-nine people." Ib sat down on the bed beside him.

"Ninety-nine—wow!"

Ib dug into his pocket and pulled out his beads, thirty-three amber ovals. *Kaan ma kaan*...it was, it was not," he began, rocking slightly as he clicked the beads one against the other. Apparently some time later, the murderer of the ninety-nine thought of the Day of Judgment, and so he consulted a holy man, who said that with such a record, the murderer would never earn Allah's forgiveness."

"So what did he do?" Fawzi asked.

"Killed the holy man. A few days later, he went to another holy man in the City of Sin and asked if he could repent after having killed one hundred people. The holy man said people in there were not the forgiving sort, so the murderer needed to go to the City of Kindness, where people were God-fearing. He gave the murderer a map and he started out."

What an inappropriate bedtime story! Sarah stared at Ib's slim fingers and the dangling beads, the amber the same color as the henna on his mother's hands. *Click*. Malika the mighty. *Click*. Malika who would murder Ib's love for her. *Click*.

"What happened when he got there?" Fawzi asked.

"He never did. He died on the way and the angels arrived to gather his soul. 'This fellow belongs to us,' the angels of punishment cried. 'Oh no, he doesn't,' said the angels of mercy. 'Of course, he does! Didn't he kill a hundred men?' the angels of punishment yelled. 'Yes, but he was headed to the City of Kindness with a heart full of repentance,' said the angels of mercy. Therefore, God sent another angel to judge the case. This angel said that if the murderer was closer to the City of Sin, then the angels of punishment could have him, but if he was nearer to the City of Kindness, then the angels of mercy had more right to him. So the two teams of angels took out their tape measures and started to measure." Ib spread his arms wide to mime the angels measuring. "Guess what? The murderer was closer to the City of Sin."

"Did the bad angels chop off his head?" Fawzi hooked his good arm around Ib's waist and snuggled close. A few hours ago, she had resolved to marry him, but now she faltered. How could she raise their children in a place where everything was black and white, with no shades of gray, and with an obsession with punishment? She lifted her hands and put her face in them.

"Sarah? Dear heart, what is the matter?"

"It's such a grisly story." She frowned and looked up into his eyes.

"Auntie Sarah is right."

"But it is not finished. Listen to what comes next. Allah ordered the City of Sin to move back and the City of Kindness to approach. Can you imagine? Buildings, parks, and trees moving? And that, Fawzi, is how God saved the murderer."

"Time to go to sleep now." Ib got up from the bed and went to sit beside Sarah. "You can look at your new comic book, but no more talking. Auntie Sarah and I will watch over you."

When Fawzi fell asleep, Ib switched off the fluorescent light overhead. It felt peaceful in the room with only the glow of the night-light. As he sat down again, she took the string of beads from him and pressed them against her cheek. They felt warm. She looked at the empty glass of orange juice on the bedside table and made her decision. "Put your arms around me," she whispered, her heart knocking in her chest. "I love you. Marry me. Please, please, let's get married."

"My betrothed! For so long I have wanted to call you that."

"Such an old-fashioned word." She ran a finger along his lip.

"What made you decide?" he whispered.

"Oh, I don't know exactly." She hugged him, flooded by a deep gladness. "I want to go with you—to the City of Kindness."

The next afternoon, Layla and Tisam came to pay a call. "Sister Sarah," Layla laughed, holding out an armful of white lilies. As Sarah arranged them in a green vase, they chatted about the wedding preparations—the band, henna party, and reception.

"Your family, what are they saying?" Sarah said.

"Oh…my father is so delighted."

Yesterday he had come to her in the ER and said, "Ah, my dear, my son has given me the good news. I liked you from the first moment." Playfully he poked at her water bottle with his cane. "Ah, foreigners. We Arabs can suck water from mud. Never mind, my dear. You will become one of us." He quoted a line from Rumi, something about lovers singing, their eyes brilliant.

Sarah turned to Layla. "Shaheed disapproved, didn't he?"

"I suppose so. He said that the world, all of it, is property, and the best property is a virtuous woman. So, of course, I told him that you were this virtuous woman."

"Touché. And Malika? She had her heart set on Ibrahim's marrying Tisam."

Tisam waved her hand to dismiss the idea. "I never wanted it."

"Don't worry about Mother," Layla said. "God willing, you and Ibrahim will make babies, and then everything will be all right."

"Are you sure you want to do this?" Tisam put her hand on Sarah's arm. "Oh, America seems so far. If I were there, I'd never leave."

"Don't discourage her," Layla tutted.

"Your happy home, where women are free. As for us, we rub on lipstick for a bright smile, eye shadow for a gleam in our eyes and blusher to make like we're happy. And then, what do we do? We hide behind our veils and weep."

Layla lit a cigarette. "Tisam, please. Sarah will think we have pain and hopelessness in our souls."

"I exaggerated," Tisam said, laughing. "My life is easier. I have no husband."

"That's unusual, isn't it?" Sarah said.

"Perhaps, but a girl cannot be married against her will. Maybe I will tell you something." She had a strange look on her face and lowered her voice. "You're a doctor, and so you keep confidences."

"I do." Sarah leaned forward.

Tisam picked at a loose thread on her sleeve. "Well, you see. I am what you call 'femme,' but God alone is my judge."

Sarah sagged in her chair. Poor Tisam, a lesbian in the worst place in the world to be one.

"God wouldn't create gays only to condemn them, would he? The Qur'an says not even a leaf falls off a tree without his consent. If he created so many of us, then what right have others to point the finger at us?"

"Darling Tisam." Layla put an arm around her. "Remember what I said. It may be a test from God for you. Pray to God for him to change you. If you were to marry, maybe—"

"It wouldn't be fair. How would a husband feel when he found out?"

"I wish you would. Imagine what people would say if they knew. We'll find a man for you who is already married, someone who'll understand and not come to you often. Who knows? Maybe you might even start to like it."

A look of distaste flitted over Tisam's face. "I doubt it. I'm not a bad girl. I put my trust in God. I fulfill my religious obligations. Maybe on the day of judgment, people will be shocked to see gays in paradise." She turned to Sarah. "Auntie Malika doesn't know, which is why she pushed me on Ibrahim. Silly, isn't it when he's crazy in love with you?"

"I'm lucky," Sarah said softly. She felt abashed, all that energy she had so stupidly wasted being jealous.

"You have lots of suitors. You should choose one," Layla said to Tisam.

"No, I shouldn't. It would be unkind. He would feel such shame when I turned from him in bed. Soon, God willing, I'll be old and men won't want me. What a blessing that will be!"

After Sarah got home, Ib called to say he was emailing her a draft of the letter he wanted to send her parents. Her mind was on what Tisam had shared with her, and she answered him distantly. Now that they were engaged, she did not want to keep any secrets from him; and he was the kind of person she could trust not to pass it any further. However, Tisam had told her in the intimacy of confidence and certainly it was not for her to disclose the secret. Perhaps Ib already knew, for he had told her that Tisam would not have him. She did not tell him. A few moments later, she went to her computer to retrieve the draft of his letter.

Dear Mr. and Mrs. Moss,

I am writing to request your blessing. I have proposed marriage
to Sarah, and she has accepted me. It is my dearest wish that you will
accept me into your family. As you know, I first met my beloved Sarah
at Thanksgiving almost a year ago when your son Peter invited me to
your home. I cherish your generous hospitality and kindness.

Sarah and I love each other. Thank you for raising her to become
the woman she is. Although we are of different cultures and religions,
is it not true, God willing, that love conquers all?

Yours faithfully,
Ibrahim Suleiman

Sarah called back to say the letter was perfect, and he arranged to have
it sent by courier so her parents would receive it the very next day.

When she called home the following evening, her mother came on
the line, a bit out of breath.

"Did you get the letter?"

"Yes…Yes…Oh, Sarah, how could you? I should be so happy for you.
But…but are you really certain?"

"Mom, we're going to be the happiest couple in the world. You like
him; I know you do."

"Of course, but it's not simple, not simple at all."

"Please, Mom, don't make things any more complicated than they are
already."

"I'll get your father."

Sarah bit her lower lip, and gripped the telephone, her hands clammy.
She never knew when her father's temper would explode. Her chest felt
tight and her stomach queasy.

"Sarah, for the love of God…" He roared across the ocean, and she could picture him bouncing on his toes like a boxer, cheeks red with rage. "You've no idea what you're doing."

"Please, Daddy, it'll be okay." She willed him to sit in his recliner.

"What about his family?"

"I'm not marrying them. I'm marrying Ib," she said, her voice shaking. "I love him. I need your—" She remembered the word Ib had used and said firmly, "We need your blessing."

Daddy's voice was flat with suppressed anger. "Have you set the date?"

"We were thinking of August 18."

"Two weeks? Why the big hurry?" He gasped. "Holy shit!" he exploded. "Are you—"

"Daddy, of course not, nothing like that. That's as soon as Ib can get permission."

"Permission! Why the hell does he need permission?"

Sarah took a deep breath, for it was not going at all well. "Just a bureaucratic thing. Any Saudi who wants to marry a foreigner needs it."

"And doesn't that worry you? Here, talk to your mother," he said, sounding disgusted. "Maybe she can talk some sense into you."

"We're losing you. What did we do wrong?" Her mother whimpered. "Why aren't we good enough for you anymore?"

"Will you become a Mohammedan or whatever they call themselves?" Daddy snapped and hung up on her.

A few moments later, she called back. When there was no answer, she went to her desk, opened her laptop, and typed quickly.

Dearest Mom and Daddy,
I know this isn't easy for you, but it'll work out. I doubt I'll become Muslim,

but I'm studying Islam so I can understand it. For me it's not a question of
which faith is better, but whether I can believe in any faith at all. Remember
how Jesus said that there are many rooms in my Father's mansion? Maybe
Islam is the one for me.

She reread the sentence and realized it would just anger her parents, so
she deleted it and continued:

Please don't focus on Islam. Religion is just one part of Ib. That's not what
matters. It's Ib and me. I feel so lucky to have him in my life.

Hugs and kisses,
Sarah

From: Rollawaythestone@aol.com
To: sarahMoss@ash.org.ksa
Subject: Concern

Dear Sarah,

I feel so disappointed and hurt. I always imagined you walking up the aisle
on your daddy's arm. Pastor Mallock always says just the right things at
weddings. Perhaps it's none of my business and forgive me if I am butting in.
I want all of God's blessings for you and I don't see that you're going to find
them in that Muslim country. Please come home. Your father agrees with me.

Mom

Later, when Sarah offered to send plane tickets so they could come
to Khobar for the wedding, they refused, repeating that they could not
bless the marriage. Ib was unpleasant about it, which was unfair of him.
"Why do your parents have to be so blunt, hurting your feelings like
that?" he asked. "Why can't they beg off, saying that the journey is
too long? Don't they care about you at all?" Then, to make matters
worse, his father offered to fly over to meet her parents so they would

trust Ibrahim's intentions were honorable. She pictured Omar Suleiman walking down Illinois Avenue in his robe and red-and-white checked headdress. Everyone would gawk, and he would feel insulted. "But your father has emphysema," she said. "The flight, the waiting, all the hassle and exhaustion would be too much for him."

Ib planted his hands on his knees, a pained look on his face. "But it is our custom. That way your family will know that we treasure you."

"They'll just think it's odd."

"Sarah, be reasonable. My father, speaking man to man, can persuade your father to relent and come be your witness. You do realize that you need a witness?"

She smiled up at him. "I was thinking of Layla."

"Sarah," he said, laughing unpleasantly. "Surely by now you realize it's better if it's a man."

"All right then. If that's the way it is, I'll ask Pete."

"So it's settled."

"Yes," she said a little sadly for it was not turning out the way she had hoped.

CHAPTER 11

LAYLA WAS OF THE OPINION that since Sarah was starting a new life, she needed all new clothes, and this evening Annie was helping her choose a dress for the dinner welcoming her to the Suleiman family. It was a Tuesday, and bachelors who were forbidden at the mall on the weekends, were on the prowl checking out the girls. Sarah and Annie drifted from one shop to the next, all of them full of the latest designer fashions from New York and Paris. It was similar to a high-end mall in Chicago except for the cordoned off prayer areas, plastic palm trees and large number of extravagant fountains. Sarah found the perfect dress, designed by Yves St. Laurent, in aquamarine silk with a cowl neck and long, transparent sleeves. They went next to Delilah's Boutique. While Annie checked out the racks of thongs and red teddies, Sarah select-ed a satin nightgown with matching ivory peignoir and a few pairs of lounging pajamas. The lingerie sales staff was men, which seemed sur-real. Sarah, who wanted a few new bras, felt odd giving her cup size to a man. There were no changing rooms so she tried on the clothes in the restroom. The place was jammed with women, wriggling in and out of clothes while screeching youngsters jumped up and down on the heaps of discards. Squeezed up against the bank of mirrors on one wall, women of all ages troweled on mascara and eye shadow and admired themselves. They were not like her friends in the States who moaned over every little pimple and fussed if they were five or six pounds over-weight. Women here all believed they were gorgeous.

After Delilah's, Sarah and Annie decided to eat at the Aladdin Café down the street. As they left the mall, Sarah noticed a woman take a pen from her bag, jot something on a scrap of paper, and toss it to the ground. Instantly a man swooped down, pocketed it, and flashed the woman a dazzling smile.

"See that?" Annie nudged her. "She just got herself a telephone boy-friend. Now you tell me, how can the faith cops ever stop that?"

The café was a pleasant place with gold-and-white embroidered table-cloths. They found a table in the women's section in back and ordered lentil soup and lattes. As they waited, Sarah told Annie about the wed-ding which was to be the traditional three-day affair with family dinner, henna party, ceremony at the mosque, and finally the reception. The food arrived.

Annie took a sip of soup. "Mmm. Spicy. Any last-minute snafus?"

"The invitations. Get this. Here's the wording, and I quote, 'We in-vite you to the marriage of our son Ibrahim to the daughter of Malcolm and Gloria Moss.' Notice whose name is absent?"

"Uh-huh." Annie took a bite of bread. "Yours. And you got upset."

"I'm afraid so. Layla said her mother was just following the custom."

"Layla's right. It's taboo to include the bride's name. Go figure." The next moment Annie looked puzzled. "But my invitation was in English."

"I didn't want to upset Malika—she's touchy— so I sent Ib's family the ones without my name. But I also ordered some in English, Miss Manners style. That's what you got." She drained her latté. "Still, in hindsight, I regret it. It's more duplicity."

"It's not important. Have you guys prepared the marriage contract yet?"

Sarah brushed biscotti crumbs off her lap. "Frankly, it turns me off. It makes the whole thing sound so businesslike."

Annie set down her cup. "Don't you get all starry-eyed. It's important to stipulate what you want."

"You sound like Ib. I had the lawyer insert conditions." Sarah ticked them off her fingers, feeling like a cop reading a crook his Miranda rights: "I have the right to work. I have the right to travel unaccompanied anywhere in the kingdom and the world. I have the right to invite anyone I wish into our home. I have the right to automatic divorce with custody of any children if Ib takes a second wife."

"I wouldn't think they'd allow all that. You're lucky he's such a great guy."

"He wasn't very nice about my parents. They're not coming."

"Bummer. So if your father isn't coming, who's going to be your witness?"

"My brother. He arrives tonight. Guess what he wants to see? Camels."

"No surprise there."

"I suppose not." Sarah glanced at her watch. "I don't want to be late for my shift."

"Don't worry. Tell me about your brother coming."

"Shaheed can't abide the idea that Pete might sneak a glimpse of Susu at the family dinner. He thinks that if Pete sees her, he'll fall for her, Susu being in Shaheed's eyes the one desirable woman in the universe. So Layla suggested Susu veil. That way she would be there but not there. Know what I mean? Shaheed said he'd consider it, but then Layla insisted it was up to Susu to decide, not him."

"Quite the feminist Layla is. I bet Shaheed had a fit. So what do you think will happen?"

"I guess we'll find out tomorrow night."

"I wouldn't bet on Susu's coming. That crazy husband of hers sounds like a lunatic. So where's the honeymoon?"

"Lebanon."

"What! Not Hawaii? Not Paris? Well, at least you'll be out of town. Safe from Big Mama." Annie leaned in close and lowered her voice. "Sometimes, the groom's mother checks the sheets the morning after."

Sarah shuddered. She could not imagine a more humiliating way to begin a marriage. She checked her watch again. Her shift began in a half-hour. She spotted the waiter, but it took several minutes to catch his eye, and several minutes more for him to bring the bill and for them to pay. At last, they were able to go. Sarah started for the door.

A waiter stood, arms crossed in front of the padlocked door, barring it. "Madam, it's prayer time. During prayer time, nobody enters, nobody leaves."

"I've got to go now."

He repeated his mantra. "During prayer time, nobody enters, nobody leaves."

"We need to leave. Now!" Sarah said in a louder voice.

"It's prayer time. Please be patient, Madam."

Sarah felt herself getting stubborn. She looked for an emergency exit, but did not see one. "Who has the key? Go get him."

"No worry, Lady. Prayer is soon over. Just a few more minutes."

"Find the person who has the key. Now!" She yelled and glowering, took a step toward him.

He backed down. "Yes, madam. At your service. I will go right away."

Sarah became increasingly anxious as he did not reappear. A full five minutes later, a white-bearded man appeared, dug deep into the pocket of his robe, and extracted a key. He pushed it in the keyhole, swung open the hasp, and informed them that prayers were over. Sarah shot out the door. She was livid, but Annie took it in stride. "Happens all the time," she said. "You'll get used to it. Just ask yourself if that's the sword you want to fall on."

In fact, Sarah made it to the hospital in plenty of time.

The next evening, she accompanied the Suleiman menfolk to the airport. All was the same as when she had arrived two months earlier in late June: the gleaming marble, the massed flowers, the scent of rosewater, and the cry of the zaghareet as women welcomed their loved ones—but she herself had changed. Then she had been untried. Now she had less freedom, but each free gesture counted for more.

As the passengers drifted out in groups of two and three, she could not help but worry. If Pete was caught with an illicit joint or bottle of whisky, he could be imprisoned. Finally, to her immense relief, there he was, a dazed expression on his face as he scanned the arrivals hall. She waved at him, and he looked blankly at her. "Pete," she called, taking off her head scarf. "It's me. Over here."

"Wow! Look at you in that get-up," he said.

"It's what we wear here." Feeling her cheeks flush red, she added in a nonchalant tone. "I must look like a witch."

Ib flung his arm around Pete's shoulder. "Welcome to the family."

"Hey, man," Ahmed gave him a friendly jab in the arm. "Glad to meet you." Ib's father shook hands too, and then they all piled into Ahmed's van and sped through the sticky August night toward Sarah's apartment in the Western Compound. "Wow. Is that ever cool," Pete kept saying, impressed by the skyscrapers, the water towers, and the engineering of the highway interchanges. Sarah felt pleased. He was staying with her and they sat at her kitchen table and talked late into the night. "Oh, another thing, last week I ran into your ex," Pete said, his voice casual.

"Oh *him*." Sarah grimaced. "Still doing the church thing?"

"Yeah, youth pastor. Married with four kids."

"Well, bully for David." She felt a little resentful.

"He sent you guys this." Pete handed her a heavy box, covered in silvery paper. Inside was a hammer, a tool she and Ib had no use for. How dare David send her a present as if he were a friend, someone who had never hurt her? For a moment, she imagined life as a pastor's wife: church politics, parishioners, and all their multiple needs. She might be expected to lead prayers; that was out of the question. Marrying David would have meant living an entire life of duplicity. And David himself? Good riddance. After sex, occasionally he would ask, "On a score of one to five, how was that for you?" It was demeaning. She could not describe passion any more than how a peony bud opens, darkening into red at its base, its petals unfurling. Some things were better honored by being kept secret. She threw the wrapping paper in the wastebasket and stuck the hammer in the junk drawer. "Hungry?" she asked Pete.

"Scrambled eggs and rice would be nice."

As they ate, she coached him on the etiquette of Saudi dining: to keep his feet tucked under him as he sat on the floor; to accept whatever he was offered, and to use only his right hand.

"Sit on the floor? Eat with my hands? You're not serious."

"Just think of it as a picnic. I'll show you." She scooped a bit of rice in her fingers, pressed it into a ball, and flicked it into her mouth with her thumb. "See, it's easy."

Pete mimicked her and then wiped his fingers on a napkin. "Greasy."

"You'll do fine. Just remember, don't look at the women, especially not Susu, assuming that crazy husband of hers lets her come."

Pete gave her a quizzical look. "Sure is strange here."

"Just different," Sarah said loyally.

The next day Ib took Pete to see the camel market in Hofuf, while Johnny drove the women to Qatif, where the dinner would be later that evening. Sarah and Layla spent the late afternoon at the tell. Sarah found a spot on the stony ledge overlooking the baths and sat with her hands clasped around her knees. Here at the foot of the tell, she felt as if she were proclaiming to past generations of women, that yes, she was risking it.

"I don't know why you and Mother like it here." Layla took off her cloak and brushed a fly off her cheek. "There she comes. She can't keep away." Layla gestured toward the figure lumbering their way.

"Ah. You." Malika pressed a leathery cheek against Sarah's. "So my daughter told you about our place?"

"Ibrahim told me. It is as beautiful here as he said it would be."

Malika scowled. "How would he know? He has not been here. Men are forbidden."

"I misspoke. He meant its reputation for beauty."

"So. And is our water pure enough for you?" Malika said in a sarcastic voice.

"Mother, don't be like that, please don't. Sarah, now that we're here, let's swim." Layla stripped to her slip, hovered a moment at the edge, and did a cannonball, splashing into the water. "Come on in," she yelled. "It's nice and cool." Sarah dived in and swam toward her. They loitered first in the shallows and afterward swam sidestroke around the perimeter. After they climbed out, Layla went off to talk to a neighbor. Sarah knew what she had to do: to court Malika the way one would a queen. Stomach churning, a smile plastered on her face, she ventured closer, but Malika remained absorbed in pushing her dozen gold bangles back and forth from her wrist to her elbow, clicking one against the other. Completely ignoring Sarah, she pulled out the bobby pins tucked in the tight bun at the back of her head and a mass of iron-gray hair fell to her waist. She took a tortoiseshell comb from her black bag, parted her hair, separating it into hanks, and began combing it.

Sarah sat cross-legged opposite her and tried to make conversation. "You have such beautiful thick hair."

"So you say," Malika grunted.

"Ibrahim took my brother to see the camel market this morning."

"Just to see it? He does that, does he? Just like you?" She scowled and raised her eyebrows.

"You must be glad that Fawzi is out of hospital." Feeling desperate, Sarah tried to keep up the farce of a conversation. "He's a sweet boy, isn't he?"

Malika bent over and rubbed the turquoise ring on her third toe.

"Lulu's very pretty."

"So they say." Malika massaged her toes.

Sarah bit her lower lip. She should feel pity for the poor woman, who was in such a foul mood that she could not get out of it by herself. She tried to think of a conciliatory remark that was neither boring nor irritating. "I'd like us to be friends," she said, reaching out to touch Malika on the arm.

Malika brushed off Sarah's hand as if it were a roach.

His mother was so sullen, so unlike the woman who had smiled at her after the procedure on Fawzi's arm. "I wish you'd smile," Sarah cried out in desperation. "You really should. You have a radiant smile."

"So you say." Malika looked her in the eye and yawned loudly, showing her gold molars.

They sat in glum silence until Layla came hurrying up a quarter of an hour later. "Can you believe how late it is?" She smiled at Sarah. "Ibrahim will be waiting. "

"Ah, yes, my son will be wanting me," Malika said in a loud, proprietary tone.

Layla draped her abaya around herself. "Mother, you talk as if you have only one son. Poor Shaheed. I think he acts the way he does because that's the only way he can get your attention."

"Girl, you talk such nonsense. I have done no wrong. It's his boss, that Kabeer. The man is a snare. I've told Shaheed a thousand times, but will the boy listen to me? He is in peril and I can do nothing. Nothing."

Sarah lagged a few steps behind as they strolled toward the town. Just outside the bakery at the end of the footpath, she noticed a girl standing, bending to adjust the strap of her pink sandals. A youth darted up, snatched her head scarf and ran off, waving it in his hand.

"See that?" Layla said. "He got away with it."

"What?" Malika said. "See what? What are you talking about?"

"Oh Mother, one of those awful Eve-teasers. Really, didn't you see? You're blind as a bat."

"If anyone ever tried a trick like that on you, I'd tear his flesh apart."

Sarah felt sure that was exactly what Malika would do. Like a tigress, she would protect her cub.

CHAPTER 12

MUCH LATER THAT EVENING, Sarah entered the Suleimans' salon on
Pete's arm. A diamond bracelet sparkled on her wrist and emeralds on
the cuffs of Ib's thobe—their presents to each other. Everyone was there
including Susu, her face veiled and her red dress covered by her abaya.
The wedding gifts were displayed on a side table. The Bedouin necklace from his grandmother did not surprise Sarah; or the two swans
in Lalique crystal from Layla and Ahmed; or the gold-edged Qur'an
from Shaheed and Susu. The other presents she might have expected
too: the sterling picture frame from Tisam with a promise of a portrait;
the antique clock from Pete; the sterling flatware from her parents; the
brass candlesticks from Uncle Tom, the hammock from Annie, and the
illuminated globe from the hospital staff. Only Malika and Omar's gift
took her aback—it was a small wooden chest inlaid with mother-of-
pearl; in one of the red velvet compartments was a heap of gold coins
and in the other three bangles in yellow, pink and white gold. Did his
mother intend the gift as a peace offering? Ib smiled at his mother and

gestured for her to slide the bangles onto Sarah's wrist, but Malika drew
her furry eyebrows close and shook her head. Ib slipped on the bracelets.

A maid tinkled a bell, and they lined up to wash their hands, the
men in one of the bathrooms and the women and children at the
old-fashioned kitchen sink. As they all sat down at the table laid with
freshly pressed linen and gleaming silver, the men rolled back their
sleeves, and in unison, they murmured *Bismallah*, "In God's name." Ib's
father raised a flute of Saudi champagne and proposed a toast to Sarah
and to Pete, "her brother and guardian." They would love and respect
Sarah as their own daughter, Omar said. As Sarah lifted the glass of
apple juice and Perrier water, she felt lucky. Blessed, her mother would
say. Pete offered a toast to the absent ones, and she yearned for her parents. She had called them earlier that day, but the connection was poor;
there was static on the line; she and her parents talked over one another,
interrupted each other, or paused too long for fear of interrupting, and
there were painful silences. The conversation was so stilted that she was
glad when Daddy said, "Good luck to you both. You'll need it." Mom
said, "God bless you, God bless you all the days of your lives."

Sarah was glad to have Pete here, an ally in the room scented with
the fragrance of burning sandalwood incense. He kept his eyes off Susu,
who lifted and lowered her veil before and after every forkful. It was all
delicious: ten different dishes including spiced fish stew, stuffed koosa
in yoghurt sauce, and Bukhara chicken. After a while, even Shaheed
relaxed and everyone ate heartily except Malika, who was busy pressing
food on Pete. He actually seemed to enjoy her attention. At the camel
market, he had met a tribesman whose camel was branded on the cheek

with what looked like the letter M. When Pete asked how much the camel cost, the man said he was planning to keep it for his own wedding.

They went into the salon, and the maid entered with the coffee tray. Sarah went to sit on the sofa beside Malika, and Ib smiled approvingly.

Malika served Pete first. Poor Pete. He hated coffee. Dutifully he drained the tiny china cup almost as soon as he was offered it. Even as a kid, he was like that, taking his medicine fast.

"More coffee?" Malika took his cup and dropped in a sugar cube.

"He doesn't like sugar," Sarah said.

Malika's dark eyebrows shot up. "What is life without sweetness?"

Ib glanced warily at Sarah, and she remembered how Saudis drank their coffee unsweetened only after a death.

Pete told them how he had seen a crane winch up a camel, the beast hovering and snarling in mid-air before it was lowered to the back of the pick-up truck. According to Ib, Pete charmed everyone he met, managing in his easygoing way with only his three words of Arabic, *marhaba*, *mabrouk* and *shukrun*.

"You don't get to see something like that market everyday, old and the new together," Pete said.

"The new, that's what counts. We must look to our future," Ahmed said, which set him off talking about his research. Pete finished his coffee, and Malika refilled the cup. He shot a despairing look at Sarah.

"Just wiggle your cup," Sarah whispered in his ear. "Watch me."

Later, when Malika approached her with the coffee pot, Sarah caught Pete's eye and in exaggerated fashion wiggled her hand. The next thing she knew, two drops splattered the skirt of her new dress. "Oh," she cried, covering the brown stains with her hands.

Malika screamed something in Arabic and ran out of the room.

Ib rushed to Sarah. "Darling, are you burned?"

"No, but my dress—look at it." She stood up, holding the silk with both hands.

Layla darted to her and led her to the kitchen where she found a bottle of spot remover in a cupboard. "It was an accident, darling Sarah," Layla said as she dabbed at the spots.

"She did it on purpose."

"Oh, no. Mother's as blind as a bat. She can't even see to pour straight. Everyone knows that. And yet, will she have that simple little surgery? She annoys me so much. Still I better go check on her."

A few minutes later, Layla came back and said her mother was sobbing in the bedroom and could not be persuaded to unlock the door.

The next morning, Sarah held Pete's arm as they entered the imam's oak-paneled office in Khobar's central mosque. On the desk lay two copies of the marriage contract, one for her and one for Ib.

Pete put Sarah's hand in Ib's. "Take care of her, okay?"

"I will protect her always." With Shaheed standing at his side, Ib looked into her eyes and said: "In the name of Allah, most Gracious, most merciful. With his help and guidance; with all my trust put in him; with my full awareness of responsibility; and with my free choice, I, Ibrahim Suleiman, solemnly propose to marry Miss Sarah Moss, and take her as my wife, in accordance with the teachings and laws of the Qur'an and the Sunnah of the Prophet Muhammad, Peace Be Upon

Him. I declare this solemn proposal before the present witnesses, praying to Almighty Allah to be my witness; Allah is the best of witnesses."

As Sarah repeated, "Allah is the best of witnesses," her voice shook and her whole body trembled. The imam gave a short sermon in Arabic, little of which she understood except for his prayer that Allah shower blessings on them and unite them in goodness. Ib signed the contract, passed the fountain pen to her, and the nib scratched against the heavy paper as she signed her name below his flowery script. At last, they were man and wife.

Two minutes later, she watched him walk away from her, flanked by Pete and Shaheed. She would not see him until the following night.

Layla took her home. Later after they had had long siestas, the masseuse arrived. A heavyset woman with indigo tattoos on her forehead, she went into the old-fashioned kitchen, where she mixed sugar and lemon juice in a pot, which she set on the stove and stirred until it caramelized. She spread a foam mat and white sheet on the large kitchen table and motioned Sarah to lie down. The custom was to have no body hair below the eyebrows, but Sarah said the masseuse could remove only the hair from her legs and armpits. The masseuse predicted something terrible—repudiation by the groom— would ensue if Sarah did not offer him a smooth hairless body.

"Well, it's my body, and I don't want to," Sarah said.

"Everybody knows Americans don't remove their body hair. Her husband will forgive her," Layla said.

The masseuse shrugged. Using both thumbs, she smoothed a strip of the sugaring down Sarah's leg and waited a moment for it to set. Then with a quick upward jerk, she pulled it off. "Ow!" Sarah yelped. Layla brought her a pot of sweet mint tea and Sarah took a sip after each painful yank.

"Such sensitive skin." Layla showed her the bits of auburn fuzz left in the sugaring. "You are so delicate, sister-in-law. Apart from that you are perfect."

"Nobody's perfect," Sarah said, her legs smarting.

Layla hesitated. "There is only one thing about you that worries me."

"Oh? What is it?" Sarah asked, trying not to sound too anxious. "Please tell me."

"I'm still not sure that you'll be able to...Will you..." Layla's voice trailed off. "Oh, how I wish you would find it in yourself to be more patient with my mother. If only you would call her Um Ibrahim. Oh, don't frown like that. Do it to show respect. Nothing more."

Here, that was how women with children were called—Mother of so and so—relegated to the status of a breeder. Earlier, Sarah had refused the seventy thousand dollars Ib had offered in dowry. Scandalized, Malika had shaken her finger and said, "Money from the husband, children from the wife. That is the tradition."

Now Layla tactfully shifted the subject to her own wedding, before which she had to rest forty days at home, not seen by anyone. That put the masseuse in a better humor. She placed a large towel under Sarah, dipped a brawny hand in a tub of dark liquid soap, and rubbed it all over, scrubbing her with a loofah. She kneaded her back, slapped up and down the length of her spine, and smeared a yellow cream over her back, then sluiced her down with water and pronounced her as soft as a turtledove. She sprinkled her with attar of rose, each drop distilled from the petals of twenty roses gathered when still wet with dew. Meanwhile Layla prepared henna for the traditional henna party. She emptied an envelope of fresh henna powder into a bowl, and added lemon juice, mixing it until it was the consistency of pancake batter. She poured the dark green glop into a plastic bag and set it on top of the old marble counter to wait for the henna to release its dye.

Layla went off to pray—it was already past nine-thirty— while Sarah drank a glass of milk and ate a peanut butter sandwich; she tried to steady her nerves. It seemed surreal that here she was, legally married yet kept from her husband and subjected to these strange ministrations when what she wanted to do was to make love to Ib.

After prayers, Layla helped Sarah into one of her new dresses, green satin with orange and black ribbons, and led her into the salon, where some fifty guests were assembled. She recognized various cousins and aunties, her Arabic teacher Munira, her interns, and female colleagues who brought along their teenage daughters. There was the usual passing of rosewater, belly dancing and light gossiping; as was traditional they ate cardamom flavored chicken *seleek* and sticky rice. About eleven, Layla brought out the henna and sat Sarah down on a bolster and cushions. "Henna brings luck to a marriage," she said; she dipped each of Sarah's fingers up to the second knuckle in the bowl of henna. She traced a floral design on the back of each hand and offered to continue the pattern all the way up her forearms, but Sarah demurred.

"You're right. We mustn't exaggerate." Layla squeezed lemon juice over Sarah's hands to keep the henna from smearing and then turned her attention to Sarah's feet. She painted the dark brown paste on Sarah's right instep, wrapped the foot in white cloth, and then did the same with the other foot. Meanwhile the women sang songs praising her beauty and later, a few of them cracked dirty jokes.

"Ah, such a lovely bride," Tisam said. "Such sparkly eyes. I dislike those brides who sit with their chins tucked in the palms of their hands like sad little birds that can't hold up their heads." She patted Sarah's wrapped hands, broke a piece of baklava, and fed it to her. Sarah felt self-conscious, but nothing could upset her tonight. The aunties gossiped about how much better life would be for her now that she was married. Now she could go walking with Ibrahim, even at night, and no Eve-teaser dare harass her; she could eat with him at any restaurant; and he would take her places and run errands for her. Oh, yes, such a lucky girl.

They clustered around her as Layla removed the cloths, rubbed off the green crust of henna, and poured rosewater over her hands. Sarah stretched out her fingers. The pads of her fingertips had turned a deep orange, which Layla called, "the color of joy."

"The bride! The bride! So beautiful is the bride," the women cried and sounded the *zaghareet.* "Sister Sarah," they called; gaily she waved her hennaed hands at them. Again, they howled. Nothing on earth could match the joy and power of this cry. Surely, it could waken the dead.

On the third and last day of the wedding celebration, Sarah slept in until four o'clock in the afternoon when the hairdresser arrived. She pinned strings of seed pearls, a gift from Layla, into her hair, and when

Sarah moved her head, the pearls swung back and forth.

"Perfume is the best aphrodisiac." Layla opened a mother-of-pearl chest lined with vials. Floral scents were best around the face, so she dabbed gardenia behind Sarah's ears, lily of the valley on her neck, and attar of rose on her throat. "Now you put on the rest—a different perfume for each part. You might like spicy around the breasts, woodsy for the arms and legs, and musk for…you know where," she giggled.

To please Layla Sarah tried them all. She dabbed the carnation scent under her breasts, touched a drop of cloves at her navel, cedarwood on her wrist, sandalwood in the crook of her arm, and musk to her pubis. Behind each knee, she dabbed on a scent like grapefruit and on her ankles a lemony one.

"Ah! Such heavenly fragrance," Layla said.

"It's not too much?"

Layla laughed merrily. "Impossible. Perfume is one of God's blessings. And now the dress." It rustled as Layla lifted it out of the tissue lining the long box. She fingered the ivory taffeta appraisingly, noting the heft of the fabric, the elegance of the design, and the bustle at the back of the long skirt. Sarah stepped into it, and Layla fastened the ninety-nine taffeta-covered buttons along the back, working them into the stiff loops that ran down the length of the dress.

"My mother, grandmother and great-grandmother all wore this dress," Sarah said. Layla, who never wore an outfit more than three times, looked surprised.

"This, this bustle, as you call it. It gives you a most beautiful form," Layla said.

Reminded of Malika's hurtful remark about her "boy's behind," Sarah touched the folds of the centennial gown. "About your mother," she said. "I know I'm not her choice, but I'll do my best."

"She feels badly about staining your dress. It's just that she's blind and can't see."

"I should have told her right away that I knew it was a mistake." Full of remorse, Sarah vowed that she would make Malika like her. It might take effort and time, but she would be patient. This very night, she would go to her.

The men and women celebrated separately in two different halls of the International Hotel. The men's party began after Isha prayers about eight, and at midnight, Ib called Sarah on her cellphone to say that he, his father, brother, and Pete would meet her outside the hall where the women were gathered. She slipped away from the women to meet her groom. Over his thobe, Ib wore a silk *bisht*, and a white headdress instead of the usual red-and-white checked one. Tisam snapped dozens of pictures of the bride and groom, and then some of Sarah and Pete, who joked he would have liked a picture of him eating camel meat. After the men of the family returned to their party, Ib took Sarah's hand, and they entered the women's reception followed by a procession of young girls bearing platters of fresh garlands and small candles and singing, "Peace be with you." The women of the Burqu'a Band pounded their drums, and Malika led the high-pitched keening of the *zaghareet* as the bridal couple progressed to gold thrones set on a spotlit dais. As Sarah arranged the train of her dress, her hennaed hand made a splash of orange against the ivory taffeta.

The drummers ceased, and a hush fell as Ib spoke. "Sarah!"

Layla had coached her on what to do, and she kept her head bowed. A second time Ib said, "Sarah!" She kept her eyes fixed on the arabesques of the Isfahani carpet at her feet. As the trilling of the *zaghareet* reached a frenzied pitch, he lifted the lacy bridal veil; she tucked her head down; he cupped his hand under her chin, tipping it up. She kept her eyes downcast until she felt his fingers touch her cheek. The moment she met his eyes, the drone of grumbling came from the assembled women, whose faces had shone with interest just minutes ago.

"Darling Sarah, you're supposed to play harder to get," he said, laughing. "They miss the suspense."

"Too much for me," she said, smiling at him.

A hundred kohl-rimmed eyes peered at them from the slits in their facemasks and veils. She felt rapturous, knowing she was linked with him forever. About two in the morning, the waiters wheeled in the six-tiered wedding cake and set it on a table between two bouquets of birds-of-paradise flown in from Kenya. His hand felt warm over hers on the ribbon-trimmed knife as they cut through the stiff icing into the wedding cake. His fingers grazed her lips as he fed her the first piece; she put a morsel on his tongue and felt the softness of his mustache.

The Nubian women of the Burqu'a Band slapped their tambourines and belted out the tribal rhythms. Layla sprang to the dance floor. Fresh greenery glistened in her hair, and she stamped her bare feet, her ankle bracelets jingling. As she tossed her head to the music, her hair cascaded down one shoulder and then the other. A few other women stepped onto the floor and Layla bellydanced up to Tisam and persuaded her to

put down her camera. Tisam loosened her hair and swung it from side
to side in a widening arc and when she got going, it flew out like a flag
and the women clapped and cheered. She took the crimson scarf from
her waist, and waved it, so it unfurled and floated. Again, the women
ululated, and the Burqu'a Band banged their tambourines louder as
Malika undulated to the center. She swayed trance-like; she rippled her
tummy, but the necklace of silver balls big as tangerines barely moved.
She raised a scabbard above her head and metal scraped against metal
as she drew out a gold-handled sword. Tisam danced up and took the
sword. Her bare arms gleamed in the light of the chandeliers, and she
danced, twisting her hips, advancing and retreating from the bridal dais.
A girl in red chiffon took the sword and danced with it licentiously;
with the blade flat on the palms of her hands, she wriggled to the floor
and laid the sword at Ib's feet.

"Let's go," he whispered with a little catch in his voice. She had intended to spend time with Malika, but she forgot all about her as she
and Ib made their way from the dais toward the door under a cascade of
rose petals.

A few hours later, in the honeymoon suite of Beirut's best hotel, above
the crashing waves of the Mediterranean, he brushed her eyelids shut
with his lips. " Such fragrance, the perfume of paradise," he murmured
as he stroked her breasts, murmuring, "dunes, beautiful dunes." He lifted her onto the bed and caressed her thighs. In her ears was a whirring,
a rhythm like the ocean enclosed in a seashell, the waves low-pitched
and continuous. The candles smoked and guttered, and they moved as
man and wife in the thick-scented darkness.

CHAPTER 13

ON SEPTEMBER 1, THEY RETURNED. They were on their way toward
Firdaus, a suburb of Khobar where the water company had reassigned
Ib to a bungalow in the family quarters. A few minutes from Firdaus, he
pulled off the highway and parked by the seaside. When they stepped
out of the car, it was so hot that it was hard to breathe normally. They
strolled toward the shoreline, where hermit crabs scuttled sideways and
mud snails nose-dived into the wet sand. Ib, who was a few steps ahead,
stopped abruptly to gather sand in his cupped hands. When he stood
up, a billion grains fell. She was reminded of last winter in Madison
when she went to his room and he trickled the rust-red sand over her.
Now he pressed his face into her hair. "I'm so glad to be back. And you?"

"I loved Beirut, the cedars, the mountains. Everything." She thought
of the bookstores, cinemas, theatres, the umbrella pines in the mountains, and the beaches with women in bikinis. "Nice for a vacation,"
she said.

"I thought you liked it too. It felt so free. We could hold hands and
nobody even noticed. Remember dancing hip-hop at the Kit Kat?"

"Sure, but there I'm just another rich Saudi. Nothing better than a dog. This is where I need to be. It's a larger world here. Look over there." He pointed to the west.

"Look at what? There's nothing."

"Oh, but there used to be. A dune, a hundred feet high, right here. One day it was here, the next, poof—gone." He gave a sharp breath as if blowing on the fluffy seed head of a dandelion. As they ambled back to the car, he told her how in prehistory the entire region was verdant, as green as Qatif, and even now, if you dug deep enough, you found water. A few hundred thousand years ago, his ancestors had migrated from sub-Saharan Africa, walking north, settling here and there for a generation or two, then traveling again, halting only when they reached Arabia. "*Arabia Felix*, Happy Arabia," he said.

Sarah looked at the emptiness where the dune supposedly had been. If she went far enough back, her ancestors also must have originated from Africa, and undertaken the same journey, but hers had kept on, crossing the Mediterranean, Daddy's forbears settling in Ireland, before emigrating during the Great Potato Famine. Almost a hundred years later, Granny, a proper English girl from Plymouth fell in love with Desmond Moss, the red-headed American soldier-grandfather Sarah had never met. Granny too had moved for love, a war bride. She told Ib about it as they got in the car and drove toward Firdaus.

When they reached the compound, the guard at the security barrier waved them through, and Ib drove down the wide streets past manicured lawns. "Firdaus" means "paradise," and she could see why the name had been chosen. Red-blossoming fig trees filled the medians and hedges of pink oleander lined the clean streets. All the buildings were long and low, nothing higher than the minaret of the compound's gold-domed mosque. Ib said that in ten years if things went according to plan, there would be fifty thousand residents in two neighborhoods, each with its own mosque, school, mall, and recreation center. He rounded a corner, slowed down and parked at the end of the cul de sac in the carport beside a stucco bungalow with a palm tree in its front yard. Clumps of periwinkle and zinnia edged the path leading to the green front door. On the doorstep, he put the brass key in her hand. She turned it in the lock and the door opened to the smell of fresh paint.

As in most Saudi rooms, white drapes shut out the light; the salon was dim, and overstuffed armchairs lined the white walls. He had placed a photograph of her family on the coffee table. In the picture, Mom's glasses had slipped halfway down her thin nose; Daddy was wearing his green baseball cap and had his arm around Mom's waist; and Pete was smiling his quirky smile. She put down the photo and glided across the room to the tall bookcase. Scattered among the Arabic books were a few poetry anthologies, the *Encyclopedia Britannica*, a stack of *Aramco World* magazines and a few hydrology textbooks. She ran her finger along the spines of the books. "Have you read all these?"

"Not yet. I mean to." He waved his arm around. "Well, is it all right? Layla sent Eliza over to get things ready for you. You will want to put your own touch on it—whatever you like, get rid of the company furniture, put up wallpaper—"

"Oh, yes, I'd like that."

"And we will need someone to help with the housekeeping."

"A maid? I'd rather not." She went to the kitchen. It was not unlike hers in the western compound: Corian countertop, porcelain sink, array of gleaming pots, and three taps— one for hot water, two for cold. One ran brackish water and the other drinking water.

She followed him into the bedroom, which was simply furnished with the Oriental rug from his room in Madison, an oak chest of drawers, and a queen-sized bed. She bounced lightly on the bed, fingering the gold-trimmed spread. The room's single painting was a calligraphy with swirls of gold leaf and blue flowing lines which Ib translated as, "I believe in the creed of love, wherever its stagecoaches may go, as love is my religion and faith." The saying reminded her of the night when she had decided to marry him so they could share the journey toward the City of Kindness.

He said she must be tired after the flight and went to draw a bath. When she went into the bathroom, she saw that he had taken a rose from the vase on the counter and was stripping it of its petals and setting them to float on the bathwater. He got up from the stool where he was sitting, sat her down on it and brushed her hair. When the tub was full, he checked the temperature of the water with his elbow—he knew she liked it hot. She slipped off her robe, rings, and bracelets and stepped in. The ceiling fan turned lazily, and as she reclined in the hot water, pleasant thoughts drifted in and out of her mind. He rolled up the sleeves of his thobe and sat on the edge of the tub to soap her back, running his thumbs along her shoulder blades and making little circles up and down either side of her spine. He soaped her feet, the insteps still orange with henna, but fainter than on her wedding night. With his knuckles, he rubbed the soles of her feet, and then he toyed with her toes, pushing his fingers in and out between them. He glided his hands over her breasts, and placed red petals on her nipples. He gathered her, dripping wet, in his arms.

"I want to pleasure you," he said, his voice catching.

She put her cheek to his chest, and they clung together, wet skin against dry. She stepped out of the tub, and his soft greedy mouth was on her, sucking her fingers, lips, ear lobes and nipples, and she knew how much he wanted her and, not a moment too soon, he took her in strong strokes and a single cry. In the night, they awakened and made love again. Afterward, she sat up in bed and turned on the small light on her bedside table. "Ib, I need you to do something."

"Anything."

"That vow we took; it's not the same as ours. The words are different. You will think I'm crazy, but I don't quite feel married. If we had been married at home, you'd say that you were taking me to be your wife." She knew the words by heart and said them in slow cadence: 'to have and to hold, for better, for worse, for richer, for poorer, in sickness and in health, to love and to cherish, till death do us part.'"

"I understand," he said. Phrase by measured phrase he repeated the words after her, and a need deep in her soul felt satisfied.

In the morning, they made love again. But at breakfast—eggs sunny-side up, hot buttered toast with strawberry jam— they disagreed about how to receive his family who were coming for the midday meal. Ib wanted to entertain them as was customary—with the men in the salon and the women and children in the family room.

"Oh, but we're newlyweds! I want to be with you."

"Shaheed will not like it."

"I'll cover up. Wear a head scarf, pants, long sleeves, the whole deal."

"My mother will think it is strange."

"But this is my home now. I should be able to live the way I want. I follow their rules when I go to them. It won't bother your father, or Ahmed or Layla."

Ib gave in, but she could tell he was irked because he left the house. That was something she had learned on their honeymoon—he evaded her when she did not see things his way. He would go off and come back in better humor. Now as she chopped parsley and mint for the tabbouleh, she pondered whether avoidance, although not desirable, was preferable to confrontation. Still, in this case maybe he was right. His way she would not have to deal with Shaheed, but she would be stuck with his mother.

When he returned she was still bent over the kitchen table slicing tomatoes. "We need a maid," he said as he sat down at the table. "Wouldn't you like that?"

"I guess. But what about Ali?"

"Ali? The houseboy?" Ib looked surprised. "Oh, I assumed you'd feel more at ease with a maid, so I found him another job."

"We won't need a maid if you help me." She smiled beguilingly. "We could cook together. Remember that delicious lasagna you made back in Madison?"

"That was *there*. Me cook *here*?" He pushed his chair back, scraping it against the terrazzo floor. "I'll set up the grill and do the barbecue, but as far as my cooking here, that's it."

She stopped chopping as she remembered how Annie had said Saudis changed when they came back from the States.

"Another thing," he said. "There's dust everywhere. I felt it on my feet the moment I came inside."

He was right. They had been back only two days, but already every surface was covered with a film of sandy dust. His mother would be sure to notice. Sarah went to the hall closet, took out the broom, began sweeping, and said she did not mind a bit of housework.

"You work too hard. I do not want you to get worn out."

"You could help. In Madison, that one time I was at your place, it was so tidy."

"I had a cleaning service. Here it is better if a woman has a maid."

"Well, maybe. So long as we treat her right." She emptied the dustpan.

He tightened his lips. "You think it is slavery that we pay so little?"

She was not going to concede the point entirely. "Two hundred and fifty dollars a month, that's the going rate, isn't it? It's not enough. A living wage—everyone deserves that."

"We pay for her air ticket, her visa, her medical expenses and her room and board. Everything."

"I don't like the idea of another woman living with us."

"As if I could be tempted by anyone else!" Pleased, he put his arms around her. "I will ask Layla. She may have an idea." He went off to read the newspaper and left her to set the table, steam the rice, stuff the grape leaves, roast the eggplant, and cut up the chicken for the kebob.

The Hollandaise sauce she would do at the last minute. Two hours later, she was finished, but she was in a bad mood. She did not want to see his snooty mother and his jerk of a brother. And it was not fair that she was the one doing all the work.

She was changing into white pants and a long-sleeved pink blouse when she heard the squeals of the twins. Lulu followed, clutching her Barbie.

"The bride returns," Layla said, kissing her three times on either cheek. She brought along Shadow whom she'd been cat-sitting while Sarah and Ib were on honeymoon, and when she unlatched the door to the cat carrier, Shadow daintily set out one paw, then another, and came up to sniff at Sarah's pants leg.

"Oh, you did miss me, didn't you," Sarah crooned as she bent down and stroked the soft fur. A moment later, she felt someone hovering. Malika. The older woman pressed her leathery cheek against Sarah's and made kissing noises into the air. Smiling brightly, Sarah invited her into the salon.

"Women should stay in the family room," Malika intoned. "Shaheed will be here any minute."

"Susu just called," Layla put in. "They're not coming. "The baby is colicky, and as for Shaheed, well you know the way he is."

Sarah felt relieved, but she imagined that Ib was annoyed. Probably he felt he had lost face at Shaheed's standing them up. As if to comfort him, Malika was squatting at his feet, her head against his knees. Meanwhile his father sat on the sofa and opened the newspaper. "One of your compatriots." He showed Sarah the photograph of Chief Little Eagle. "He's at the Marriott Hotel for American Week."

Layla peered over her father's shoulder at the newspaper. "Oooh, he's cute. Look at that feather in his braids." The conversation then switched to Beirut.

"Everyone said they never heard an American speak such good Arabic as Sarah," Ib said proudly.

"And did you ride around Pigeon Rocks in a motorboat?" Malika's rust-brown eyes gleamed. "And sit at the outdoor cafés on Hamra Street? Remember that summer we spent in Chemlan in the mountains? How we hunted under the pines for piñon nuts?" She reached for his hand and squeezed it.

"Sarah and I did all those things. Now, you and my bride have something in common. You both love Lebanon."

"Who wouldn't love Lebanon?" Layla cried. "The shopping. The restaurants. Skiing at Faraya. Dancing the *debke*. Nothing's better than Lebanon. Ah, those Lebanese. '*Au revoir, ya habibi*, I'll see you *bokra*.' Yes, one of them actually said that. And Lebanese designers, they are the best."

"Now, now, Layla," her father said. "No ladies' talk."

Sarah picked up the paper that was lying on the sofa. On the front page was a photo of bulldozers smashing Afghanistan's monumental Buddha statues. Why did the Taliban do that? Why couldn't they live and let live? She noticed that Malika was looking at her and politely she passed her the paper and asked if she would like to read about the Indian chief.

"No," Malika snapped. "I don't read such stories. They are so boring."

Feeling rebuffed, Sarah said she was going to make the Hollandaise sauce. Malika, her mouth in a hard straight line, said that was unnecessary, as she had brought Ibrahim's favorite garlic and lemon sauce to accompany the chicken.

"Mother, Sarah is the mistress of my house, and she would like to please you by making this special sauce."

"Make the sauce then," Malika smiled regally. "Make it if you'd like, Sarah."

In the kitchen, Sarah opened the fridge and took out eggs and butter, grated the zest of a lemon and squeezed out the juice. As she was separating the eggs, Malika entered, anklets jingling. "Please don't trouble yourself so on our behalf."

"It's no trouble," Sarah cut a wedge of butter and melted it. She was not sure she had the right quantity as the butter did not come in calibrated half-cup sticks. Malika hovered over her as she separated the eggs and whisked the yolks over low heat. What a relief—they didn't scramble. Now for the tricky part: Drop by slow drop, she dribbled the melted butter into the yolks. Just as she was about to declare the Hollandaise a triumph, disaster struck; the creamy pale sauce curdled.

"Tch, tch. Such a pity." Malika's eyes gleamed.

"I must have measured wrong. Too much butter…Just a drop too much."

"The feather that broke the camel's back," Malika chuckled, her heavy shoulders shaking. Ib came in to the kitchen to get the tongs, and Sarah showed him the curdled yellow mess. "He who eats of her sweets must also put up with her misfortune," Malika sang out.

Sarah grabbed the tongs from the drawer and handed them to Ib. "I'll scream if she spouts one more proverb," she hissed. She followed him out into the yard, his mother trailing behind.

Above, high in the frangipani tree, Farouk was plucking flowers and tossing them down to Lulu who scampered about screeching as she picked them up. Fawzi, his arm still in the cast, was helping Ib monitor the chicken on the grill. When Lulu had amassed a small stack of blossoms, she ran up to Malika and asked her to make a necklace with them. Malika went inside to get a needle and thread. She returned, settled on the grass, snapped off a length of thread, and holding the needle an inch from her face, poked the thread toward the eye. She missed. She tried again several times. Sarah watched as Malika wet the thread and pressed it between her thumb and finger to flatten it. It did no good. Each time she tried, she missed the eye. "Here, let me help you," Sarah said, taking the needle and threading it.

Without a word of thanks, Malika poked the needle through each of the blossoms. When she finished, she cut the thread with her teeth and knotted both ends. "For you, my princess," she said as she placed the garland around Lulu's neck.

"Barbie needs a necklace," Lulu said.

"It's not a necklace that doll needs," Malika scowled. "It's decent clothes. Shorts? And that pink, that...what do you call that?"

"Tank top," Layla said. "Cute isn't it."

"Never mind the name. Bare arms. Bare legs. They're lewd."

"Mother, it's just a doll."

"Shaheed is right, wanting to ban them."

"Oh, let's not argue. Doesn't that chicken smell yummy? It must be ready." Layla offered to help Sarah. They went into the kitchen and brought out the food: platters of fish and saffron rice, spinach turnovers, *tabbouleh, hummos, babaghanoush,* the cucumber-mint-and-yogurt salad, and a fruit bowl.

"*Sahtayn.* To your health." Ib passed around the skewers of garlicky chicken.

Layla took a bite of eggplant dip. "Mmm. Oh, Sarah, you are a very good cook."

"So many different things to eat," Malika said politely.

"Well, what if you don't like some of it? I don't want you to go hungry." This was the time to smile warmly and say, "Mother of Ibrahim, please let me honor you," but the words stuck in her throat. Still, she did her best. When Malika raised her hand to shade her eyes, Sarah took off her sunglasses and offered them to her; Malika shook her head. Sarah changed places with her so her mother in-law-would be in the shade next to Ibrahim.

With the others, it was easier. "Try a little more chicken. May I pour you another glass of water? Another helping of fish? It's fresh today." At first she felt pushy, but she began to enjoy playing hostess, asking if Layla wouldn't like a little bit of this, a little bit more of that, if Ib's father was at ease, or if there was too much sun for the twins.

After the meal, she broached the subject of a maid, and Layla offered to have Johnny drive Eliza over a couple of times a week. So that was settled, and Sarah was glad. There was simply too much chopping in Arab cuisine. And far too much dust. Dust everywhere, seeping in at ev-

ery windowpane and under every door; dust coating every book, every
table; dust on every flower and leaf.

The afternoon was going well, probably the effect of all the good
food. Layla was browsing a copy of *Vogue*, the twins were playing leapfrog; both Lulu and her grandfather had fallen asleep, her Barbie in
the crook of Lulu's arm, and Omar's mouth open showing his yellow
teeth; Ahmed and Ib were playing chess in the shade of the banyan
tree. Meanwhile Malika sat by herself. She had taken an orange from
the fruit bowl and was fondling it in her hand as she leaned against the
trunk of the frangipani tree. Sarah went inside to fetch a cushion and
placed it behind her. Malika smiled, her face radiant. She lifted the
orange up to her nose, sniffed it, and closed her eyes in pleasure. "Bring
me a knife," she called out to no one in particular.

Sarah jumped up, ran into the kitchen, and came back with one. She
watched as Malika scored the orange and peeled each segment out from
the center so they formed petals. How Malika could eat another bite,
Sarah could not imagine. She felt overfull.

"For you, my daughter." Malika handed the orange to Sarah.

"Thank you," Sarah said. "I can't. I'm stuffed."

Malika's face darkened; she stumbled toward the house. "She is not
one of us. She will never understand our ways. *Abadan.* Never."

"Mother, don't go." Layla ran to catch up with her.

Sarah dropped her head in her hands, horrified.

"Mother was just trying to be nice," Ib said, coming up to her.

"I don't know what got into me. It was so stupid. Stupid! Still, she
always makes me feel she's the queen and I'm some obnoxious little

beetle."

"Nonsense. She was trying to please you."

"Why does she have to make such a big deal of it?"

"It was not just the orange. She felt stupid when you asked if she wanted to read the paper. She hates being illiterate. Hates it with a passion."

"Illiterate? Why didn't you tell me?"

"Didn't you know? There were no schools for girls then."

Sarah picked up one of the frangipani blossoms lying on the grass and pulled off the star-shaped petals. "No matter what I do, it goes wrong. I'm just not like you."

He ran his fingertip along her lips. "Such perfect teeth," he murmured. "Mother is right. You will never be like us."

"I'm going to find her and apologize." She would not give up. She went into the house to look for Malika, but she had locked herself in the bathroom.

CHAPTER 14

September 11 was the day for the fashion show at the Marriott Hotel. It seemed a long time since Sarah had gone to anything frivolous and she dressed carefully, deciding finally on an ivory suit of pongee silk with a slit up its long skirt.

"Darling Sarah, you are too cute," Layla said. "At least cover your hair. Here, I'll lend you something."

"But my outfit. It'll spoil the effect."

"You can take it off as soon as we're inside, away from wicked men." She opened the hall closet and took out several scarves, all black. "Here, pick one."

"Do I have to?" Sarah rolled her eyes as she took a scarf.

"Why is it so upsetting to you if we cover our hair?" Layla said sharply. "Really, why do you have this hang-up?"

Sarah flushed at the rebuke. "I'm sorry. I apologize."

That mollified Layla. "Don't you know? The *mutawwa* will go crazy and kill us if we are too beautiful." She giggled and flashed open her cloak to reveal a yellow organza top and skintight pants. "What do you think? It's Ahmed's favorite," she said as they went out the door.

Johnny dropped them in front of the Intercontinental Hotel. It was blustery, and Sarah who hated wind-blown hair was glad to be wearing a head scarf. She took it off inside the lobby, where the plush carpet was pockmarked by women's stiletto heels. The ballroom was packed, but they found seats at one of the round tables under a crystal chandelier more glittery than the one she had seen at the Waldorf Astoria Hotel in New York. When the music started up, a pencil-thin woman in a black Channel suit and floating black chiffon scarf strode down the catwalk.

"Ladies and dear fashion devotees. A thousand welcomes. Today we celebrate couture, both our heritage and our aspirations. Our silks are from the Far East, our piping from Paris, and our trimmings from Italy, but our heart is Arab." She spoke first in Arabic, then in clipped, British-accented English.

Layla nudged Sarah. "That's Jasmine Hussein. She used to be a news broadcaster on Lebanese TV. Oh, she is so glamorous and clever." Sarah nodded, wondering what could have induced Jasmine to leave Beirut.

The lights went out. From the inky darkness came the roar of a rushing wind, then a sudden hush. "The north wind," Jasmine announced, and a model in combat pants strode jauntily down the catwalk, whipped off a magenta vinyl jacket, turned, and stomped back, bondage boots crushing the rose petals at her feet as a tape played the thuds of rockets and rat-a-tat of machine gun fire.

"Jackets, dresses, and pants, all on lines drawn from the Arab past. They've proved right for thousands of years. Ladies, look to your past. Ladies, listen to the peaceful wind of the south." The haunting melody

of a Bedouin flute sounded. A model appeared in a flowing purple caftan, the sleeves of which were adorned with peacock feathers. She raised
her arms as if in supplication or benediction, and Jasmine dramatically
lowered her voice. "Ladies, listen to the peaceful wind of the south and
look to your past. These simple lines have proved right for a thousand
years and will be forever fashionable.

"Now the east wind," Jasmine said, and a girl appeared in a pink-and-
turquoise turban, a colorful peasant blouse and shirred pantaloons.

"And now, dear ladies, the daring wind of the west, the wind of the
avant-garde." A model, lean and angular, her hips swinging to a souped-
up soundtrack of the Dixie Chicks flaunted her way down the catwalk
in white leather shorts with red satin piping and a halter-top under a
transparent abaya, face veil, and six-inch stiletto heels.

"Her hair. It's pink," Layla gasped. "The *mutawwa'in* will get her for
sure."

"Now for our sparkling party clothes," the MC continued, ignoring
the scandalized looks of her audience. "Ah, dear ladies, who would want
to live without parties?" The beat of the Dixie Chicks intensified. A
platinum blonde in a red silk dress, slit up the thigh, belly-danced down
the catwalk and with a small self-absorbed smile contemplated her left
hip as she moved it in small circles. Behind her strutted a model with a
Cleopatra haircut in slinky black pants and an off-the-shoulder blouse
with gleaming silver sequins. Many of the outfits were designed by Lebanese couturiers, the others by familiar names like Valentino, Kenzo,
Hermes, and Ralph Lauren.

"I wish they'd show clothes we could actually wear," Sarah complained.

"Oh, don't say that. We want to dream. Nothing's better than fantasy."

"And let us not forget our mothers," Jasmine continued. "For them, our inspiration is all Arab." An elegant gray-haired woman appeared, silver pendants and jeweled headgear swinging with each twist of her hips. She raised both hands and held them above her spangled gray silk dress. "Ladies, note the long pointed sleeves of the Najran."

The music switched to Rimsky-Korsakov's *Scheherazade*. "And now, ladies, we present our selection of cloaks and scarves. Please admire the draped fabric. It has a noble lineage and is one of the most enduring elements of fashion." Three models appeared, standing stock still side by side. The first looked straight ahead, her face uncovered, a loose black mantle softening her jawline, so she resembled a Madonna in a medieval painting. The second model was veiled, with only her jet eyes and a single strand of black hair visible until she dropped the silver-sequined veil to reveal tattooed cheeks. The third girl stared with intelligent, kohl-rimmed eyes from the slits of a mask as shiny as a scorpion's shell. "Sheba, Cleopatra, and Scheherazade are our glorious past. Grace and mobility, these are our heritage, but ladies, the winds of change are swirling. Now let's look to our future."

To the strains of Beethoven's "Ode to Joy," models in cloaks of orange, fuchsia, and electric blue undulated down the catwalk. Some of the abayas were accordion-pleated, while others were smocked, tasseled, or slashed on the diagonal. Not one girl had her face covered. Their lipstick was fire-engine red, their smiles triumphant and their cloaks took on a life of their own, swirling and billowing.

"Look at her," Sarah whispered as a model in a cloak of gold lamé raised a flaming torch. The draped folds shimmered in its light. "She looks like the Statue of Liberty."

"Tisam would like that one. You see, fashion conquers all." She lit up a Winston and gestured to the cloak of cobalt blue worn by an elegant Nubian. "I'd like that one. Or maybe that one over there." She gestured toward a model in simple black silk, tucked in at the waist and bosom. "Except it's got darts. The Sheriff would have a fit. I keep telling him we need abayas of different colors to make it easier for the children to find us in a crowd." She wrinkled her nose and made sniffing sounds. "That's how they find me now—by scent. Or by my Jimmy Choo shoes." She giggled and flexed a foot, clad in soft blue calfskin. "Cute, aren't they?"

"Very."

"I gave my old ones to Eliza. By the way, how are you two getting on?"

"Eliza? She's wonderful. She's always smiling."

The public address system crackled. "Aramco ladies, report at once to the front desk for transport home," a male voice boomed. "At once, ladies." The abrupt announcement led to a rush of grumbling. "Oh, no! Do we have to? What a nuisance! It's not over yet."

"Poor things. Back to home, the prison," Layla said as the westerners pushed back their chairs and left the hall.

The final number was a wedding gown in pink and green satin. As the bride proceeded down the catwalk under a canopy of white silk, she kept her head bowed; the moment she raised her veil of Chantilly lace, the audience broke into the same trills that Sarah had heard at her own wedding, at the airport when she first arrived, and at the hospital when a patient died. It seemed peculiar that the *zaghareet* served to express both joy and grief.

"You were a much prettier bride," Layla said as they waited for their ride.

"Rashidis," the doorman bellowed as a Cadillac pulled up in front of the hotel. A young woman squeezed through the crowd, and her driver opened the car door.

"Umbargis," the doorman roared. Another shape enveloped in black pushed her way to the curb and climbed into the Mercedes waiting for her.

Khalidis…Farags…Sultans…and finally the shout, Suleimans. Layla and Sarah set off, their heels crushing the husks of sunflower shells underfoot. Johnny approached, his face grim. "Have you heard? About New York?" He fingered the crease of his crisply pressed khakis. "A plane crashed into the World Trade Center."

"Pardon?" Sarah said, not believing. "What did you say?"

Johnny opened the car door. "Yes, it seems the plane collided into one of the towers. I just heard it from one of the drivers."

"How awful." She turned to Layla, "I hope nobody was hurt."

They were silent for a while and then Layla suggested perhaps the pilot had had a heart attack. A few minutes later, she was again prattling about fashion and exactly what Shaheed would and would not let her wear.

Sarah tugged at Layla's veil. "Say, aren't you going to take that off?"

"Please don't talk like my husband," she said crossly. "Ahmed insists I'm crazy to wear it in our own private car, but I say the streets are full of men."

"It's almost dark. No one can see in."

"Oh yes they can. At the traffic lights, they can. Better play it safe. That's what I tell Ahmed."

When Sarah arrived home, Ib sat her down and told her the full story. "No. No. No," she kept saying. She could take in only snippets of what he said, just words: carnage, towers, smoke, fireball, airliners, hijackers. She clutched her throat, feeling she would throw up, and staggered to the telephone. It would be noon in Wisconsin, but even if Mom had already left, she could talk to her father. She dialed the number. "Answer, answer," she begged silently, but a recording said that all circuits were engaged; she called Pete in Madison and received the same message. She could hear the CNN anchor in the background. "America is under attack," he said, enunciating A-ttack as if it were two words. She sat in front of the television, eyes glued to the screen. She saw the heavy towers toppling, the woman with blood streaming down her legs, the twisted carcass of the towers, the businessmen fleeing. Every quarter hour she dialed home in vain. She e-mailed three acquaintances who lived in Manhattan, asking, "Are you all right?"

Doctors would be needed right away, so many doctors. She went online and checked the Saudi and American Airlines schedules. She could catch the overnight flight via Jeddah and be in New York tomorrow; all she needed was an exit visa. She went to ask Ib to help her get it. He was sitting in front of the television, and when she saw the rows and rows of empty cots in a rescue center, she realized there was no help she could give.

At midnight, he turned off the television. In bed, he kept his arms around her until he dozed off. She could not sleep so she got out of bed and found some candles in the kitchen drawer. She went out to the patio, and arranged them in a circle on the small metal table. The night sky was bright with shooting stars. She breathed in the scent of beeswax, and began to hum and then softly to sing: "O beautiful for spacious skies, for amber waves of grain; for purple mountain's majesty above the fruited plain. America! America! God shed his grace on thee." Unable to remember what words came next, she sat in the lawn chair and listened to the chittering of crickets until she fell asleep.

When she awakened, it was 5:30 a.m. Ib had already left for morning prayers at the mosque. She tried to reach her family again on the phone, but as usual heard the "all circuits are busy" recording in the tinny voice. She turned on the television and switched channels back and forth between Al Jazeera and MBC, the independent Arabic satellite television station. She yearned for the usual morning trivia, but the sickening news had not changed. She felt overcome by a sense of futility, and it occurred to her to go to the bedroom and take from her jewelry box the wavy flag pin her mother had given her at Chicago O'Hare Airport. "So you don't forget who you are," Mom said. Sarah felt better as soon as she pinned it on. She looked back at the television screen, which showed a man and a woman jumping, hand in hand, through a window, followed by a pink mist that rose from the pavement. At 6:00 a.m., the local news came on: all the kingdom's airports and schools were closed. At 6:45 a.m. the consulate telephoned—not a personal call but a recorded message, urging Americans to exercise caution in their movements and to secure extra supplies of cash, water and non-perishables. At 7:00 a.m., the phone rang again. It was Malika saying how sorry she was with what sounded like genuine grief in her hoarse voice. "Thank you," Sarah said, her eyes welling, but later, she could not help but wonder whether Malika had called on her own initiative or if Ib had put her up to it.

In the hospital, the orderlies, physicians, techies, and nurses all offered condolences. "How terrible it is when innocent people die," they said, shaking their heads. Annie sat beside her in the cafeteria, hardly saying a word. Her silence was a solace. After Sarah's shift ended, Johnny drove her downtown to load up on the extra supplies. At the bank, the line snaked from the counter to the door, and the money-counting machines were spinning. Sarah went to the end of the line. "Lady, lady, no need to wait, you go to the front," someone called out.

"Oh, Missus, I am so sorry for your country," a laborer in a soiled khaki shirt said.

"God bless America," the teller said as he counted out her riyals.

At the checkout counter at Safeway, the clerk scanned her bottled water, peanut butter, cans of soup and tuna and he too said, "God bless America." When she returned home, the light on the answering machine was blinking. Layla, Tisam, her father-in-law, Munira her Arabic teacher, the Egyptian anesthesiologist, the Syrian dermatologist and four nurses had all asked God's blessing on her and on America. Blessing— what did the word mean? Perhaps that they liked her and the States. Or something more? Was it any different than Mom's breathy

"Bless you," said so often that Sarah never paid attention?

Their next-door neighbors, the Yaqubs, brought over roasted lamb, rice, and tabbouleh and said she must keep up her strength. Sarah was pushing a bit of tabbouleh around on her plate when the telephone rang again. "My parents—maybe that's them." She bolted out of her chair.

"Who was it?" Ib yelled as she slammed down the receiver.

"Some creep." It happened so often, guys calling random numbers on the off chance they would find a telephone girlfriend.

That evening she and Ib watched the thousands of soccer fans in a Teheran stadium rise for a minute's silence. "You see, Sarah," he said. "The whole world grieves."

"Maybe. Maybe not." Shaheed had not called, and she pictured him rubbing his hands in glee.

She was still awake when the phone rang at two in the morning. She snatched the receiver on the bedside table. "How are you?" Daddy asked.

"OK, I guess," she said, her voice tremulous.

"Come home. It's too dangerous over there."

"But, Daddy, it's the U.S. that's in danger."

"You may be right," he said, a waver in his voice. He'd been listening to the 700 Club and had heard Jerry Falwell and Pat Robertson say that God was angry with the U.S., and that He had withdrawn his blessing and was no longer protecting it.

"What?" she cried. "That's crazy. It doesn't make any sense."

"They say it's because we've sinned. We put up with gays, abortionists, and the feminists."

"Oh, Daddy. That's crazy."

"Come home," he pleaded.

She swallowed hard. In a steely voice, she reminded them she had a husband. She had a contract. People were depending on her, and she could not just up and leave. "Just listen to me. Daddy, I wish I could but I can't."

The line went dead. She was not sure whether he had hung up or whether they were simply cut off. She tried to call back, but could not get through. "Damn Jerry Falwell!" she yelled. She clamped her hands over her ears, stretched her mouth wide to howl her grief. It came out as a scream, nothing like the *zaghareet*, but a relief all the same.

CHAPTER 15

OVER THE NEXT FEW DAYS, Sarah remained in shock. She could not take in the tragedy and like a zombie, she moved listlessly at work and kept her eyes riveted on the television at home. When it was reported that fifteen of the nineteen hijackers were Saudis, she felt aghast. She knew Saudis, or at least she thought she did, and they did not seem violent—but perhaps she had been mistaken. When Layla called suggesting a drive in the country, Ib immediately agreed, saying that it would do Sarah good to get away.

It was harvest season in date country, and Ib wanted to show her the family grove of five hundred date palms. More than a hundred varieties grew in the area, but the Suleimans cultivated only *khlas*, which were sweet and dry and received greater care than the varieties which were meant for fodder. Sitting on their haunches, the workers picked dates off the strands and spread them on circular palm mats to dry. According to Layla, the dates flourished because they had their feet in the water of the canals and their heads in the fiery sun. Sarah could not take her eyes away from the emaciated men in red-and-white checked sarongs, knives clenched between their teeth, as they shimmied up to the crowns of the palms.

"It looks dangerous," she said.

"Not if you're experienced. I used to help out when I was a boy." Ib kicked off his sandals and called for a hemp belt. He hitched his robe up above his knees, fastened the belt against his buttocks, planted his feet on opposite sides of a male date palm, and climbed from the stub of one leaf base to the next until he was fifty feet above, hidden in the shining green fronds.

Layla touched Sarah on the arm. "See, he wants to impress you with his courage. Don't watch. You'll get nervous."

Feeling afraid for him, she put her hand to her mouth and watched as he slashed off clusters of dates. A whoop sounded from above. "Watch out," Ib shouted. He placed clusters in a basket, lowered it to the ground, and shimmied down, holding a date sheath. He gave it to her, and gingerly she stroked its long, smooth surface to the tip of creamy flowerets, which had no scent and were dry as dust. "The heat must agree with them. I feel a little queasy," she said.

"Let's go, let's go." Layla herded everyone back to the van as if she feared her delicate sister-in-law might again collapse with heatstroke. Within a quarter of an hour, they were in central Qatif. The sun glared off the white buildings on the long straight streets. At an intersection, a billboard urged parents to inoculate their children; further on another encouraged people to refrain from smoking—not that it made any impression on Layla. When they arrived at *Bayt Shajra*, Ib parked in the shade of the tree. His parents and grandmother lived in the larger of the two houses with Shaheed and Susu who were due to move to the other one as soon as it was completed. Sarah climbed out of the van and took in the adjoining vacant lot, just the size for another house, and thought how fortunate it was that Ib's job required him to live in company housing.

"My house is your house." Malika pressed against Sarah and pecked her on both cheeks. When Malika asked how she was, Sarah answered politely, "Fine, thank you, praise Allah." The glimmer of a smile passed over her mother-in-law's face. "And your parents and your brother?"

"Fine, thank you, praise Allah." Sarah said demurely. She had vowed to try to fit in and to disrupt her in-laws' life as little as possible. She would use the rules of etiquette to help her.

"Come!" Malika ordered.

Susu was not there, probably because Shaheed did not dare let Ib see her, given his conviction that his wife was sexually irresistible. As for Shaheed himself, he ignored Sarah, staring into space a foot or two from her face.

Sarah followed her mother-in-law to the hall closet and hung up her cloak. She was wearing her flag pin, but Malika did not notice, or if she did, she did not object. Still, in her presence Sarah felt back at square one, that torrid day in the tent when Malika had insulted her, saying she had a "boy's behind." Sarah let the conversation roll over her: Malika's failing eyesight, the grandmother's deafness, Omar's emphysema, and the international school where Layla had just refused a job offer. It sounded like the one where Annie's son Joey went. After the midday meal, Ib's father went off to nap. In the corner of the room, the twins were building a log cabin with blocks. Lulu was playing with her Barbie, draping a black cloak over the long-legged plastic body and shiny blond hair. "That's my good girl," Malika beamed. "Such a nice modest doll."

"Three billion dollars a year the U.S. sends Israel," Shaheed was say-ing in his high-pitched voice. "I tell you, those crashes are the price America is paying."

"Terrorists used those planes as bombs to kill innocents," Ib said, an-ger lacing his voice.

Shaheed played with the curls in his beard. "Box cutters, that's all they had. Obviously, Allah approves. They could never have accomplished what they did if he did not."

"Ahmed! Shaheed! Don't fight. Don't fight," Layla jumped up. "You've both got it wrong. No Arab could have done it. It was too organized. Everybody was on time. Does that sound Arab to you? It was the Moss-ad, and they made it look like Arabs. Maybe the Mossad stole Saudi passports or bought them from forgers. A Muslim could never do some-thing so evil."

"A *good* Muslim wouldn't," Sarah said. "But I still think Bin Laden did it. He may be a bad Muslim but he's still a Muslim. He calls himself a Muslim. He quotes the Qur'an. And he's so horribly charismatic." She looked to Ib for confirmation, but he seemed not to have heard her.

"How can we be sure who those wicked, wicked men were? They were at a bar drinking and lap dancing the night before," Layla said. "Mus-lims don't do that. It makes no sense. I'm sure it was the Mos-sad."

Shaheed and Ib ignored Layla too. Was it because they were women? Mere women?

"Those men are martyrs, who gave their lives," Shaheed shouted.

"Men who committed suicide which God abhors," Ib said in a low intense voice.

"Mark my words, brother, it was martyrdom, and I approve of it," Shaheed shouted back.

Upstairs the baby started howling. The twins looked up from their blocks, and Malika, Layla, Sarah, and Lulu all cried out, "You woke up the baby."

"I didn't mean to fight," Ib apologized. "I'm sorry."

"To you is your way and to me is mine," Shaheed said, unperturbed as little Saladin screamed on. "Only Allah can guide us aright."

"My husband is perfectly right," Sarah said in a low, fervent voice, looking into Shaheed's insolent eyes. "I know because—"

Shaheed turned his back on her. "Your wife shouldn't talk to me."

"And why not?" Ib said irritably. "The prophets' wives were always talking to men."

"Yet are we not their guardians?" Shaheed yelled over the baby's screams. "Do we not spend of our wealth on them?"

Ib laughed. "Look at Sarah. She earns more than I do."
Shaheed flung up his hands. "Well, then, let her spend it on whatever she wants."

"Why should we worry our souls about politics when we can do nothing? Nothing, I tell you," Malika said.

Upstairs Susu must have picked up the baby, for there was silence except for the noise of the occasional wooden block falling on the terrazzo tile floor as the twins continued to raise their towers of blocks. Malika brought in tea and dates, and the truce seemed to hold for a quarter-hour or so when the men started arguing again, this time in lowered voices. Lulu left her Barbie and joined the twins as carefully they placed more blocks on their two towers. "More. More. More!" she yelled.

Abruptly Farouk grabbed a toy plane and screaming, "Twin Towers! Twin Towers!" he rammed it into one of them and it crashed to the floor. One of the falling blocks hit Sarah on the ankle. She cried out, and Shaheed's eyes glittered with triumph.

"Bad boy." Malika grabbed Farouk and slapped him on his face.

"Then the police should kill them," Fawzi said, sticking up for his twin.

On the television, Al Jazeera was showing pictures of the usual misery in Palestine. Youths in bloody shirts hurried through the streets carrying a shrouded corpse under the black, red, green and white flag of Palestine.

"I hate the *Yahoodis*," Farouk screamed, his hand on the cheek Layla had slapped.

"Don't say that," Sarah said. "The Israelis had nothing to do with September 11."

"How many died in the World Trade Center? Three thousand. Not one child. But do Americans remember our precious children? No, they do not." Shaheed beckoned to Farouk and the boy rushed into his arms.

"I hate the Americans too," he said.

"Don't talk like that," Layla scolded. "Remember Disneyland and Sea World? You liked them. And Auntie Sarah is American, and she's good, isn't she?"

Ibrahim started praising the virtues of American life, but Sarah thought instead of what a passenger had said to his wife on his cell phone as United Flight 93 plummeted: "I love you. Don't be sad. Take care of our daughter. Whatever you do is okay with me." The man's attitude and faith in his wife seemed heroic. It reminded her of a poem she had heard at a Black History Month celebration last winter, but she could not recall the exact words—something about freedom.

Her period was late, and she hoped it would not come today, as she had not brought tampons. She excused herself and left the room. She could not recall the Islamic protocol about bathrooms—was she to enter with her right foot and leave with her left, or vice versa? Nobody was around to check on her, so it did not matter. Inside the spotless room was an Oriental toilet, a hole set in the white tile floor. She squatted and relieved herself. There was no toilet paper, only a spigot set low on the wall with a red rubber tube attached so people could clean themselves the traditional way—with water. Instead, she reached into her pocket for a tissue, wiped herself, and pulled the chain on the wall. She had never been late before with her period. Perhaps it was the stress of being in Malika's presence.

As she walked back toward the salon, she overheard Malika say, "Poor thing, she doesn't know Allah, the glory of Islam and the joy of prayer." Embarrassed, even mortified, Sarah cleared her throat, pasted a fake smile on her mouth, and sashayed into the dark salon. The moment she came in Malika left with the children and told Layla to hurry along, which she did. The air was stale and Sarah wanted to fling open the windows. Ib and Shaheed were arguing. On and on they went —Ib citing the need for patience, Shaheed ranting about Bush and the Israelis. After listening to them for what seemed an eternity, the words she had been trying to remember came to her.

"Listen, I've something to say. You both think you know everything about how to live. But listen to me. I've got something to say."

Shaheed kept on blathering; she went and stood beside him, and placed a hand on his shoulder. He shook her hand off and glowered at her. "Listen to me," she said. "It's no good going on this way, just arguing. It's no good rehashing the past." She spoke quickly and confidently from the heart and without embarrassment. "Going on this way won't solve anything. A black American poet wrote about how we have tomorrow before us, and how it is bright like a flame. I'm not sure if those are his exact words, but we need to have hope. That's the gist of it. We need to forget the past and look to the future."

"Forget the past?" Shaheed snapped. "How could we be so foolish? In any case, your people are free while Palestinians live under occupation. It is our sacred duty to fight for their freedom."

"Well, I'm all for freedom. Freedom for women, too. Here and now." Taking her time, she unknotted her head scarf and her dark red hair tumbled onto her shoulders. "Another thing, Shaheed. I don't like the back seat. I'm sick of it. It's time to change."

His eyes dropped to the flag pin. For a moment, she thought he might rip it off, but that would mean he would have to touch her, which he would never do. Nonetheless, she pressed her hand protectively over the small wavy pin.

Later, on the drive home, Ib asked what had happened to make her speak out so boldly. She did not know, but she felt glad she had. She wished Malika and Layla had witnessed it.

CHAPTER 16

AT THE END OF SEPTEMBER, Sarah's pregnancy test came back positive. All the gloom from New York City paled, and she floated. Ib was overjoyed too, and those first precious days of her pregnancy, it was as if the tragedy of September 11 had never happened and nothing mattered but the miracle in her womb. Her bliss lasted until October 7. She and Ib were taking afternoon tea in Qatif with Malika when she heard the tip tapping of Omar's cane in the hall. He stumbled toward them in his haste, the deep mahogany of his forehead furrowed. "There's bad news," he said, wheezing. "The bombing has started. May God be merciful."

It felt unreal to her; it could not possibly be happening, she felt. That night she cried out in her sleep. Ib awakened, and held her as she told him about the nightmare. She could not remember the details, only the image of little girls, bare arms sticking out through barred windows. When she told him that pregnant women have crazy dreams, he said that attention must be paid to any dream because it might contain a revelation. She looked askance because she had not thought him superstitious, and then she snuggled against his warm chest and went back to sleep, only to be awakened by another nightmare, this one of Layla crouched at the feet of a bearded man brandishing a scimitar. Ib slept on and Sarah got out of bed, went into the salon, and turned on the television. American Tomahawk cruise missiles had been launched from ships and submarines in the Gulf, the attack aircraft speeding thousands of miles from the U.S. in order to bomb Kabul and Kandahar. There were pictures of the royal palace, the TV towers and the airport, all of which were targeted by the Americans. Al-Qaida training camps had been hit too. It made her feel glad, especially when skinny, sinister Osama Bin Laden appeared on screen to praise the attack on the World Trade Center and to accuse the west of hypocrisy.

She was very tired but afraid that if she went back to bed, she would have more nightmares. She thought of the dream catchers the Winnebago Indians made by stretching a bright web of yarn across a hoop, leaving a hole in the middle for the good dreams to slip through. She wanted to speak to her parents, who would be worrying about her. She could cheer them up by telling them the good news about her pregnancy. She decided against it as she was in the very early stages when she might suffer a miscarriage. But she yearned to talk with them. Glancing at her watch, she calculated that it would be evening in Wisconsin when they would be home. When she got through on the telephone, Mom was in hysterics. She told Sarah to apply for her exit visa right now, and if she could not get it on her own, Ib should pull strings and get one for her immediately. She should take a European airline and not an American one, anything to stay safe. "You're right next door to Afghanistan," Mom said. "Don't you understand? It's dangerous."

"Mom, it's okay. Look at a map. It's as far from Khobar, as I don't know exactly, but it's very far away."

"We're getting back at those cowards," Daddy said, picking up on the other phone. "About time too! Don't you worry, we'll get 'em. How are you holding up?"

"I'm okay. Really. There's no terrorism here."

Her father told her about a prayer vigil where the names of those who died on September 11 were read. She did not ask if the names of the hijackers were included. In her parents' religion you were supposed to love your enemies—as if one could— but those men did not deserve anyone's prayers. She made herself a cup of hot chocolate and settled down with a novel. Unfortunately, she could not concentrate on it, so she went to comb out Shadow. She had a bout of morning sickness, which cheered her up for it meant the baby-to-be was really there, alive inside her. At five a.m., she went to the porch and picked up the morning paper. She was surprised that the lead story was not about Afghanistan, but a report on how Saudis and expats were donating blood to show their support for Palestine. She glanced through the rest of the paper: a feature story on a deaf mute artist in Riyadh; the stock market; a page of comic strips including *Dr. Morgan, Dagwood, Peanuts and Dennis the Menace.* The police blotter on page two had a local brief about the execution of a teacher who had locked a student in a closet for chattering and gone home forgetting to let her out. Layla had told her earlier about the incident, which must account for the hideous dream Sarah had had. At the bottom of the page, she noticed a paid advertisement from the Filipino Embassy warning its nationals to avoid wearing t-shirts with pro-American slogans. Therefore, she thought, Americans were now to be reviled. Feeling disgusted, she put down the paper and went into the kitchen. She set out croissants and orange juice for Ib, and when he came down for breakfast, she scrambled some eggs for him. She told him about the Embassy's order, and he quipped that it would halve Johnny's wardrobe, a joke she thought was singularly tactless.

He turned on the radio to the BBC. The U.S. and British attacks on Afghanistan were continuing. "The Americans are making a mistake," he said.

"We have to do *something*," she said, a squeaky little rise in her voice. "Bin Laden's there. We can't let him get away with it. If the Taliban won't hand him over to justice, we have to go get him."

"A revenge attack solves nothing. A wise leader would patiently track down the individuals involved rather than bombing an entire country. Now there are two tragedies instead of the one."

She hated it when he was so smug. She told him not to be such a pessimist and that maybe everything would get better. After he left, she went upstairs to make the bed, pulling the spread taut over the pillows. As usual, he had left his boxer shorts—yellow printed with green cacti— on the floor for her to pick up, and she kicked them under the bed.

When Johnny came to drive her to work, he had on a Hawaiian t-shirt, and Sarah felt much better.

In the staff locker room, she donned her white coat, clipped on her badge, and hung her stethoscope around her neck. The day started quietly with only three patients in the waiting room, one of them a diminutive crone about four feet tall who perched on the edge of one of the blue plastic chairs. Mid-morning brought a man who presented

with chest pains. As he sat on the examining table, she attached monitor wires to his chest and asked the usual questions: *When did the pain
start? Dull or sharp? Have you ever had this pain before? On a scale of one
to ten, how bad is it?* As Sarah left for lunch, the old woman was still
waiting, hands clenched in pain over her stomach. Sarah left it to the
triage nurse to sort out.

In the cafeteria, she selected a dish of kebob and rice and headed for
the physicians' dining room. She saw Annie eating with a few Arab colleagues and made her way to them. The instant she sat down, everyone
stopped talking; they must have been discussing Afghanistan. Annie
removed her handbag from the table to make space for Sarah's tray, but
not before Sarah noticed the red maple leaf decal stuck on the black bag.
It made her angry. Annie was playing it safe, making a big fuss about
being Canadian so the locals would not blame her over Afghanistan.

Annie went on the attack. "Why is your George Bush so bent on
revenge? Who does he think he is? Killing ten thousand innocents to
catch one terrorist."

The Arab doctors looked down at their plates. Had they all turned
against her just because she was American? "Don't lecture me about
Kabul and Kandahar," Sarah said. "Think of all those people who died
September 11. We had to do *something*." She hated the squeaky sound
in her voice. She took her tray and went to sit by herself near the window. She swallowed a mouthful of rice, chewed a piece of kebob, and
felt sick. She rushed to the staff bathroom where she locked herself in a
stall, put her arms around her stomach, and rocked back and forth on
the toilet seat, trying to stifle her sobs. She did not want anyone to hear

her blubbering. By the time she had composed herself, her lunch break was over, and she started back. To get to the ER she had to pass John Hunter's office and she hoped she would not run into him. Yesterday after staff meeting, he had said in his prissy Oxford accent that instead of "cozying up to the Yanks," Tony Blair should be sorting out terrorism in Northern Ireland. When she was close enough to see the brass "Chief of Staff" plaque on his door, she overheard a familiar voice. "She seems to be falling apart. I'm concerned. She's under a lot of stress. She's having trouble concentrating, and it may affect her judgment. Don't you think she should talk to someone?"

Sarah bit her lip, mortified. What kind of a friend was Annie anyway? First that Canadian smugness and now this!

"Surely you don't mean our Sarah?" Dr. Hunter said.

"Yes, she's jumpy and depressed, haven't you noticed? That's not like her."

She slipped past the open door without their noticing her. In the ER waiting room, the old woman had still not been treated. Sarah took one look at the brown blisters above her swollen left eye and marched over to the triage nurse. "Can you tell me why the old lady is still here? It looks like shingles. The sooner she gets acyclovir the better."

"We can't do a thing," the nurse said, her forehead creased with worry. "Her son brought her in and disappeared before signing the consent form."

"Where's the husband?"

"She's a widow. We can't locate the son. We keep calling."

"Keep me in the loop," Sarah barked. An hour later when she had finished her charting and paperwork, she returned to check on the woman. If the cornea was infected, it could become damaged and scarred. She considered treating the woman without authorization the way she had Fawzi, but she did not dare rock the boat again. She decided to skip the chain of command and go straight to the top to Ib's father. She found him in his office reading a medical journal. He did not look well. He was coughing and thinner than when she had last seen him. As he set down the journal, she noticed how his hands resembled Ib's, the same coloring and suppleness. But Omar's fingernails were gray-blue, which was a bad sign. She asked how he was feeling, and he rested his jowl on his hand and said he felt a little tired.

"And you, dear Sarah? This bombing, how awful it must be for you right now. I am so sorry. Ten years ago when Iraq invaded Kuwait, that war was over swiftly. God willing, this one will be quick, too. And now, my dear, how may I help you?"

She told him about the woman with shingles, and he picked up the telephone, spoke a few words, wheezing slightly, and replaced the receiver. "It is taken care of, my dear. You may treat the woman on my authority. Such a selfish young man to go off and leave his mother like that. Really, I don't know what is becoming of the new generation."

On the drive home, she noticed Johnny had changed out of his Hawaiian t-shirt and now had on a plain red one. So like Annie he too was distancing himself from America. *Coward. Fair-weather friend,* she thought. As she went into Safeway to buy some meat for supper, she noticed the line of men standing waiting by a dozen orange phone booths. They were Afghans calling home worried about their families.

Back home in Firdaus, she went to the kitchen and started making the meatloaf for supper. She was chopping onions when the front door-bell rang. It was a courier with an advisory from the U.S. consulate. At the top of the page was the word URGENT in bold capitals. A paragraph down, the report advised Americans to take "necessary precautions." They were to limit their movements, keep their doors locked, and to stay away from malls.

"Ib," she shouted. "Have a look." She thrust the advisory at him.

He had the saddest look on his face as he read it. "So it's come to this," he said, shaking his head.

She pushed a heap of onion chunks to one side of the chopping board. "God, it's awful!"

"Sarah, darling, the warden is right."

She wiped her hands on her jeans. "It's like they're telling me I have to act ashamed of my country. I can't wear my flag pin. Remember the look in Shaheed's eyes when he saw it? And at work today everyone was horrid. Your father was the only one who was kind."

Ib touched her cheek. "This thing, it is making you cry. It must be awful for you."

"I'm not crying. It's not just this—this thing, this problem. Really it's the onions."

He put both his hands on her shoulders, but she pulled away. "Listen to me, listen just a minute. American bombs are killing Afghans, and as Muslims, they're our brothers. That changes things. Osama has thousands of sympathizers here. I wish I could convince Shaheed—"

"Fat chance. What's he up to?"

"The usual. Flogging Eve-teasers, that sort of thing."

"What a creep." She sighed loudly.

"But he is my brother," Ib said in a surly voice.

She rolled her eyes and sighed dramatically.

"I wish you would not do that thing with your eyes."

"I can't help it." She sliced another onion. He sat there, hunched over and silent. She wanted to make things better between them and wished he would ask her about the pregnancy; then she could blame her roller-coaster emotions on being pregnant and say that her moods would stabilize in the second trimester. She imagined how he would put his head on her belly, saying how he loved the baby, how Sarah was taking good care of it, protecting it from the heat, breathing and eating for it.

The next day was her day off, and after he left for work, she decided to go to the zoo because that was what she did to cheer herself up at home. Perhaps the next time she went, it would be several months from now and Ib would be pushing their baby in a stroller. She checked that it was Women's Day, and it was. She was glad for it meant that men would not bother her.

"I'll take the bus back," she told Johnny when he dropped her off. Following the stream of women and children past the sign, WOMEN ONLY, she meandered down the path under the pergola covered with purple bougainvillea. She took off her cloak, folded it into a small square, and tucked it in her backpack. She was wearing her white Capris and a t-shirt with diagonal stripes of red, yellow, and green. An Asian worker was pushing a squeaky wheelbarrow heaped with bloody hunks of meat. As he tossed some into the lion's cage, she wondered what he was doing here on Women's Day, and then she remembered that servants, in particular Third World Nationals, did not count as male. It was as if they were eunuchs. Knowing that he would not shout at her to cover up, she took off her headscarf and shook out her hair, feeling free again. At home, the weather would already have turned nippy with kids in windbreakers scrunching through piles of leaves, but here it was still so hot that she could feel the sweat gliding down her sides and thighs. For a while she stared at the companionable apes grooming each other, just as they had when she and Ib had stood in front of them at the zoo in Madison and chatted about Darwin and evolution. She made her way along the trail to a grassy enclosure, which held a corps of giraffes; she admired the elegant, supple creatures with their long necks and legs and the velvety brown nubs on their heads. She strolled on until she came to a smelly lagoon where an alligator lay so still that she assumed it was a log until she saw the sign, "Visitors throwing litter into this pit will be required to retrieve it." She frowned for she hated that sort of nasty humor. At the snake house, she gazed through the glass at an enameled rock python, coiled gem-like and unblinking. Beside it was a viper, whose distended jaws were icky with a milky gelatinous substance. Feeling slightly nauseated, she left the snake house. Outside she passed the caged gazelles, wolves, and baboons and studied the signs giving factoids about each species: habitat, diet, and length of life. Most lived less than twenty years. Poor creatures bred in captivity and caged for the duration of their short lives, all out of their natural habitat, just as she was. She crossed a wooden bridge over a creek where silver-flashing minnows leaped continuously up a two-foot dam. Not one made it to the top. She continued on to the aviary, where a small bird ruffled its yellow feathers, and with legs thin as pencil leads, it gripped the green netting that crosshatched the sky. Larger birds flew in the aviary's upper reaches. Outside, the free birds dipped and circled, warbling and hooting through the palms, and a chestnut-headed duck shot by her, flashing yellow in its tail. Beyond the aviary were various cages. In one, a caucus of crows cawed raucously; in another, a bald eagle beat its wings against the bars.

A wave of melancholy overcame Sarah. No other woman had come alone. The others were all laughing and talking with friends or family. She was about to leave when she noticed a sign for the tigers and she decided to go look. On her way she passed a couple of bears, and then oryx, gazelles, wolves, and a gray barking baboon, all of them caged. The tigers were caged too, and a gang of youngsters gawked at a powerfully built Bengal tigress, with dark stripes and amber eyes. Abruptly one of the boys yelled, and they raced to an overflowing trash can and pulled old newspapers, which they balled up and hurled at the tigress. They missed, but she tossed her head from side to side and growled menacingly. Two of the brats unscrewed their water bottles. "Attack. Attack. Bombs away," they shouted as they aimed streams of water at the big cat. One of them picked up a stone from the sandy ground. Sarah dashed toward him and knocked it from his hand. She grabbed him by the arm and dragged him away from the cage, but he shook himself free and ran off to join his pals. Trembling, she made her way to a nearby bench. What had gotten into her to treat a child like that? She must leave that instant. She rummaged through her backpack, found her cloak, threw it over her shoulders, and hurried toward the exit.

Outside the gate, a bus going toward Firdaus was parked at the bus stop, but it pulled off just before she reached it. She was less than two miles from home so she decided to walk, in the hope that it would calm her. As she crossed the street, she noticed a man seemed to be following her. He had a sallow complexion and was dressed in a drab olive t-shirt and khaki pants. She continued at a brisker pace until she reached the traffic light at the next corner. Suddenly he was so close she could see the purple zigzag of a scar on his left temple. She grabbed her head scarf from her backpack and put it on, pulled her cloak close, and walked faster. Halfway down the block, she glanced back. He was the same distance as before. "Stop imagining things," she told herself, but she felt afraid. She entered the first shop she came to, a stationer's, and lingered before the magazine racks, feigning interest in the latest *Newsweek* as she debated whether to tell the clerk about the stalker. She decided against it because she was not positive the man was pursuing her, but the clerk would most certainly lecture her about how a woman needed an escort. He might even sic the faith cops on her. Outside again, she glanced left and right and breathed a sigh of relief: the stalker was gone. But at the next corner, there he was. She rushed ahead, breathing hard, her sandals flapping on the sidewalk. She hurried across to the shady side of the street and kept within the shadow of the walls. At the next intersection, she turned into the souk and pressed her way through the crowds. Confident that she could lose him here, she barely noticed where she was going. She did not see the dresses hanging on racks or later the pyramids of oranges in the vegetable souk. She turned again and yet again. She was lost, with a stalker at her back, twenty feet behind. Or was he a terrorist? He would have seen her hair. He would know she was American. Maybe he intended to kidnap her, stuff her into the trunk of his car, and hold her for ransom. Finally, she came out of the warren of alleys and lanes into a broad avenue, and she rushed ahead, crossing against the light. Sweat trickled down her sides. She jerked her head backward. The stalker was gaining on her. She ran, stumbling and panting until she found herself on Sixteenth Street. A hundred yards away stood the British bank of the Middle East, with a contingent of National Guardsmen standing in front, armed with rifles and bayonets.

"A man, a stranger, he's following me," she blurted out in English.

"*Arabee. Arabee,*" he snapped.

"There, can you see? That way?" She gesticulated to the shadowy figure fleeing from them.

"There," she yelped, pointing. "That's him."

The guardsman unshouldered his oily-looking machine gun. "He Sa-ooo-di man?"

"What difference does that make?"

He narrowed his eyes, swiveled the machine gun from side to side, and set out after her stalker.

"No! No!" she screamed. "Don't shoot him!" She stretched her arms in front of her, hands flailing. "*Malesh.* It doesn't matter. Put down the gun." But the guardsman raced down Sixteenth Street in hot pursuit, machine gun leveled and ready to fire.

"*Quf*! He's Saudi," she yelled. The guardsman stopped and turned back toward the bank. Ahead of her loomed the high ochre wall of the Boeing Compound, and at last, she had her bearings. The Firdaus compound was a mere two blocks away. Every few steps she turned around, and to her relief she did not see the stalker.

When she arrived home, Ib was waiting. "You are late," he said as she came in. When she told him why, he clenched his fists. "I told you to be careful. You never listen to what I say."

"Don't be crazy. You make it sound like it's my fault."

"Well, you should know the basics by now. You are asking for trouble if you do not cover your hair. It is not the same here as in the States."

"Well, that's for sure. No fun here."

As she went to hang up her abaya in the hall closet, he followed her. "That does not matter. You are here. You must act accordingly."

"Oh, don't be so condescending."

"All I am asking is for you not to go out alone. Go with my sister or my mother. This is a bad time for Westerners."

"And when isn't it?" she said scornfully. "Oh, just stop nagging me." She turned away from him, went to the window, and looked out. The sky was filling with pink clouds, the streets amassing the faithful headed to the mosque.

He came and stood behind her and put his arms around her. "I was half-sick worrying about you. Sarah, you are like a lost soul. If only you could embrace Islam—"

She pulled away. "Why? Because Shaheed would like it?"

"No, that is not it at all. Life would be easier for you."

"I'm not even sure there is a God."

"Do not say that." Ib paled and murmured, "*Bismillah ar rahman ar rahim.*" He took his string of prayer beads out of his pocket and turning away from her, fondled each amber bead as if it were a talisman. They did not speak for the rest of the evening, and that night, for the first time, feeling like the loneliest person in the world, she slept with her back turned to him.

CHAPTER 17

IB'S FATHER WAS RIGHT ABOUT THE WAR. It was short, with the Taliban effectively removed from power before the fast of Ramadan began. Now instead of depictions of U.S. bombed hospitals and mosques, Saudi television showed American acts of charity—C-17s air-dropping food and medical packs and convoys of trucks lumbering across the stark mountains. At work too, things were easier between her and Annie, who apologized for holding her responsible for every stupidity of her crazy president. Despite the flight of the Taliban into Pakistan after their losses in Mazar-I-Sharif, Kabul, and Tora Bora, Osama Bin Laden was still on the loose. And even though they no longer *had* to, the Afghani women she saw on television were *still* wearing their burqas, those billowing robes of palest blue with pleated sleeves and crocheted lattice-work over the eyes.

"What do you expect?" Annie was putting on her scrubs in the physicians' locker room "We cover up too, don't we? All of us, even your U.S. servicewomen when they go off base. And drive? No Sir. It's the back seat for all of us. You know what the fundos say—how everybody is equal under Islam, and if we don't like it we should hightail it for home."

"But we have to wear it here. Women there don't have to. Not anymore.

That's the law."

"You wait and see. I bet they stay covered up."

That night Ib said it was not easy to legislate, for in their hearts few Afghans wanted to change the system. They liked to keep their women secluded; it was as simple as that. It bothered her that he was so listless; she wanted him to be passionate about it, like Tisam.

The next morning, the first day of the Islamic month of Ramadan, which fell on November 16 of the Western calendar, the cannon boomed before dawn, awakening Sarah and Ib. Quickly, they made love on the satin sheets in the dark of night, and afterwards, he had beans and rice while she went back to bed. He would eat nothing until dusk, but she was both pregnant and not a believer, so she was not expected to fast.

Work was interesting that day. An asthmatic came in trying to tough it out without his inhaler, and she called Dr. Nabeel to persuade the woman that it was a form of medicine and thus permissible. In the afternoon, she examined an American student with stomachache and vomiting. When she pressed the right lower abdomen, he exhaled sharply and she noted he had rebound tenderness. The blood tests and urinalysis confirmed the need for an appendectomy. The boy's father nervously ran his fingers through his blond crew cut and fussed. "What if the surgeon is Muslim? He might get the shakes or faint from lack of food. I don't want to sound prejudiced or anything, but—" Sarah checked the surgery rotation list and arranged for Dr. Brown from Vermont to operate.

That evening, they were invited to Layla and Ahmed's for the *iftar* meal that ended the day's fast. At the door, Sarah slipped off her turquoise sandals and lined them up between Eliza's black plastic flip-flops and an elegant pair of platform ankle-straps belonging to Layla, who came to the door in a satin dress in a floral print; she had her hair in a shiny new look, center-parted, and with her ringlets straightened. As they entered the salon, Omar was complaining that materialism had ruined Ramadan with people just telephoning greetings or sending text messages on their cell phone, not like in the good old days. Sarah smiled politely, bored already.

The cannon boomed, the children raced in from the courtyard, and Eliza passed around glasses of juice. "Ah, the taste of the first sip, how it explodes in the mouth with sweetness," Omar said. Then the conversation turned to soccer and stayed there right through dessert, a syrupy sweet pastry of shredded wheat. Sarah covered her mouth as once again she yawned.

"Bored?" Layla asked.

"No, just sleepy," Sarah said.

Layla giggled and poked her in the side. "Too much lovemaking," she whispered. Sarah was thinking how pleased Layla would be to learn her secret when the telephone rang; it was for Layla. Sarah flipped through an old copy of *Elle* while Layla chatted, the twins roughhoused, and the men talked politics. Malika was not there, and it was a relief not to have to deal with her, but she missed Lulu, who was with her grandmother. After a while, Sarah put down the magazine and went to help with the dishes, but Eliza shooed her away. Layla was still gabbing on the telephone. Feeling left out with no one to talk to, Sarah hoped they could leave right after coffee, but when Shaheed steered the conversation to the ninety-nine most beautiful names of Allah, she knew it would be a long time before they could go. Not in the mood for theology, she glanced over at Layla, who was chattering to her friend about the new abayas they had seen at the fashion show. "Life is short. Dare to be cute," she was saying in her tinkly voice as she played with the golden charms on her bracelet. Meanwhile, the men were deliberating the attributions of Allah. Shaheed's favorite was *the just*, Ib's father said his was *the source of peace*, and Ibrahim liked best *the knower of subtleties*.

"And you, Sarah?" Ib asked.

"*The light*," she said, the word springing from her mouth.

"And God knows best," Ahmed said approvingly in English.

"Talk English if you must, but whatever language you use, call our Lord, Allah," Shaheed snapped. "God is not his name."

"Make no mistake, it's the same God," Ahmed said.

Good ole liberal Ahmed, Sarah was thinking when she heard the boys squabbling. Farouk had again called Fawzi "Fatso."

"Now, now, boys, no fighting," Ahmed said, separating them. "Let's have Auntie Sarah tell us the story of Jesus and the dead dog."

"Dead dog? And Jesus?" She looked up, surprised. "I don't know any such story."

"No? Then I'll tell it," Ahmed said. "One day Jesus and his disciples passed the corpse of a dog."

"Corpse? What's that?" Farouk piped up.

"Remember that dead bustard on the camping trip?" Ib put in. "That's a corpse—something dead."

"The disciples said, 'How foul is the stench of this cur!' Jesus replied, 'How white are his teeth.' And do you know why Jesus said that, my sons? To teach us never to insult anyone, not even a dog."

It was an interesting story, but Sarah could not place it. However, since Muslims claimed Jesus as a prophet, it stood to reason they had their own stories of him. She glanced at her watch and saw it was nine o'clock. The twins should be in bed, but it was not her place to say so. Instead, she suggested they illustrate the story of the dead dog, and they went off to find Fawzi's colored markers.

No sooner had the twins stopped fighting than Ib and Shaheed started, as if discord were a family gene.

"The fast helps me understand what it means to be poor," Ib said. "And no one but God knows if we are fasting. It's a way to come closer to him."

Shaheed sliced his hand through the air. "We fast so we will not go to hell."

"Brother, it's a blessed time." Ib gave a hard laugh. "I certainly don't do it because I'm afraid of hell."

Layla, who had finally hung up the telephone, came in and plunked down on the sofa between them with a box of chocolates. "Don't fight, Shaheed. Please don't, Ibrahim. I go away one instant, come back, and find you quarrelling. Here, have a chocolate. I heard that Muhammad learned about fasting from Christian monks in the desert." Sarah stifled another yawn as Layla went on about the Prophet, how he swept the floor and mended his clothes to save his wife the trouble, and how once when a toddler was crying, he shortened the prayer so the mother could console him. This family seemed to have no end of stories about Muhammad. It was like Mom going on about Jesus.

The evening dragged on. The twins showed her their pictures of a pitiful-looking dog, with lolling pink tongue, pointy white teeth, and maggots on its black coat. After Ahmed and Layla took them off to bed, Shaheed switched on the television. A nature program was playing— long-horned oryx bounding across the desert—and he flipped the channel to Al Jazeera news. Sarah groaned. Now they could not leave until it was over. On the screen, a boy howled, his chest covered in burns, a victim of an attack on a Palestinian refugee camp.

"*Amrikiyi*," Shaheed spat out. "They give the money to the Isra-ee-lis; those dollars buy the bombs."

"Yes, the children suffer," she said, unable to sit still a moment longer. "Sometimes they die. That happens in wartime."

"Sarah, you sound so bitter." Ib said.

"Well, perhaps I am. I hate what's happening there. I hate the way people here go on and on about it but do nothing to help the situation." Ib went to turn off the television. Just as he was about to flick it off, the image of a doctor with a blond mustache bandaging a girl's eyes came on the screen. "Ib, wait a second!" Sarah cried. She turned to face Shaheed. "See that! That's what I believe in. Healing."

"Turn it off. Now!" Shaheed shrieked, and Ib clicked off the set.

"Get lost, Shaheed," she said. In carefully enunciated Arabic, she quoted the proverb, "Go tile the sea."

On the ride home, she stared out of the window. Ib looked sullen and did not speak. He was angry with her for fighting with his brother. As they passed the shop with the neon sign that flashed MIXED NUTS, she thought with a sinking heart how different he was becoming in this, his natural habitat. As soon as they reached home, she went straight to bed. She would not apologize. However, in the night, she reached out for him, and he was not there. Her parents never to her knowledge slept apart. Kiss and make up before bed, was their rule. Thinking of that reminded her of another habit they had, one that embarrassed her. A few times she had come into their room late at night and seen them: Daddy had his big hand in Mom's freckled one, which lay on the Hudson Bay blanket, which they had pulled up to their chins. Their eyes were shut, and she could hear them praying, first Daddy and then Mom. Once Daddy prayed she would find peace, whatever that meant. She slipped out, relieved they had not noticed her.

At dawn when the Ramadan cannon boomed, Ib was still gone. The day dragged, giving her plenty of time to worry. She contemplated how rarely Ib's parents were together, and how often Ahmed absented himself from Layla. She did not want that pattern for her marriage. Ib was inspecting one of the outlying water plants and would spend the day in the broiling sun. He would be thirsty, but because of the fast, he would not take a single sip of water. She remembered how she had suffered heatstroke on the camping trip in July, and worried he too might faint. After work, she dialed his cellphone number. There was no answer. She listened to a CD of American folk songs, flipped through an old Vogue Layla had lent her, and played with Shadow. She took a long cool bath, but all she could do was worry about Ib. Eventually, she decided to make his favorite eggplant casserole; she started chopping vegetables. By the time the cannon boomed to signal the end of that day's fast, the casserole was ready. Twenty minutes later, she was still waiting. She rested her face on the cold enamel of the refrigerator and wept. No one was ever late for meals during Ramadan.

An hour later, the kitchen door creaked as he opened it. He stood before her, an enormous watermelon in his outstretched arms like a peace offering.

"I was at the mosque. It was no use being there. I could think only of you," he said, his voice made odd with emotion. He set down the watermelon on the counter, and she went to him and hugged him hard. From the refrigerator, she got out the pitcher of orange juice and poured him a glass. When they finished the simple supper of lentils, eggplant casserole, and tomato salad, they went out to the patio where he sliced off hunks of the huge round watermelon, juicy red and delicious. Laughing, they spat out the glistening black seeds, seeing who could spit them the furthest onto the patch of grass.

That night in bed he said that he had a confession to make: When he had asked her to marry him, it was partially because he wanted her as a souvenir wife, like a pretty and very alive Statue of Liberty. She replied that her motives had not been a hundred percent pure either, and one of the reasons she had wanted to come was because she was tired of home. She told him about being in the bar in Milwaukee and how as they were enjoying their brats and Schlitz, Pete had accused her of liking Ib because she was tired of her own culture. She had denied it, but now she admitted to Ib that he had been partly right.

"It's a better life there, there's freedom," she said.

"You're right. But it is even better to live and fight for it here," he said.

In December, the week she finished her first trimester, Ib and Sarah announced to his family that she was expecting, and even Malika hugged her and said the child was a gift from God and would bring joy and light to their home. The weather was cooler now, and they ate their meals at the round wood table in the courtyard. It was pleasant there with the breeze in the frangipani trees, the scarlet bougainvillea cascading down the wall and Shadow hunting in the green undergrowth.

Then came a week-long spate of bombings in which six Westerners were killed on the streets of Khobar.

"Do you think it'll get worse?" Sarah asked as she licked her fingers after eating pizza for supper.

"Maybe. Shaheed and his gang, they are like hounds," Ib said. "On 9/11, they caught the smell of blood and they will not let go of the trail."

"Surely, it's not that bad." She blew out the candles on the table and left him reading the newspaper while Johnny drove her to the hospital for the late shift. About eleven p.m., the paramedics brought in a girl, her cloak blood-splattered, her face slashed. In the next hour, twenty more girls and women were admitted, all with bruises and lacerations. Their fathers, uncles, and brothers crowded into the waiting room. Some shouted for help for their girls, others for revenge on wild youths. One father banged his head on the wall; another beat his chest and groaned that his reputation was lost, his honor sullied. The chaos made it difficult for Sarah to attend to the women, and she paged for help.

"What the hell is going on?" Dr. Nabeel raced in, stethoscope bouncing on his chest. "Get the visitors out. Get out, I tell you. Get out! *Yalla.*" Most went docilely. A few jostled the orderlies and once out, tried to shove their way back in, but gradually a semblance of order was restored. Sarah doled out Valium and sutured cuts as women continued to arrive, all dazed with shock and terror. One of them told her how a gang of teens stopped her husband's SUV as it slowed to enter a round-about. They dragged her behind the juniper bushes in the roundabout. When her husband tried to pull them off, they beat him with their sticks.

Sarah immediately thought of Layla. When she was with Ahmed, she did not veil. Sarah snapped off her gloves, sprinted to the nursing station, and telephoned their number. Ahmed answered, his voice grog-gy, and said Layla was asleep. As Sarah hung up, three police officers came through the swinging doors into the ER, pushing two manacled young women ahead of them. The girls were dressed in— of all things— Bermuda shorts. Blood trickled down their slim, tanned legs, and the pink-striped tank top of the shorter girl was ripped at the breast. The taller girl, her chestnut hair caught in a ponytail, was sniveling. They were followed by a Saudi woman, cloaked but unveiled.

"*Amrikiyeen.*" The officer curled his upper lip in disdain as he re-moved the handcuffs. Sarah was wondering what had possessed them to go out in shorts, during Ramadan of all times, when the girl with the ponytail tugged on her white coat. "Doctor, you've got to help us. Like, call the consulate. Call somebody, even the MPs. We're with the Army."

"First, let's take care of you." She picked up a needle from the suture tray. "Now then tell me what happened."

It was a prank gone awry. They were on their way to the souk to buy souvenirs when one of the G.I.s jumped out of the jeep in front of an ice cream parlor and came back with two ice cream cones. He dared the girls to take off their cloaks and walk a block in shorts in return for the cones. Laughing, they agreed. They climbed out of the jeep and strolled, licking their ice creams, along Sixteenth Street.

"It was for fun. That's all. Just fun," the shorter girl said. "Then these Saudis came after us and our guys vanished. The Saudis kept coming, wolf whistling, and yelling." She dropped her face in her hands and burst into tears. "We were scared they'd rape us."

"They started throwing stones," Sarah said quietly.

"Yes, and then the cops came and shoved us into a paddy wagon and took us to some jail and threw us into a cell with no bed or chair, nothing, just the cement. We waited like forever until this nice lady brought us here."

"I'm the warden of the women's prison," the Saudi woman introduced herself. "I tried to bring them in earlier, but you know how slow things can be. I've called their commanding officer."

After Sarah treated their cuts and abrasions, the police officer put back on the handcuffs. "Ouch. They're too tight. Ouch. Loosen these damn things," one of the girls yelled.

"Silly, silly girls. What they did makes it harder for all of us," the Saudi woman said in an angry voice.

The next morning there was nothing about the incident in the newspaper, but at the senior staff meeting at the desalination plant that afternoon Ib learned what had happened. The two Americans were said

to have performed a striptease on the street; another *mutawwa* claimed
they had insulted the Prophet. The fury of the *mutawwa'in* spread like
wildfire, and those patrolling Sixteenth Street did nothing to stop the
youths who had assembled at the perimeter of the roundabout, had set
up a roadblock there, and were stopping each car. If an unveiled woman
was inside, they smashed the windows and pelted her with stones. Some
of the women were dragged out of their cars and beaten for wearing un-
authorized abayas, cloaks identical to those she and Layla had admired
at the fashion show. It was sheer chaos, but what happened later was
bizarre. Young thugs pushed their way into the family sections of restaurants; there they yanked cloaks off the pretty young girls and wrapped
themselves in them, whirling like dervishes, while the girls cowered
against the walls, covering their faces with their hands. Their menfolk
did nothing, catatonic with shock.

"Shaheed? Was he there?" Sarah asked. They were sitting having
chicken and rice for supper in the courtyard.

Ib put down his fork and took his prayer beads from his thobe pocket.
"If you must know, yes he was. He reproaches the women for being out
so late."

"Blame the victims? That figures." She rolled her eyes and huffed a
sigh.

"I wish you would not do that, that thing with your eyes."

"Sorry, can't help it." She looked at Ib, who was fiddling with his
beads. What was the matter with him? He should be livid the way he
had been in Madison when a rapist got off with a light sentence, or
when she had told him about David Ritter. If David deserved to be

flogged, so did those thugs, especially Shaheed.

"It's not right for those creeps to get off scot-free. It makes me sick. I can't eat another bite." She pushed away her plate.

"I blame myself." Ib reached for her hand on the table.

"Don't talk nonsense. You've always opposed him."

"Not always. When Shaheed came back from Afghanistan, I should not have let him go to that *madrasa*. If I had objected, Father would never have permitted it."

"Why did he go to Afghanistan in the first place?"

"Try to understand." He told her how Shaheed as a teenager had been caught driving drunk in the outskirts of Riyadh. The religious authorities summoned both Ib and his father Omar. The cure for alcoholism is Islam, they were told, and Shaheed would be forgiven if he atoned for his mistakes. After only two weeks in prison with several prayerful visits from clerics—no lashes for him—Ahmed was released to go fight for the Mujahiddin in Afghanistan.

The phone rang inside and she went into the house. It was the American vice-consul. With a clipped New England accent, he explained to her about the consulate's emergency phone tree; she gave him her email address, her office and cell phone numbers, and assured him she had voice mail and an answering machine. She asked if the craziness caused by the two army girls had been reported in the States, and he told her that sort of news was censored. He urged her to keep a low profile the next few days and predicted that the crisis would blow over, but if not evacuation plans were in place.

The next afternoon, she and Ib drove around the Western Compound. Newly strung coils of concertina wire stretched along the high perimeter walls. With the concertina wire glittering in the sun, her old neighborhood now looked like a penitentiary. Al Firdaus felt safer. She half-hoped there would be an evacuation as that would give her a face-saving way to leave. Her pants felt tight in the tummy now, and she had trouble zipping her jeans. This was no place to wait out a pregnancy. She consoled herself by remembering that in only three weeks she'd be home for Christmas.

The school vacation at the end of Ramadan started December 17. Layla, Ahmed, and the children had abandoned their plans to go to Hawaii and had taken a plane earlier in the day; they were off to ski at the Cedars in Lebanon.

That evening Ib and Sarah joined the rest of the family in Qatif, where Malika greeted them by the ancient blackened tree. Under her abaya, Sarah was wearing a maternity dress in black taffeta, one she had ordered from England for the "just showing" stage. Usually she did not wear black, but she could not resist this one with its sparkles at the bust and a bouffant skirt that ended just below the knees. "Very short. Very seductive," Ib had said when she first modeled it for him. "Better not let Shaheed see you with that on." She promised to wear the abaya while he was in sight.

When she went to the kitchen to drop off a plate of brownies, she overheard him in the hall. "You are running back again. You see, you prefer it there," he said in his shrill voice.

"My wife wants to spend Christmas with her family. And yes, I do like it there," Ib said.

"Christmas, that's for Christians. You should hate America. For fifty years, they've allowed Israel to occupy Palestine. Israel is nothing without America." She knew what was coming—how the U.S. let Israel demolish houses, assassinate elected leaders, and shoot children who threw stones. Did not American tax dollars subsidize the military jets, missiles and bombs? It was true, but she had heard it so many times before.

"To fight the real enemies of Islam, you should tackle illiteracy and poverty," came Ib's voice.

They were at it again.

Sarah waited until she could no longer hear them, and then she went to the cloakroom where she hung up her abaya. She joined the other women in the family room. Malika looked regal in a gown of gold and brown, and Sarah greeted her first; then she went around the circle of women, kissing each one. Tisam had gone off somewhere, which was a disappointment. Sarah sat and made polite conversation with the women, most of them distant cousins who wanted advice on various and sundry medical problems. She would not have obliged in the States, but here she was glad to be able to help. Eventually the fumes of frankincense and the perfumes—Opium, L'Air du Temps, Anaîs, and Chanel— made her queasy so she decided to go outside and get a breath of fresh air. She slipped out of the salon and sneaked down the hall to the closet to get her cloak. She was almost there when she heard a light tapping behind her. She turned and saw it was Shaheed. In his hand, he held a slender cane, no thicker than her little finger. He flexed and bent it; he swished it on the terrazzo tile. "Sister, you are a distraction," he said.

"And you are rude."

"Woman!" He tapped the cane again. "Where you go?"

"Out."

"Cover your legs." He switched her bare legs— *whht whht whht*— three times, so fast his stick whistled.

Smarting, she touched her hand to her calves; they stung with pain. She grit her teeth because to whimper would be to let him win. She raised her hand to slap him, but he had already turned and was slinking off in the direction of the salon. She ran to the closet, grabbed the first abaya she saw, and made for the front door. She had her hand on the doorknob when Malika appeared. "Where you going?"

"Out." Sarah flung the black abaya over her short dress.

"Why?"

"For a walk. It's a lovely evening. Maybe I'll see stars." She smiled a bright fake smile. She would not give Malika the satisfaction of knowing how Shaheed had humiliated her.

"Hrrmpf. Have you so soon forgotten the night of stones?"

"I'll risk it."

"Your place is here. A pregnant woman should rest, not rush about."

At that moment Tisam appeared. "Oh there you are, Auntie." She draped one arm around Sarah and the other around Malika.

"Alone. Alone," Malika grumbled. "Always she wants to be alone."

Tisam patted her on the arm. "Everyone is looking for you. Do go to them, Auntie. You leave for one instant, and everyone asks for you."

As Malika lumbered off to tend to her guests, Tisam winked at Sarah. "She's old, poor auntie, so we humor her. Shall we go back in?"

Sarah bit her lip. Her calves stung where Shaheed had switched her, and she felt ashamed, angry, and disgraced.

"We'll go to the sunroom—no one's there— and listen to my new CD. It's the Indigo Girls. Auntie Malika calls it decadent although she doesn't understand a word."

Sarah begged off, but in the end she allowed herself to be persuaded, and they sat on cushions, listening to "Power of Two" while Tisam chatted about the fun Layla must be having in Lebanon and how inventive their cartoonists were, almost as good as the Egyptians. Sarah asked to see her latest work, and when Tisam left to fetch her portfolio, she checked her calves. The skin was not split, but three red straight lines marked where the cane had lashed her soft flesh. She knew that Shaheed had caned Layla, at least once. Layla had not showed her the welts, but had made light of it, saying, "Oh, it's just a little spanking. That's our sheriff for you."

Tisam returned with her portfolio, and Sarah picked up one sketch after another, admiring their economy and freshness. "This is my favorite," she said of a cartoon that portrayed a *mutawwa* reaching out with his stick to cane a bird in the sky.

"My friends say no one dares publish my work. Too provocative. Too insulting. Too insensitive. Too this and too that. But when I have enough for a series, I'll self-publish. If we don't fight back, men will think we accept our sad little lives." She slipped the sketches back in the folder, and a solemn look came over her face. "What happened on the night of stones must never happen again. *Abadan!* Never."

"Tisam—something happened to me just now. Look." She lifted the hem of her skirt and showed the red welts on the back of her calves. "Shaheed did it."

"Oh darling Sarah, I'm so sorry. Oh, the shame of it. I don't see how Susu puts up with him." She clenched her jaw, and her green eyes turned hard and stony.

"In the States, he'd go to jail."

"As he should." They talked about the night of stones and how the crazies, the "fundos" as Annie called them, had become more audacious since 9/11. "One day you get away with something, but the next they cart you off to prison. In Jeddah, it's one way and in Riyadh, it's another. Dhahran, Qatif, everywhere it's different. Our men say we are no better than sheep. But whose fault is that? Our cartoonists poke fun at the bureaucrats and that's good and brave, and they express the desire for peace, and that's good too, but for me, I want to fight for women. The men say if we had freedom, there'd be…oh, you know what they say. There's something else too. Sometimes I am near despair." She buried her head between her hands.

"What is it, Tisam?" Sarah put an arm around her shoulders.

"What I think about all the time."

"What? What do you think about?"

"Immorality." Tisam touched a red hibiscus in the vase on the side table. "I think about immorality a lot. Remember what I told you? About me?"

Sarah nodded.

"If Shaheed knew…" Tisam shuddered. "Last summer, Layla and Ahmed took me to London. At an Internet café, I found sites like, well, sites they block here. Don't look surprised. It's to be expected. After all, they block thousands of sites. It's to preserve our values, of course."

Sarah's gray eyes widened. It was the first sarcasm she'd heard from a Saudi. "But aren't you afraid? I've heard, well, that gays are sometimes…" Her voice trailed off.

"Don't believe everything you hear." She tapped Sarah on the wrist. "Execution is for murderers or rapists, and they deserve it. What we worry about is how to meet others like us and how to keep it secret. Thank God, I'm not a man. It is harder for them. People say that it is sinful for a woman not to need a man, but I can share a bed with a friend, and people won't suspect anything."

"But if they do?"

"Well, then it's very bad. So I keep my little secret, and when the mothers of my suitors come begging for my hand, I jump in their faces like a wild cat." She laughed hysterically, rocking back and forth.

That night Sarah went to bed before Ib. She lifted her nightgown and looked at the back of her legs: the three lines were there, still red. Still feeling incredulous that Shaheed had dared strike her, she smoothed lotion on her calves. Once she was back home in Deep Lake, she might stay put, at least until the baby was born. She would not mention it to Ib, not now when he had so many concerns.

CHAPTER 18

CHRISTMAS EVE, SARAH AND IB LANDED at Milwaukee's Mitchell International Airport. Her parents were waiting at the gate, Daddy in his sheepskin jacket and Mom in her puffy down coat. It had only been six months since Sarah had seen them, but they had more white in their hair and she embraced them gently. Light snow fell throughout the two-hour drive to Deep Lake, the fluffy flakes hitting the windshield as she and Ib sat holding hands in the back seat. She pointed out the skiers on the lit-up steep slopes near Hartford, the barns bigger than the houses along highway 23, and the billboard outside the city of Ripon, "The birthplace of the Republican Party...a nice place to live." Twenty minutes later, they arrived at Deep Lake. They passed the courthouse, school and library, the grocery store and the shops selling souvenirs for the tourists from Chicago. In the park with the plastic Santa and bandshell, a boy was pulling a red sled with another kid in it.

They turned up the familiar red brick drive. Electric candles glowed in the windows of the graceful Italianate home. Red ribbon twisted around the porch's white pillars, and the evergreen in the front yard twinkled with blue, red, and yellow lights. When they piled out of the car, it was so frigid they could see their breath. "Invigorating, isn't it?" she said, laughing and grabbing Ib's hand. A few squeak-crunch steps through the snow, and they were inside, enveloped by the scents of mulled cider, cinnamon potpourri and lemon furniture polish. As she took off her heavy jacket, she wondered if either of her parents would notice that she was pregnant.

"You're so tanned," her mother marveled.

"I only realize it when I take off my watch." Sarah removed it to show the strip of pale skin at her wrist. "I've had the tan so long now that it seems my natural color." She felt a little disappointed her parents did not notice that she was pregnant; she reminded herself that she was in the barely showing stage.

In the living room, the tree was trimmed with tinsel, icicles, and glittery ornaments she'd made in grade school. When they were alone, Ib again admired the Raphael Madonna and Child painting and predicted she would be a mother just as tender. Flattered, she smiled and toyed with one of her gold hoop earrings. She remembered how Ib had said the Madonna resembled Layla, and she wondered if perhaps his sister was pregnant again and would have that fourth child.

"Sarah. Come here a minute," Mom called from the kitchen. She asked if she should make the BLTs they traditionally had on Christmas Eve. Sarah said Ib did not eat bacon, and Mom said she would make grilled cheese sandwiches instead. The dishwasher was broken, so Sarah helped do the dishes, her hands in the deep tub of suds while her mother dried with a thin dishtowel. It felt intimate and pleasant being together, and when Mom invited her to the Christmas Eve service, she said that she would come if Ib did too.

Mom's brown eyes went beady. "Well, dear, do you think that's a good idea? You know how people are about Arabs after 9/11."

Her mother was right. In any case, Ib would have gone only for her sake, so she suggested he stay home to wait up for Pete who had not yet arrived from Madison.

In the narthex of the Sunshine Community Church, two lengths of butcher paper scotch-taped to either side of the sanctuary doors listed the names of some of those killed in the 9/11 attacks. The Sunday School children had printed names in purple and yellow crayon while the adults of the congregation penned the other names in longhand. Pots of red poinsettia lined the steps to the choir loft; white tapers burned at the stained glass windows; and in front of the elevated pulpit was a Christmas tree festooned with scarves and mittens the congregation had collected during the Advent season. As Sarah followed her parents to their pew toward the front, she noticed the flag up front and felt relieved that Ib had stayed back. He would think a flag did not belong in a house of worship, and that it made the creator of the spinning galaxies seem like a trivial tribal god. But she liked seeing the bright stars and red stripes. Anywhere!

Mom nudged her. "I should have warned you," she whispered. "David Ritter is here."

As the organ played the processional, he marched up the aisle beside the senior pastor. Although David's black clerical gown was as loose as an abaya, it was clear he had not lost any weight. On the chancel steps he called for the cherub choir to sing "Away in a Manger." Then came two more carols and the senior pastor's sermon, of which she could not remember one word, followed by the prayers of the people:

"Healing for my cousin Joe who had a heart attack."

"Lord, hear our prayers."

"For the unemployed."

"Lord, hear our prayers."

"For my sister Ann who needs a job."

"Lord, hear our prayers."

"For my dog Squish who died."

"Lord, hear our prayers."

"For those in hospital." Images from the ER crowded in on her: the drowned girl; the crone with shingles; the teenager who miscarried Sarah's first day, the multitudes of women in double-thickness veils. "For the women of Arabia," the words bubbled up in her and she felt as if she might burst if she did not say them, but just then a strong male voice from the back of the church called out, "For those who lost loved ones during 9/11." Close to tears, she prayed for them, instead. As the service came to a close, the deacons passed out white candles and the congregation rose to sing "Silent Night." Sarah and her mother leaned in close to each other as she tipped her candle toward her mother's to light it. "Sleep in heavenly peace," she sang in a tremulous voice.

On the way home, they talked about David Ritter. She had not seen him since all those years ago when he had jilted her, and she felt angry that he was able to continue on to seminary, graduate and then win this job as youth pastor in her home church.

"How he can stand up there in front of everybody is beyond me," Mon said. "Everybody knows now. Everybody."

"Knows what?"

"About the affair."

"Really? With whom?" Her voice rose with genuine incredulity.

"The confirmation class teacher. He got her pregnant."

"Not again! Is he getting away with it?" Sarah clenched her teeth, feeling furious.

"Thank God, no. He pleaded to finish out his contract, but we gave him just a month."

"Serves him right," Sarah snapped.

"He'll be gone in two weeks. After all, how can we have a man with his lifestyle lead the True Love Waits classes?"

It was so preposterous that Sarah laughed aloud.

Christmas morning the blue spruce outside the window of her bedroom was flocked with new fallen snow. Ib handed her a small package tied with a pink ribbon. Nestled in the white tissue was a heavy heart-shaped crystal, which fit in the palm of her hand. She went to the window and raised the crystal to catch the sun's rays. The flickers of green, pink, and purple light that shimmered across the ceiling reminded her of the northern lights. Shyly she gave him her gift, a portrait she had painted of Layla, working from a photograph Tisam had taken.

"It's perfect," Ib said.

They went downstairs, and after coffee and Christmas kringle, everyone opened gifts by the tree. Ib gave her parents a nativity set, carved by Palestinians in Bethlehem.

"Just what I've always wanted." Mom touched the smooth figures of olive wood: the shepherds, three kings, a donkey, a cow, and the baby Jesus with his stiff, outstretched arms. Sarah helped arrange the crèche scene on one of the end tables, and as she placed the baby Jesus in the manger, she touched her belly and wondered whether she could really raise a child in Arabia, so far from home. Mom brought down the family Bible, the one with the red leather cover, and as he did every Christmas morning, Daddy turned to the Gospel of Luke and read the nativity story. It might be good for their child to have a faith— either Islam or Christianity. If she could give a child that gift, why not? Why deny it the gift of faith just because she could not swallow every bit of theology?

After Daddy closed the Bible, Ib mentioned that the Qu'ran had a similar story. In the Muslim version, the angel Gabriel appeared to Mary with the same good news: she would bear a son to be named the Messiah, Jesus, who would be "noble in this world, in the hereafter, and among those who are closest to Allah." Sarah touched the wooden figurine of Mary, kneeling with her arms folded over her breasts. There was more to the Islamic version, but it was unpleasant, which was perhaps why Ib had omitted it. Lucky Christian Mary had kings and shepherds, oxen and angels rejoicing with her while poor Muslim Mary had to face snarling neighbors, who were about to throw stones at her.

"Well, I'm glad they respect Jesus in your country," Mom said. "But he is more than a prophet." She put her hand on her heart. "Praise the Lord. He is our personal savior." Ib stiffened; his eyes glazed and he kept a fixed smile while Mom went on about God being everywhere, making it sound as if he were like a celestial waiter at their disposal.

Sarah wished Mom would not talk like that. Personal savior…personal trainer, what was the difference?

She remembered Tisam's request and asked Mom if she could take a Bible back for her friend.

"Absolutely. That's marvelous," Mom said. She took Sarah up to her bedroom to choose one from her small collection. When they came back, Daddy was telling Ib the story of the prodigal son, of how the father ran stumbling, arms outstretched to meet his swinish boy. Ib had a peculiar look on his face, half puzzlement, and half horror. He told her father that God would forgive, but that God should lose his dignity was unseemly, even ungodly. When Daddy went on about how Jesus had died on the cross for his sins, Ib said that God would not allow his beloved prophet to die such a shameful death. "The crucifixion did not happen. Jesus was raised alive to heaven by God," he said. Daddy glared at him, and Ib tried to be conciliatory, saying that both Christians and Muslims were People of the Book, and thus had much in common.

"It's not the same." Daddy shrugged, went off to the den, and turned on the television to the 700 Club.

Sarah tapped Ib on the shoulder. "Let's get out of here. Want to go for a walk?"

They pulled on their boots and coats and headed down Illinois Avenue. Snow was falling, and Ib kept blinking his eyelashes to ward off the flakes. As they crunched through the snow, she told him about her Uncle Tom and Aunt Helen who were coming for Christmas dinner. Ib looked glum. He wished he had met them before 9/11 because now they would assume that as a Saudi he was in some way responsible for the attacks.

Everything was harder for him than it had been a year ago. This time it had been an ordeal getting to the States. After 9/11, visas were no longer issued at the consulate in Dhahran, and he had to fly to Riyadh to get one. He had left Khobar at three a.m. in order to be there when the doors opened at seven because only seventy visas were being issued each day. At seven a.m. seventy-three people were already ahead of him in line, so he had called to say he had to stay in the capital overnight. The next morning, he reached the consulate shortly after five a.m., but for security reasons those waiting for visas were not allowed to assemble until six a.m. He had to wait outside in the sun for six hours, and the American vice-consul, whom he saw for all of three minutes, had offended him by being arrogant. Yesterday when they arrived in New York, the immigration official at JFK fingerprinted Ib, which he found offensive. He was wearing his gray Armani suit, but his passport photo showed him in a thobe; this led the official to question Ib's identity and to grill him for two hours almost causing them to miss their connecting flight to Milwaukee.

Now, as they looked out on the frozen expanse of Deep Lake, the white unbroken except for the occasional ice-fishing shack, she told Ib not to worry about Uncle Tom and Aunt Helen, because she was sure they would like him. When they returned from their walk—her cheeks flushed from the cold, his ears tingling with it—her relatives were already there.

"So you're a Saudi?" Uncle Tom said as they shook hands.

"An Arabian." It was Ib's standard response. He disliked being called a "Saudi," and although he never criticized the kingdom when he was beyond its borders, he did not think it right to have an entire country named after a single family.

"I see." Uncle Tom shook Ib's hand. "It's quite a controversial country, isn't it?"

"So it may seem. We are trying to change, but feeling our way. It may take time."

"And what do you make of 9/11?"

Ib's face darkened; he stiffened.

"Uncle Tom, really! He's no terrorist." Sarah put her arm around Ib's waist. "Do you know what he did, long before anyone knew that Saudis had anything to do with it? He sent off a check for the families of the victims."

"Hear, hear," Uncle Tom said.

Mom brought in the turkey on her Granny's blue willow platter, and Sarah offered to carve, but Daddy said it was a man's job. Aunt Helen started on Saudi women, "Those poor things…"

"You mustn't think that just because they don't live the same way we do, there's something wrong with them. Women who cover up can still work and study. Lots of women in New York City don't drive, either. It's not an issue, at least not for me. I've got a driver."

"That sounds nice." Aunt Helen poked her husband in the ribs. "I wouldn't mind not being allowed to work. That'd be just fine with me."

"You might not feel the same if you didn't have the choice." Realizing that she was speaking on both sides of the issue, Sarah felt torn and frustrated.

"Those poor dears. Pass me a little more of that dressing." Aunt Helen heaped two spoonfuls on her plate. "And the bigamy. How can they stand it?"

"It doesn't happen much anymore."

"Just imagine, four wives."

"It's up to *them* to decide how they change," Sarah said.

"Well, young man, whoever civilized you, certainly did a very fine job." Uncle Tom gnawed at the turkey leg in his hand.

Ib flushed and the tic in his neck throbbed, and she knew he felt humiliated at this condescension. Pete came to the rescue by saying, "Really, Uncle Tom, you should thank his parents for that." Gradually, with the abundance of food—creamy mashed potatoes, gravy, and thick slices of turkey—the mood grew convivial. After they finished the main course, Sarah took the plates to the kitchen and left them stacked on the counter because the dishwasher was still broken. When she came back with the plum pudding, the men were engrossed in a conversation about the best bait for catching walleye.

"Attention everybody," she said as she struck a match to the pudding, and a blue flame rose. "We've something to tell you."

Ib pushed back his chair, lifted his glass, and proposed a toast: "To my bride, a mother-to-be."

"Sarah sweetheart! Ibrahim," her mother gushed, "That's wonderful news." Everyone clustered around to hug her and to shake Ib's hand and made what Daddy called a real hullabaloo, and Sarah felt a whoosh of love for her family.

The next day a brisk wind was blowing out of the north. The bait shop was closed, but Pete had already bought minnows and gold shiners. His face half-hidden under the furred lid of the parka, Ib helped pack the mobile fishing shelter in the trunk of the pickup truck.

"Got everything?" Sarah asked.

"Yep. Auger, ice picks, cleats, spikes, and flotation devices," Pete ticked them off his fingers. "Don't get your hopes up," he warned Ib. "Fish are sluggish in winter. It could be a while before we get a bite."

As a child, she had been mystified as to how fish could swim in ice. Her father explained that below the ice, there was water, and when the lake froze over, the fish swam deeper. One day he had pulled her on a red sled, skidding along the icy surface of the lake to the green shanty, warm and smelly from the kerosene heater. With his awl, he punched a pancake-sized hole in the ice and she peered into the dark blank swirl. He set up her lines, letting them out hand-over-hand over the hole. "Don't let the bait just hang there. Troll," he said. For a long time she jiggled the line without anything happening. Suddenly there was a silent Z-shaped ripple in the water—a fish.

She would have liked to go with Ib and Pete, but she had offered to get the dishwasher fixed. She spent two hours on the telephone, being put on hold, transferred from one operator to the next and listening to Muzak and assurances that her business was very important to the company and her call was being monitored for quality control. Exasperated, she located the copy of the warranty and headed to the hardware store to see if the manager would help, but even he was given the runaround. She could not resist saying that in the kingdom she would have made a two-minute call and that same day a smiling repairman would have appeared to do the job. The manager gave a look as if to say, well if it's so fine over there, just go back.

After she came out of the store, she ran into David Ritter on Main Street. His shoulders were hunched, his fat arms crossed against the cold, and his black coat flapped against his legs in the frigid wind. She felt he had been lying in wait for her.

"Sarah," he said.

"David." She forced herself to look at his face. His eyes were tired and anxious. He had flecks of grey in his hair, and did not look at all well. For a few moments neither spoke.

"So you know? My disgrace."

"Yes."

"Have a coffee with me? Just coffee. Just to talk?"

"I don't think so." She shook her head.

"Please." He gestured to the Starbucks across the street.

She relented. "Okay, ten minutes. Then I've got to go." They sat at a table and she kept on her orange down jacket while he shrugged off his dark coat. His sweater was black too. She traced the Formica table with her finger while he sat there, hands clasped around the mug. She took a sip of coffee and waited for him to speak.

"I'm sorry about how it ended between us," he finally said, looking into his cup of black coffee.

"I hardly ever think of it. Not anymore." She asked about the confirmation class teacher. He had been counseling her, he said, and they got carried away. She was planning to give the child up for adoption, and the church was footing the bill for his therapy—a month with other lapsed clergymen. No, his wife would not be going with him.

"The pain I've brought her. That's what hurts most of all."

"That's easy to say." She pushed aside the half-empty cup and remembered the day she had had the abortion.

"Perhaps if we'd stayed together, none of this would have happened," he said.

She stood up. "I never thanked you for the wedding gift, the hammer."

"I hope your husband didn't mind."

"It surprised us."

"Remember that spiritual we used to sing, 'If I had a hammer.'" He hummed the tune and then said the words in a lowered voice, "'I'd hammer out justice, I'd hammer out freedom all over this—'"

"Stop it!" What right did he of all people have to talk about justice and freedom? She felt livid and had to look away from him to regain her composure. On the counter, there was a red velvet cake, a single slice cut from it. When she turned back to face him, his eyes were red around the rims. "You know, David, you can change."

"It's nice of you to say so. Nice to think so."

"But next time, don't forget the condom," she said, her voice harsh as she went out the door. It was not so easy to forgive as she had imagined.

When she arrived home, two walleye trout lay glistening and pink in the stainless steel kitchen sink. "Yours?" she asked Ib. "What a fisherman," she said, kissing the nape of his neck.

'Hey, you two," Pete yelled. "Cut it out."

That weekend she and Ib spent at a hotel in Madison. They went shopping on State Street for things she could not find in Khobar: tubes of paint, scented drawer liners and some layette items; in the afternoon they went to the zoo and for a walk along Lake Monona; that night they went hip-hop dancing at the Goose Blind Café. They felt a sweet nostalgia at revisiting the sites of their courtship. But when they returned to Deep Lake, it was difficult. A neighbor gave them the cold shoulder, and Sarah did not know whether Mrs. Schmidt was anti-Saudi or simply inhospitable. Daddy kept the television tuned to Fox News, quoted Rush Limbaugh and argued politics nonstop. Daddy believed the U.S. should buy the oilfields or invade the kingdom to help the good Saudis get rid of the bad ones. Her father's ignorance irritated Ib. Always Sarah found herself in the middle, trying to mediate the two positions; it exhausted her. It was worse with her mother, who was obsessed with having their baby baptized.

"Mom, it's not even born yet," Sarah said. "And it would be hypocritical."

"But it's important. You say you want a wider world for your child. Ib can tell the child about Islam all he likes, but don't refuse me this."

Ib steepled his fingers, looked solemn and murmured something innocuous about "the Prophet Jesus, peace and blessings be upon him." Sarah looked daggers at him because he had done it again— left her carrying the spear. "Look, Mom, we're not doing it. Let's just leave it at that. You can tell it Bible stories all you like, and take it to church with you when we visit, but that's it."

"There you go again. Always criticizing. You never miss a thing. Pick.

Pick. Pick. We're never good enough for you."

It was tranquil only when she and Ib were alone in her bedroom. Plastic sheeting taped over the storm windows kept out the drafts. She would lie listening to the furnace rumble and feel safe and cozy. That night she and Ib went to bed early and snuggled under the blue-striped flannel sheets, a hot water bottle at their feet and a down comforter over them. Most nights they talked of nothing in particular, the easy unremembered chat of couples in bed, but tonight she dissected the quarrel with her mother and how despite the best of intentions she could not find the words to appease her.

"You're upset because you're not getting along," he said.

"No, not that exactly. It's just that I can't avoid these squabbles. I want to be pleasant to her, really I do. It's like the way I am with your mother. Maybe I'll feel differently once the baby has come."

"Let us hope so."

"Come on, Ib, don't you get after me too."

"Sorry." He stroked her hair and said his mother once told him a story about a poet, who deserved to go to hell, but whom God welcomed to paradise for the sole reason that he had honored his parents.

"Surprise, surprise," Sarah said dryly.

"Not at all. Here lies the surprise: the poet was unhappy in heaven; so God called in David the psalmist to chant for him, but the poet was still gloomy. God became curious and asked the poet why he was disgruntled. 'To sleep in the bosom of Abraham is nothing like the kindly breast of a mother,' the poet replied. 'That is something you have never known.' Therefore, God decided to experience this joy, and that is how it happened that the Virgin Mary conceived. A good story for a pregnant woman, don't you think?" He stroked her belly with his fingertips.

"Oh, I enjoy stories like that, but I don't like admitting it. They're exotic, but here…well, they seem awfully sentimental." She was surprised to find herself homesick for Arabia. She missed Layla. She missed the women's kisses and compliments, the incense and sticky sweets, the rose water and thirty-three varieties of olives. She missed the call to prayer and how it resonated with yearning and devotion. When Ib gave the call, he stretched out the one word "Allah" so long it seemed as if time itself were a plaything of the creator. "Allah…Allaaaah." How much gentler that sounded than "God," that harsh monosyllable. She remembered how when Shaheed sounded the call, he would clear his throat and deliberately make his voice ugly. She lifted her nightgown to look at the back of her legs; there was nothing—not the faintest pink ridge. She told Ib how Shaheed had switched her, downplaying it as much as she could. Ib's eyes blazed in anger, and he made her promise never to be alone in Shaheed's presence. It seemed like giving in, but it was also in her interest. Now, she would have only to contend with Malika.

Outside, it started to snow, and she remembered how it had snowed when they met at Thanksgiving last year. "So, tell me, what did you see in me?" she asked.

"Fishing for compliments?" He laughed. "You zipped about, so energetic and lively. I hope our child will be that way." He laid his cheek on her belly.

"It's too soon to feel motion. In a couple of months."

A look of concern flitted across his face. "Are you all right?

She heard the gravity in his voice. "Oh, everything is fine, exactly the way it should be, except…"

"Sarah, tell me."

"It's just that sometimes I get scared and have a funny feeling that something bad is going to happen. For no reason at all. It's probably nothing." She forced a smile. Looking relieved, he turned off the light and took her in his arms, and she forgot her worries.

The morning before their return flight, she was flipping a second batch of pancakes for breakfast. Ib had already eaten a stack of six, nicely buttered, and drizzled with pure maple syrup, when her mother entered the kitchen. "Look what I've brought you." She held up a tiny hand-smocked gown. "It's for the christening. Baby boys wear gowns for that too," Mom said, a nervous catch in her voice.

Ib put down his fork and knife. He was breathing in and out through his nose the way he did when he was concentrating. He stood up. "Mrs. Moss, that is most kind, and I know it is well-intentioned, but I cannot accept this gift. Our child will be a Muslim."

"But—"

"I have spoken." He smiled and left the room. Mom followed him down the hall corridor and halfway up the stairs, but he must have shut the bedroom door because Mom came downstairs crying. She put the fragile lacy gown back in its tissue.

"He's stubborn. That's the way he is. I'm sorry," Sarah said.

"I knew you shouldn't have married him."

"Mom, it'll be okay. I need to stick by him."

"Listen, as far as your soul goes, that's your business, but baptize your baby. Please, for God's sake."

Sarah pressed her lips tight and shook her head. "I'm so sorry, but I can't." She kissed her mother on the forehead and quietly walked out of the kitchen. That afternoon, her parents shunned them, delegating Pete to drive them to the airport, and Sarah felt relieved to be returning to Arabia.

CHAPTER 19

ON THEIR RETURN, IB ASKED SARAH if she would like to have an architect design them a home, one built specifically to her taste on the family
compound in Qatif. That led her to think of the homes of her past. First
came the high-ceilinged Victorian residence where four generations of
Mosses had lived, with its china door knobs, oak wainscoting and par-
quet flooring, and outside the cry of the loons on Deep Lake; then her
studio flat in Chicago's leafy Hyde Park, close to the medical school, but
dangerous for walking at night; following that, the comfortable, clut-
tered apartment in Madison close to the hospital where she had had
her first real job; and more recently, the flat in the Western Compound,
now surrounded by concertina wire, where she had lived provisionally,
her suitcases stashed under the bed. In each of those living quarters, she
had been one in a long line of inhabitants. However, no one had lived
here, which meant it was theirs to create. These white walls had no stories to tell but theirs, which might affect the stories of others to follow
them. She felt a responsibility to live here in love, without squabbling.
As gently as she could, she told him that she would prefer to live here in
Firdaus.

Perhaps because she felt homesick, she decorated the bungalow with a view to recreating her past. She had brought back with her from Deep Lake the blue willow china that Granny had carted from England to the States a half-century earlier. In the kitchen nook, she pasted a wallpaper mural she had bought when they were in Madison over Christmas, a forest scene with a muddy path and gurgling brook. Ib entertained visitors in the salon so she let him keep it Saudi-style, dark and cool, with the drapes firmly closed at the picture windows. The family room she claimed as her domain. She took down the Venetian blinds and let the sun shine in. She had the walls painted orange and placed a yellow carpet on the floor. She ordered contemporary furniture with clean light lines, and arranged and rearranged it until it felt right. For the nursery, she bought a rocking chair, a white wicker bassinette, and she hung clown curtains at the windows. In the yard, she hung a hammock between the two palm trees and set a pair of Adirondack chairs on the grass. The heat killed the flowers she loved best, delphinium, tulips, daffodils and lily of the valley, but she delighted in the mass of purple bougainvillea that tumbled down the west wall. It might be company housing, with the exteriors of her neighbors' homes identical, but she assured Ib that she was perfectly happy living in Firdaus.

Three weeks later, he was ordered to Beirut for a fortnight's consultation with the Lebanese national water board concerning an ambitious project to use the waters that trickled down the mountains to the Litani River.

"Lebanon? That's brilliant! Lucky you." She took off the rubber band circling her ponytail.

"I was hoping you would come."

"If only I could, but I can't just walk out. They'd have to get a locum, and it takes time to find one." She shook out her hair and dragged the hairbrush through it.

"It would be like a second honeymoon. Remember the Cedars? The snow on top of Mount Sanin? Remember hiking in the pine forests?" He sat close beside her and put his arm around her shoulders.

"Don't tempt me." She pulled slightly away and brushed so hard her scalp tingled. "I can't. We just got back from the States."

"Workaholic!"

"So, look who's talking!" She jabbed him in the ribs, intending it playfully, but it must have hurt for he rubbed his side.

"Your boss would understand if you asked for time off."

"John Hunter? I don't think so. It's bad enough I got my job through your father. I can't just run off whenever I feel like it."

He got up from the bed and stood looking down at her. "People think it is strange you are still working, my mother especially. I told her you had my entire approval, but even to me it seems odd. If you will not come with me, I want you to stay with her."

"What on earth for?"

He kept his voice level, patient. "It is what people expect."

She glared at him and felt how it was unfair.

"Mother does not know you, the real you. Perhaps it will be easier to get to know each other without me around."

"But I don't want to. I want to stay here. Do you think it's dangerous because of 9/11?"

"Darling, no one is going to grab a pregnant woman. But it's important to my family. All it means for you is a slightly longer commute for two weeks. Surely, you can make that small sacrifice. Please, it means a lot to me." He took the hairbrush from her, sat down, and brushed her mane. It was long now, past her shoulders, and she had grown it out for him. In college, she had worn it in a single braid, which fell to her waist, but after the hideous abortion, she cropped it ultra-short and kept it that way until after she met Ib.

"Darling?" he said.

"O.K. I don't want to stay with your mother, but I will, just so long as you don't go on about what people expect. She thought she had offended him, but he smiled and rumpled her hair.

The next day Johnny dropped her in Qatif, and she knocked on the faded turquoise door. As she waited, she glanced at the vacant lot where Ib had hoped they might have their architect-designed house. She felt lucky to have escaped that. When no one answered, she knocked harder. She was rubbing her knuckles when Layla opened the door.

Layla kissed Sarah five times on each cheek—it sounded like birds cheeping. She had just finished shampooing her mother's hair and was preparing to henna it. It was because of the henna muck that she had on this old grey t-shirt, she explained. "I hate to look like this, but you know how henna gets everywhere."

She showed Sarah her room. On the ground floor, it was large and square, its walls a dull buttermilk and its single window barred and shuttered. It was hot. It was always like that, Sarah thought grumpily, too warm in Saudi homes, too cool in Western offices and homes.

Layla pushed open the shutters, and wiped the dust off her hands. She switched on the overhead fan, and the accumulated dust drifted down from the moving blades.

"I must talk to the maid," Layla said. "She is too lazy. And smokes all the time. Oh, dear, how am I going to get through this weekend without a cigarette?"

Sarah plunked her suitcase on the bed. "Well, you could smoke here. If Malika got a whiff, she'd think it was me."

"You are too kind, but I couldn't. People think a woman who smokes does other things too. My mother would…well…" Layla searched for the right words, "Well, she'd think poorly of you."

"She already does."

Layla was flustered. "No, no. That's just her way."

Sarah shrugged. "So how much do you smoke?"

"Smoke? Two packs a day."

"That's a lot." A look of concern crossed Sarah's face. "Have you tried the patch?"

"That's what Tisam said. So I tried it. Six times! Ahmed says I should try hypnosis the next time we go to the States." A door slammed at the other end of the house. "That's Mother. I better go. She's getting impatient."

Sarah unzipped her blue suitcase, took out her maternity jeans and oversized t-shirts, folded them, and put them in the dresser. She had a canvas and oil paints with her as she hoped to work on her painting of the tell. When she finished unpacking, she went to the bathroom to wash her hands. She found several long strands of Malika's iron-gray hair coiled in the sink. Sarah grimaced, plucked the hair with her thumb and index finger, and tried to drop it in the wastebasket but it stuck to her fingers, and she had to use both hands to get it off.

She went into the kitchen to find Layla. Malika was sitting at the kitchen table, a cape around her shoulders and a white terrycloth turban covering her hair. She was barefoot and her ankles were swollen. The fresh hay odor of henna overpowered her smell of onions and sweat.

"So it's you," Malika said. "So it's you."

"Yes."

Layla pulled off her gold bangles and set them on the table beside the tub of henna. She put on a pair of plastic gloves and started to apply the henna. "Hold still. Tilt your head back. Don't move now." She slathered the gray-colored glop into her mother's hair, working in the henna with her fingers. "Your roots, they'll be such a nice color now, almost like Sarah's."

Malika grunted. Some of the henna mixture trickled down her neck, and Layla wiped it off with a towel. She complained about Ahmed. He paid so little attention to the children. If only he were more like Shaheed who cosseted little Saladin. Layla fussed for a while longer and Sarah wished she could go off by herself to the tell, but Malika would have a fit. It seemed hypocritical since she went there alone, but apparently, older women were given greater liberty. When the henna treatment was finished, Layla stood behind her mother, who was seated at the table in front of a heap of bobby pins, a brush, some pink plastic hair clips, a flat iron, and a hand mirror. "Hold still." Layla scissored off some split ends. "Isn't it pretty?" Layla patted her mother's hair, now a luscious mahogany color. Malika smiled in bliss. She must be at least fifty-five, but she loved to primp and doll herself up.

"Want to come to the tell when you're done?" Sarah asked Layla.

"I promised Mother I'd flat iron her hair. If you like, I could do yours too."

"No thanks."

Layla squeezed an inch of moisturizer from the tube onto her finger, spread it on her hands, and scrunched it through her mother's hair. Sarah was about to leave when Susu came down with the baby because Shaheed had male company upstairs and wanted her out of sight. Little Saladin was wailing, arching his back, trying to lurch out of Susu's arms, while she paced around the kitchen and murmured, "*Allaaahu Akbar …Allaaahu Akbar*. God is great. God is great." The male voices from upstairs grew strident.

"What are they talking about, do you think?" Sarah asked.

"Eve-teasers, probably," Layla said. "Thinking up new restrictions. Soon, we won't be allowed outside at all. They are too horrid."

"The reason is simple, my girl. Young men no longer fear Allah. They forget they will be held accountable on the Day of Judgment."

There it was again, judgment day. According to Ib, there would be a big bang, like the one that initiated creation, and the sun would go dark, the stars fall, and the earth roll up like a scroll in God's hand. Every person who had ever lived would be judged, a record of deeds in his or her hands. They would stand, gathered together, the rich and the poor, the weak and the strong, the ugly and beautiful, and no one would have status or power because the resurrection was the great equalizing force of the universe, the compensation offered to the poor and the oppressed, who would find joy in the garden of God. On that day, Muslims would stand behind Muhammad, Christians behind Jesus, and Jews behind Moses. Then Moses, Jesus and Muhammad would approach God in turn and state the case for each of his followers. When she said it sounded grim, Ib touched the pulse in her throat and said that God was closer to her than her jugular vein. It was normal to worry, but there was no need to panic. He told her a story his mother had told him, which was about a prostitute who gave water to a mangy dog dying of thirst, and because of this small kindness, God forgave her all her sins. And Jesus? What would he be like as an advocate? Mom thought the last judgment would be like Michelangelo's painting of it—the banners unfurling in heaven and the sinners tumbling headlong into hell.

"Sarah?" Layla elbowed her as she twirled the hank of hair in her hand. "Pass me a hair clip, will you? They're right there—in front of you on the table." She fastened the hair to the scalp with the clip and then did the same with the other three sections. When she had finished sectioning off Malika's frizzy hair, she plugged in the flat iron to warm up. "Mother, you're wrong about the Eve-teasers. They know the Qur'an by heart and all the sayings of the Prophet. That's not the problem."

"Like my husband says, flog the stalkers and Eve-teasers."

"Mother, hold still." She started in front, took out a hair clip, brushed Malika's hair smooth, then clamped it in the flat iron and pulled it through.

"It's too hot," Malika yelled.

"Mother, it's supposed to be hot. If you don't see smoke, it's not hot enough. Just wait. Soon your hair will be light and loose, shiny too, like natural straight hair." She turned to her sister-in-law. "Susu, really! Are we to flog all our young men? Do you know what I think? It's not bad upbringing. It's hormones, that's what."

"Well, of course," Malika said. "Men are like that. May Allah preserve them."

"Hold still. Don't move. I'm almost done." Layla pulled the iron through the last section, the steam rising from the flat iron, and curled the hair under at the ends. She unplugged the iron, tugged off the gloves, and gently massaged her mother's thick wrinkled neck before she pinned up a tight round coil at the back of her head and handed Malika the mirror. "There, you're done. Ah, my beautiful mother. Tell me you like it."

Malika fingered the bun and smiled. "Very nice."

It was too late to go to the tell. Grumpily Sarah followed the women into the salon. Malika plunked her considerable heft on the sofa and proceeded to take out her embroidery bag. She held up a needle to the light, squinted as she tried two or three times to thread it. She gave up and handed it to Layla.

"Father is right. You do need that operation." Layla threaded the needle.

"Nonsense. I'll see just fine in paradise."

"Oh Mother, don't. Don't talk like that. Why not have the operation? It's simple and easy. You tell her, Sarah."

"Layla is right," she said, knowing how unlikely it was that her opinion, even on medical matters, would hold any sway with Malika.

"Now about those wicked young men," Malika said. "Let me tell you what the problem is." The needle glinted in the sunlight as she pushed it in and out of the black linen. "It's the nannies. How can you have a good Muslim family when the children aren't brought up by their mothers?"

Layla squirmed. "It's so difficult to find a good Muslim nanny."

"My girl, I tell you, a good mother raises her children."

"But Eliza is excellent. And I like teaching," Layla said passionately. "I like my students. I like doing lesson plans. I'm good at it."

"Shh. Not so loud!" Malika put a finger to her lips and pointed to the bassinette. "It takes time to be a mother. You are always busy. One upright mother is worth a thousand teachers. You don't need to work, not when Ahmed provides for you so well. Why do you insist on teaching the children of others when you could be teaching your own?"

"But I do teach them. All the time. Besides, their teachers are excellent. Oh, look at that plant on the windowsill, will you?" she said, evading a fight she would never win. "It's wilting. Oh that maid of yours, Mother, she's no good. Doesn't she know that ferns need lots of fresh water"? She hurried out to the kitchen.

Sarah went to the window and looked out at the blackened tree in the front yard. She heard a car drive by, probably some man on his way home from work. By assailing Layla, Malika was attacking her too. Her colleagues assumed that now that she was showing she would quit. Dr. Nabeel and her interns joked about it. Even Mom expected it. However, she enjoyed the feeling of competence work gave her and the sense that she was making a difference in the lives of women here. She glanced pityingly over at Susu. The girl was such a doormat, letting Shaheed and Malika walk all over her. Whenever the baby cried, it was Susu's fault: she did not nurse him often enough; she did not swaddle him right; she let him get a chill. Just then, he started howling.

"He's hungry. Better feed him," Malika said.

If Malika talked to her in that same bossy tone when she was nursing their baby-to-be, it would probably dry up all her milk, Sarah thought but Susu immediately unbuttoned her blouse and calmly picked up the baby.

"Back home, most women work," Sarah said as Layla returned, watering can in hand.

"Don't talk to me about America," Malika snapped. "That land of sex wolves."

"Sex wolves," Layla giggled. "Oh Mother."

"A woman's paycheck helps," Sarah said as she sat down again. "It'd help here too."

"You don't know anything about us. Not one thing."

Layla set down the watering can. "Mother, don't. Sarah lives as one of us. She doesn't isolate herself from us."

"Then she should know that a good woman belongs in the home."

"But mother, think of all the widows and divorcées. If they find jobs, it's better for them."

"Let them go to their families instead of stealing jobs from men. Without jobs, how can men pay for a dowry and start a family?"

Sarah rolled her eyes as she remembered that it was not Shaheed but Ib who had paid for Susu's dowry—thousands of dollars in gold jewelry and cash.

"When they look for a wife, some men want a teacher, who can help pay the bills. I read it in the newspaper," Layla said.

"Ha! The newspaper!" Malika snorted. She bobbed her head up and down; she leaned forward so Sarah noticed again her dowager's hump, and she was reminded of one of the proverbs she had learned: "The camel cannot see its hump." Malika could not see what was so wrong about Saudi society. Nor could Susu, or Saudis who had not known a different lifestyle. Susu had a beneficent smile on her face as she nursed Saladin, and as Sarah listened to the baby's peculiar sucking sound, she remembered what Ib once told her: that they were all in Allah, and if people could open wide their million pores, sweet Allah would flood in, and they would be filled with compassion and act with kindness to all. Could it be that the universe worked this way? Might beneficence leak its way into humans with no more effort on their part than that of nursing a baby? Susu put Saladin to her shoulder and patted his back until he burped, and then he yawned, his mouth a small round O. Susu drew aside the lacy covering over the bassinette and tucked him in. Malika bent over him, cooed, and affectionately pinched his cheek. He started howling again, wee fists flailing.

"He's crying," Malika snapped.

"My darling, my darling," Susu crooned as she jiggled him up and down in her arms. "He's teething, poor baby."

"He can't be. He's too young for that." Malika narrowed her brown eyes and reached inside his Pampers. "He's dirty. Just as I told you, you should have changed him before putting him down."

"Yes, Um Ibrahim." Susu went to get a diaper while Malika put on a CD. "The 'Nightingale of Cairo,' we call her," Malika said as the throaty voice of Um Kulthum filled the salon. "Four million came to her funeral. Yes, you heard. Four million."

Layla yawned and covered her mouth with her hand. "You see, Mother, Um Kulthum proves my point: one can be a Muslim, a respectable woman, and yet work for a living. But she's so melodramatic, she puts me to sleep."

"It's Sarah who needs sleep. A pregnant woman must sleep. Everybody knows that."

"You're right," Sarah said, glad of an excuse to escape. At the door, she turned and looked directly at Malika. "Actually I won't be going to sleep for a while. Ibrahim will be calling. He'll want to tell me," she paused for effect, "yes, to say how much he loves me." It was a low shot—she did not know what had gotten into her to say it— but it was about time Malika realized where she stood in the scheme of things.

The fallout was not long in coming. At six a.m., the phone on her bedside table rang. Ib was calling from Beirut. It was about his mother, he said in a strained voice. She had telephoned him at three in the morning and was livid. "Why did you tell her the hospital was backward? Do you not realize how hurtful this is to my father? I didn't sleep all night worrying about it."

Sarah felt shocked and confused. "But I never said any such thing. Why would I? It's better than most places its size in the States."

"You said alley cats sneaked into the delivery room and sneaked off with the placentas."

"What! That's crazy." She would have laughed if the matter were not so serious. She sat up straighter. "She's making it up."

"But where would she get such an idea?"

"Who knows? She just doesn't like me. I'm horrible to her. I can't help myself."

"She says I love you more than I love her."

"I'm your wife. Isn't that the way it's supposed to be?"

"You know what I mean."

All she knew was that she felt lonely without him. Still, she had been nasty, and she promised that as soon as it was light, she would apologize. She must have gone back to sleep because she was awakened by a door slamming. She got out of bed, pushed open the shutters, saw the streaky pink clouds that began the days here and thought about their unborn child, her precious "clinging," as Ib called it. Already it could fit into the palm of her hand, flex arms and legs, and twitch soft fingernails. Already it had sex organs distinctly male or female. Today she would see her obstetrician and find out which. She better go straight to Malika and apologize before she lost her nerve. She would do it to keep peace in the family.

When she got to the kitchen, no one was there. She shook some dry cat food into the plastic bowl for Shadow, who rubbed silkily against her ankles. When the maid came in with a breakfast tray of tea, bread, cheese, and jam, Sarah asked her where Malika was, and was told that she had gone out to the market. Sarah breathed a sigh of relief.

John Hunter rapped the table to signal the beginning of the monthly meeting of expatriate staff. Once he had their attention, he addressed the political situation, giving them the news not found in the daily papers. According to the British embassy, demonstrators had taken to the streets in Riyadh, and a car bomb had detonated outside Safeway. Yesterday, some fanatic had spat at Dr. Tony Snare, a colleague who flew out that same night, saying he had not signed up to suffer abuse.

"Watch your words," Dr. Hunter said. "Do not, I repeat, do not discuss politics. Men, check your cars before getting in. Everyone, be on the lookout for suspicious packages. No trips into the desert to party. No dallying in restaurants or public places. And no bootleg whisky." He looked around and lowered his voice. "It is entirely possible that this spate of anti-Western activity is sanctioned by those in the Ministry of the Interior who wish the kingdom to cut its ties with the West. Let's not make it any easier for them. We must remain optimistic, but prepared for the worst."

After the meeting, at lunch, Sarah told Annie Malika's fib about cats snatching placentas. "It's such a weird story. Where could she have gotten such an idea?"

Annie shrugged. "Maybe it happened long ago in a clinic out in the boonies. Dreadful places. Know what I think?" Her eyes glinted with amusement. "Those cats got it right. Placentas are chock-full of enzymes and vitamins. Just the cure for post-partum depression. Eat up, girls."

"That's revolting," Sarah said, chuckling.

"She's out to get you. Better make nice to Big Mama. You don't want that crazy brother-in-law of yours to go to Big Daddy and charge you with disturbing family harmony." A somber look crossed Annie's face. "It's no laughing matter. I had a friend in your predicament. Well, her father-in-law directed her hubby to divorce her. The guy refused so Big

Daddy divorced his wife—the guy's mom. Get it? God, I can't stand how conflict-avoidant they are."

Sarah bit her lip. For a fleeting instant, pity for Malika pierced her. As a divorced woman, she would lose everything—her reputation, her children, and her standing in the community of women.

"Here, everybody's got to get along and divorce is no big deal, not for the guy, that is," Annie said.

"Ib says God despises divorce. And his father would never divorce Malika. You know him, he wouldn't. They've been together for years."

"So? Who'll get the boot then? If you don't want it to be you, better suck up. Kiss ass. And don't give me that hurt look. I'm telling you for your own good."

"I'll think about it." Sarah picked up her tray and pretended not to be upset as she walked off. The afternoon passed uneventfully, and at four p.m., she went for her appointment. As she lay on the examining table in her obstetrician's office, the aide smeared cool gel over her abdomen. Whether a baby was blind, deaf, or retarded, it still had a soul, Ib had told her, and a disabled child might be closer to Allah, and as such, might prove a special blessing. Now as Doctor Jones studied the sonogram, she determined that whatever happened, she would keep the child.

"Your baby looks just fine," Doctor Jones said.

"Thank God," Sarah breathed in relief.

"We'll need to grow the amnio cells, of course, but things look fine. Interested in the sex, are you?"

"Yes." The word popped out.

"Lookie here." He turned the monitor around so she could see and pointed to the teardrop form with a line down the middle.

"A girl, a baby girl," she breathed. "Oh how precious!"

The aide printed out the fuzzy outline, and Sarah held it close. If only Ib were here to see it. She felt a pang she missed him so much. For the baby's sake, she determined to make amends, and as soon as she got back to Qatif, she hurried to find her mother-in-law. According to the maid, she had locked herself in her bedroom.

Sarah tapped softly at the door. No answer. She put her ear to the crack: Malika was softly singing a plaintive melody in a soprano voice. Sarah imagined her rocking back and forth on her haunches, dreaming of the past when daughters-in-law were amenable as she slipped the yellow, cream, bronze, and rosy pearls through her fat fingers. Sarah remembered Layla saying there was a connection between suffering and pearls, but whatever it was, Sarah could not recall.

CHAPTER 20

THE SCHOOL PARKING LOT WAS BLACK ASPHALT, and the heat crept into the car as Sarah and Johnny waited. She frowned up at the iron bars over the windows on School Number 13; it was a pity that Layla had not got around to applying for work elsewhere. Why did a country with such cutting-edge civic architecture allow its children to attend such shabby-looking schools?

Layla had told her they were lucky to have schools at all. It sounded like a fairy tale. Although every girl learned the teachings of Islam at home, there were no schools for them until a few decades ago when a princess left Turkey to come marry her cousin, King Faisal. Once she had daughters of her own, she was troubled by the lack of schools and set up one inside the royal palace. She invited the other royals to send their daughters, but they made up excuses, with the result that the Turkish princess had to recruit orphans girls; only orphans had no relatives to object to girls being educated.

"And now girls' education is all the fashion," Layla summed up the story.

Sarah glanced at her watch. 2:15 p.m. They needed to hurry if they were to go to the tell before dark. She had almost finished her painting of it. Ib would return any day now, and it was to be his welcome home gift. She had done the pool, the dragonflies with iridescent wings flitting over it, and the luxuriant verdant undergrowth. The painting had felt inert until yesterday when she painted in a nude standing at the bank. She wanted to visit the pool again to get the details of the foliage. "I'm going to see what the hold-up is," she told Johnny. She got out of the air-conditioned car and flung on her abaya. As she walked, she held it above her ankles so she would not trip. Yesterday she had treated a woman who had fallen from a bus after getting her cloak tangled in the exit. Now, as Sarah hurried across the parking lot, her feet sank ever so slightly into the hot asphalt. She reached the cracked cement path that led to the school and went up the steps. The glass double doors had no handles, just a keyhole. She peered in through the dark glass and saw another set of doors with a chain and padlock looped around the two handles. She looked for a doorbell, but there was none. Scandalized, she hurried back toward the cool of the car. What was Layla doing shut up in such a place?

There were more cars and buses now in the parking lot, and as she edged her way through she noticed the pack of a dozen or so youths slouched on the east wall of the school: Eve-teasers, youth wild with desire to ogle the girls.

Johnny opened the car door for her. Absent-mindedly he touched the gold cross glinting under the neckline of his blue t-shirt, and then got in the driver's seat and went back to reading the newspaper. He had it spread open over the steering wheel at the article Annie had showed her at coffee break. The story was about the Eve-teasers arrested after the night of stones, and the accompanying photograph showed a line of men, a *mutawwa* behind each, flogging away.

"That'll teach them. Fifteen lashes each. They'll never do that again," Johnny said.

"It's awful," she said and left it at that. She did not intend to get into an argument with Johnny. "I wish Layla would hurry up," she said.

"Any minute now," Johnny said. "See him?" He gestured to a slight man with a white goatee who shuffled up to the entrance, pulled a set of jangling keys from his thobe pocket, and unlocked the double doors.

All at once, there was a flurry of veils. Girls, cocooned in black folds, strolled, laughing, along the uneven pavement and piled into the big yellow school buses lined up along the curb. A few boys raced up to the bus. Moments later, a girl opened one of the windows and let fly what looked like a paper airplane. One of the boys dashed over, plucked it from the ground, and sprinted off. Three *mutawwa'in* followed, chasing him.

"They get that boy, they'll whack him good," Johnny said.

After the students left, the teachers straggled out one by one. One of the last was Layla, a stack of papers and books under her arm. Sarah told her about the boy who had got off scot-free.

"He'll pass around her cell phone number." The faint lines in Layla's forehead creased, and she reached in her voluminous designer bag, took out a pack of cigarettes, and lit one. "Silly girl. She'll get in trouble. Like me." It had been a terrible day. She had had recess patrol, and was supposed to snoop and report any girl who was wearing anything too tight, short, or brightly colored. She had not turned anyone in, and the principal called her on it. That afternoon, she had had to send a student to the office for cheating. In the period after that, her students were acting out a skit to practice sports vocabulary when abruptly the principal marched in and reprimanded her in front of the class for not sticking to the government syllabus. "The principal wants drills: 'What is he doing? He is raising his hand. What is she doing? She is raising her hand. What are they doing? They are raising their hands.' Oh, drill, drill, drill. I hate it. What good is it? I want to teach the fun modern way. The inspectors cannot speak English, so who are they to tell me how to teach it?"

"Ahmed's right. You should find a better place to work," Sarah said.

"Maybe next year." She lowered the window and flicked the ash off her cigarette. "Have you heard? Tisam says they may allow professional women to drive to and from work. Step by step, that's what Tisam says, and before we know it, things will be delightful. Paradise itself." Johnny kept looking straight ahead as if he had not heard he might find himself out of a job. "Don't worry, Johnny. You will always be my one and only chauffeur," Layla said, leaning forward and putting her hands on the back of his seat.

"Thank you, Mrs. Layla."

"About your school," Sarah said. "Why not find a better place?"

"And leave my girls? Oh no. They need me. Did I tell you how they like *Pride and Prejudice*? Where would they be without me? In a private school, I might have to teach boys or mixed classes. Imagine! Mixed classes in high school! I will never consent to that. Never."

"It works fine in the States."

"Well, it won't work here."

Sarah looked out the window. They were at the stoplight outside the MIXED NUTS store. She kept quiet although she wanted to retort, "Layla, how can you possibly know for sure?" It irritated her, this being an outsider, her ideas discounted simply because she was not one of them. Increasingly she felt she really was different. The other day, for instance, she and Ib were discussing the Night of Stones, and how to prevent similar craziness.

"You can't just stand by and ignore it," she said. "But it's the fault of the system, more than that of the individuals involved. You've got to change the system."

"I'm afraid the system, as you call it, is too entrenched to change." He favored punishment because people had to be held accountable for their actions. He told her how at fifteen, he had stolen a bone-handled penknife, one belonging to Shaheed, and his father told Ib to stretch forth his hand and struck his open palm ten times with a pencil. It had not hurt, but Ib could hardly bear the shame of it; he could still call up the sound of those sharp taps and had never stolen again.

She told him about theories of behavior modification, and how positive reinforcement could be used to alter undesirable behaviors, and how she disliked the use of negative reinforcements. "I don't think you make people better by harming them."

"It's not as simple as that. When we are afraid of someone, we run away."

"Sure. It's the old 'fight or flight' response."

"A mystic named Rabi'a compared fear to a candle whose flame helped a person distinguish good from evil. She thought that fear of God is different. She said those who fear God flee to him."

"Fear? Come on. That's a poor motive."

"Rabi'a would agree. Once she tried to quench hellfire by throwing buckets of water on the flames; then she ran up to heaven and lit its four corners with a flaming torch. And now tell me, why did she do that?" He raised his forefinger dramatically.

"Really, Ib, I don't know," Sarah said, a little irritated.

"So that people would love God for himself alone. Now that was wise." He nodded his head sagely.

The call to prayer sounded, and she asked Layla to roll up the window. That was the major problem with living here—this obsession with religion. "We need a break," Sarah said. "Let's go to the tell as soon as we get to Qatif. I brought a maternity bathing suit. The water will be so nice and cool."

"I'd rather go shopping," Layla said.

"Well, let's do both."

"Okay. Shopping first."

The roads were still jammed with people headed to the mosque for afternoon prayers. Being stuck in traffic did not bother Layla, who pulled a magazine out of her handbag and started to flip through it. Eventually the traffic let up, and they got to Qatif about four p.m. The cloak and veil Layla had ordered at the fashion show on September 11 had finally arrived, five months later, and she took forever to try them on. She stood in front of the hall mirror and picked at the soft fabric of the abaya. The darts at the bosom and the tucks at the waist showed

off her shapely, abundant figure. "I shouldn't have bought it," Layla
moaned. "The *mutawwa'in* will get me for sure."

"Hurry up. Let's go. You look cute."

"Can't you see? That's the problem. Oh, I'll take it off right this minute. I'll wear my old one, just to be safe. Or maybe I'll borrow one of
Susu's."

"Hers are triple thickness. Isn't that a bit much?"

"Ah, the Sheriff, he's a fool in love. He thinks any man who sees her
will grab her." Layla dropped her new abaya and flung on her old one.
"Oh, how I hate it, this plain rough style."

"Then don't wear it. It's ugly."

"That's the point," she said gloomily.

Sarah picked up the new cloak. "Wouldn't Ahmed prefer this one?"

"Sure, but he's not here and Shaheed is."

"But what do you want? That's what matters."

Layla laughed as she pulled on a pair of black gloves. "It's simple. For
everyone to get along, and for me to be fashionable. *Mish mumkin.* It's
not possible." She rapped Sarah on the knuckles. "Don't let the Sheriff
catch you showing off your pretty hands."

"We better hurry or there won't be time for the tell."

"Really, what do you and my mother see in that place? Oh, I wish the
two of you would talk. I hate being the go-between. Now she tells me
to ask what you enjoy about being married to Ibrahim. Layla's voice
turned schoolteacher-sharp. "What's best about it?"

"Oh, really, I don't know," Sarah said impatiently.

"She's a good woman. It's not just because I'm her favorite that I say that. I'll tell you a secret. When Susu couldn't get pregnant, Shaheed's boss, that awful Kabeer, suggested he take a second wife who would give him babies. Every one of the aunties suggested good prospects. Shaheed refused. Susu would be too hurt, he said. No one but Mother stuck up for Susu. She wanted another grandchild badly, yet she was willing to sacrifice the desire of her heart. She saved their marriage. And Allah blessed them with baby Saladin. You see, Allah knows best."

"Maybe one day your mother will save me, too." Sarah clapped her hand over her mouth to stifle a laugh.

"Sarah, my darling. That's too funny."

At the flower souk they split up, Layla going off to window shop while Sarah went to buy saffron. They were to meet at Toyland at five-thirty p.m. Sarah glanced at her watch. That would not allow much time for the tell. She hurried past the lilies, delphinium and long-stemmed roses in tall metal cylinders in the direction of the spice souk. There she breathed in the odors of nutmeg, ginger, cardamom, and cumin that wafted up from sacks lined up outside the stalls.

"Dis best quality. From Spain," the Indian clerk said. He scooped out the orange pistils from an open sack, weighed out a hundred grams, and wrapped them in a twist of newspaper.

As she made her way back to Toyland, she admired a pyramid of apricots in the fruit and vegetable market. She glanced at the sticker —sixteen riyals a kilo. It seemed expensive, but apricots were Ib's favorite fruit.

"Tomorrow there will be apricots," the merchant joked. She smiled, remembering that the saying signified something or other. Too much in a hurry to take the time to bargain, she paid full price and hurried off to meet Layla. She found her at Toyland in front of a large display of Hello Kitty accessories.

Layla showed her the Hello Kitty doll in her hand and smiled as if enchanted. "See, no mouth. Hello Kitty doesn't need one. She speaks from the heart."

Sarah glanced down at her watch. "That's nice. Let's get going, shall we."

Layla would not be rushed and insisted on showing Sarah all the Hello Kitty accessories and paraphernalia. She had bought her a Hello Kitty diaper tote bag, insisting that Sarah needed it. Then she dawdled in front of the windows at Victoria's Secret to see the latest negligees and wanted Sarah to go in and buy one. Sarah tried to hurry her along but Layla stood her ground. "At least try one on. Your turtledove is coming. You need it."

"I've got lots. Let's get going now," Sarah snapped. She looked at her watch; it was 6:12 p.m.

"Just a moment. I'm dying for a cigarette." Layla said. She grabbed Sarah by the hand, scooted down a shady alley, and when she saw that it was empty, she lifted her veil and held it so it was three or four inches from her face. She put a cigarette to her lips, lit it, and inhaled under the black gauze.

"That's dangerous," Sarah said.

"Do you think so?" She laughed. Finally, Layla took one last drag, dropped the butt, and crushed it under her patent leather heel. She pulled a vial of rosewater from her bag and sprayed it around, the fine mist perfuming her veil. "Now, mother will never know."

Sarah grimaced. If they did not get to the tell, her painting would be the worse for it. Layla recognized some distant relative—the veil did not stop her— and stopped to talk. By the time they reached the fork in the path that led to the tell, it was six-thirty and the sun was setting.

"It's too late to go. I'm so sorry. Mother will be waiting."

"Oh, never mind," Sarah snapped. "Just never mind."

"What is the matter with you? So grumpy. You're never like that when Ibrahim is around."

As they entered the house, they could hear Malika shouting. When they went in the kitchen, she was standing by the sink with a bowl of tabbouleh in her hands. "Do you think I'm blind?" she yelled at the maid. "For shame. Stems are bitter. We do not eat them." Seeing her in such a foul mood, Sarah grabbed a Pepsi from the refrigerator and fled. She unlocked the door to her room and shut it. Shadow was curled up on the desk next to the Barbie that Lulu had forgotten and was purring with her eyes closed. Sarah scratched behind the tufted, lamb-soft ears, and Shadow yawned, teeth gleaming white against the pink tongue, tail flitting back and forth, a silvery plume. Sarah got the metal comb from the desk drawer, and as she combed the thick fur, her anger melted. She liked being here in Ib's boyhood room, surrounded by all his things. Rolled up in a corner was his red prayer carpet; he had his diplomas on the wall, and in the desk she found a box with his scouting badges and a picture of him in the Boy Scout uniform with its green and white scarf. Without a mustache, he looked young and vulnerable.

After she drained the Pepsi, she took her painting and easel from their hiding places in the closet. She studied the canvas. She liked the way the heavy black strokes delineated the nude's curves. Perhaps if the woman held a hibiscus? Yes, she would try that. She worked steadily, using a pointillist method to get the red petals and golden stamens just right. Absorbed in her art, she did not hear the door open. Malika loomed in front of her.

Sarah jumped back. "Oh! You didn't knock!" She moved to block the painting with her body.

"Layla worries that you're lonely."

"I wanted to be alone."

"So. Why is that? I see you've opened the shutters again." She went to the window and closed them. She picked up the empty Pepsi can that was lying on the desk and tossed it in the wastebasket. "He who eats alone, coughs alone," she muttered.

Sarah stood in front of the wet canvas, not budging.

"What you have there?" Malika lumbered toward the easel.

"Nothing. Uh...nothing at all," she said, her voice shaking.

When Malika's nose was less than an inch from the wet canvas, she gasped and cried out. "Are you blind? You are certainly a liar. We dress when we go to the baths. We are not whores."

"I didn't mean to offend." Sarah shifted nervously from one foot to the other. "It's a painting of me for my husband. A present."

Malika stabbed her forefinger at the canvas, a centimeter from the naked pink breasts. "For shame!" she cried. She turned and grabbed the Barbie from the desk and slapped her cheek. "Barbie's still smiling, isn't she? Maybe that's how you Christians act. Muslims don't. We fight evil." With the back of her hand, she swatted the other plastic cheek so hard it must have hurt her knuckles. She threw the doll on the floor and stomped out of the room.

Sarah picked up the Barbie and smoothed out the long synthetic hair. It was platinum blonde, not red, and Barbie's legs were impossibly long, without a single freckle. Nevertheless, for her mother-in-law, Sarah knew she was this Barbie: hard, sexy and wicked, a Jezebel who had toyed with her precious son and drawn him into her web.

CHAPTER 21

DRESSED IN FOLDS OF GOLD VELVET, her black eyes rimmed with kohl, Malika stood in the front yard by the blackened tree and waited for Ibrahim. Sarah was still not on speaking terms with her, but she was in her territory and would defer to her. Sarah stood at the window as Ibrahim clicked the gate behind him and had to restrain herself from flying to him and flinging her arms around his neck. She watched as he bent to kiss his mother's hands. When he came in, his mother was still clutching his hand.

"Hello, stranger." Sarah smiled up at him, expecting a kiss and a hug, but Malika dragged him over to the loveseat, tossed Shadow off, plumped herself down, and patted the space beside her. "Ibrahim, darling, sit here next to me."

He did so but winked and smiled at Sarah.

"I watched Beirut on the weather channel," Malika said. "Very rainy, their February. Here the sun shone every day and we pray for rain."

"Yes, Mother."

"Shaheed says the drought is a punishment for sin."

Sarah grimaced—her crazy brother-in-law and his loony ideas.

"Mother, he's wrong. Allah might punish green and fertile countries with drought, but surely not a desert place."

"Of course. So wise you are." Malika patted his knee. He smiled at her, and then got up and went to sit beside Sarah on the couch opposite.

"Remember Shaheed's boss? Ah, such a good man. He's helping Shaheed find work. They've increased patrols at the girls' schools," Malika continued. "Layla says it's dreadful how the girls flirt."

"Ah, yes." He scratched Sarah's palm lightly.

"Now any boy they catch, they flog. Whhht…whhht…whhht…" she cackled, waving her arm back and forth as if she were whipping some poor unfortunate, and then turned to Sarah. "Girl, bring some fruit for your husband."

In the kitchen, Sarah arranged the apricots she had bought in a pretty yellow bowl and brought it into the salon. She saw that Malika had moved over to the couch where she had been and was squeezed next to Ib, thigh to thigh.

"Ah, apricots." He took one, put it to his nose, and sniffed. "Heavenly."

"How much you pay?" Malika demanded.

Sarah could not remember exactly, but she figured sixteen riyals a kilo sounded about right.

"What! Sixteen! That's robbery! I can get tastier apricots for half that price."

"I'm sure you can." She sat down on the sofa vacated by her mother-in-law and reached for an apricot.

"For shame!" Malika snarled. "Use your right hand. Only the right hand for food."

Yet another gaffe, but Ib was smiling at her, so it could not be very important. Malika was rotating the apricot in her hand, as if examining it for defects. She found a brown spot no larger than a freckle.

"Spoiled rotten," Malika snapped as she put back the defective apricot. "It'll make the others go bad. Shaheed says humans are like that. One spot and they turn soft. Rot spreads. He worries about Layla. He says Tisam is a bad —"

"He's crazy. Just crazy."

"I was speaking to my son."

"Tisam is intelligent, courageous, helpful and pure. She's exactly what this place needs. As for the Sheriff, he's so—" Abruptly she stopped, re-alizing that this wasn't the time or place for such an outburst and that it made her look weak. "I'm sorry, Malika," she said meekly. "I don't know what got into me."

Malika ignored the apology. "Ibrahim, did you visit the coffee shops on Hamra Street? Are they not a marvel? I recall a little coffee shop in a side street off Hamra, Sidani Street, I believe it was, where a Turk once ground me coffee from Yemen. An unforgettable aroma. I hear they no longer serve *ghawa* at the cafes."

"Things change, Mother."

Malika tsk-tsked. "Old-fashioned *ghawa* is best."

"I'll go make some." Sarah got up and went to the kitchen. Shadow, who had been lying in a sunny spot on the carpet, stopped licking her silver fur, and got up and followed her. As the mocha beans whirred in the coffee grinder, Shadow rubbed against her ankles and Sarah recalled Malika's lie about the cats in the delivery room. She remembered the Barbie incident, that declaration of war as Malika slapped the doll on the cheek. Increasingly agitated, Sarah turned on one of the three faucets and filled the pot. She made the coffee, stirred in the cardamom, filled the demitasse cups, and set them on the tray. She hurried back into the family room, a calculated smile plastered on her face; the first cup she offered to Malika.

She took one sip and banged down the cup. A flush spread along her high cheekbones. "Taste it, Ibrahim. Is this how your wife makes coffee?"

He put the cup to his lips. "Oh darling," he burst out laughing, "you've used the brackish water."

"Terribly sorry. Terribly. I'll make a fresh pot."

"No, *I'll* make it." Malika said imperiously. She heaved herself up, set the cups on the tray, and waddled out of the room.

Ib got up and sat beside Sarah, who was nervously twisting her napkin into a thin rope. "She'll think I did it on purpose, but honestly, she makes me so nervous. I just forgot about the different taps for pure and brackish water."

"Never mind. It gives us a few minutes alone." He pressed his hand gently on her stomach. "Oh, what's that? The baby moved. What happiness!" For a while, they talked quietly about the baby—the sonograms, whom it might look like, if it could laugh in the womb, and if it would like being tickled—until they heard a raspy clearing of the throat. Malika entered, set the coffee pot on the table, and squeezed herself between Sarah and Ibrahim.

"You must be very tired to make a mistake like that," she said as she served Ib. "Tomorrow you get up early for work. Now run along while I talk with my son."

"Mother, I want to be with my wife." He gulped his coffee in two swallows, grabbed Sarah by the hand and they bolted. Once inside the bedroom, he locked the door, put a chair against it, closed the curtains, grabbed her, and kissed her deeply. He pushed her gently onto the bed, hitched up his thobe, and tugged off her panties. Without a word, he took her, and it was fast, strong and good.

"Where's Mr. Foreplay? Where's Mr. All-the-time-in-the-world?" she teased afterward.

"Sorry. I was in a hurry. Those two weeks, it was an eternity."

"For me too."

He unbuttoned her blouse, and took it off along with her bra. He caressed her breasts and marveled at how they had grown—"enormous, like melons." He sucked each nipple and edged his hand under the waistband of her skirt. She unzipped it and slipped it off. When he saw the bare skin where her patch of red fur used to be, he caught his breath. "I did it for you," she murmured.

"Now you are like our women. Such silken skin." With his fingers, he stroked her thighs and lower belly, and she moaned as he explored her, pleasuring her. Much later, she took the painting from its hiding place in the closet and propped it up against the wall. She had not been able to return to the tell, but it did not matter. All the hours she had spent on it—planning its composition, roughing in the shapes, applying the paint, even the time spent cleaning her brushes—had been a joy. This was her Arabia: the ancient tell with the sunlight piercing the palms, the red of the hibiscus blossoms, the shining foliage, and the pool of shimmering emerald water. She waited anxiously as he looked at it for a long time.

"It's beautiful, every inch of it." With his index finger, he grazed the figure of the nude by the pool, a blur of red around her head. "Especially her."

"Even though her belly pops."

"Especially because of that." He grinned. "Still, you better not let my mother see it."

"Sorry. The damage is done. She came in the other day when I was working on it, and we quarreled."

"Darling, don't be so angry with her."

"Me, angry? I'm not angry."

"Darling, just look at yourself. The moment her name is mentioned you frown and ball your hands into fists. You become totally unlike yourself."

Her throat tightened and she thrust her hands behind her back. "So what? I've good reason. She's doing every little thing she can to sabotage our marriage."

"But she is suffering too."

"That's crazy."

He went to the dresser, took the hairbrush from it, sat down beside her on the bed, and brushed her hair; he smoothed it and ran his fingers through it. "You have had a hard time, I am afraid."

"It's over now, thank God."

"I promised my mother that we would stay until the day after tomorrow." He pulled a bit of red fluff from the brush.

"I can't take any more."

"It is just one day. How can I refuse her a little thing like that?"

Sarah sighed, and for once, he did not say he wished she would not, but kept smiling until grudgingly she said it was okay, so long as it was just one day. They talked, drifting from one topic to another: his work in Lebanon; hers and Layla's troubles with their by-the-rules bosses; Malika's cataracts and his father's increasing frailty; and whether her parents might visit for the birth.

"About having hurt them at Christmas. I did not see any way out of it."

"I should have told her straight off I'd promised you could raise the child as a Muslim. I've been thinking..." She clasped her hands and noticed that her palms were sweaty; she looked up at him, wondering how he would respond to what she had to say. "It might make it easier for our child if I were Muslim too, like the rest of you."

"Are you sure? Don't let anyone pressure you."

"No one is." She had expected he would be thrilled, but he seemed anxious, even displeased. She told him that she could never believe what he did. Her mind simply could not grasp the majesty and compassion of God. Still, she liked the stories told by Muhammad although not as much as those of Jesus. She liked awakening to the muezzin's dawn call: "Come to prayer. Come to success. God is most great. Prayer is better than sleep." She liked watching Ib unroll his red and blue prayer carpet and kneel to say his prayers. She even liked the expression "to embrace Islam" because it sounded gentle and non-threatening, quite unlike the strident question, "Are you saved?"

She asked him to teach her the motions of prayer. "That way, I could join in with everyone else. Of course, I wouldn't say the words aloud. If

I did, I'd be fudging it."

He looked at her severely. "Sarah, no."

"I don't mean any disrespect. I just want things to be easy for our child. When I hear the call to prayer and listen to the stories, well, I feel I already am a Muslim. A little bit."

"Step by step, maybe that is the way." He took out his beads and clicked them one against the other. "It is a big decision. Do not do it unless you are convinced."

The next day he took her to the souk to look for a prayer carpet for her. Several hundred years old, the souk was dim and cool under the awnings, and dust motes danced in the slits of light where the sheets of canvas joined overhead. They wandered through the dry goods section with its bolts of Egyptian cotton, Irish linens, and gleaming Thai and Chinese silks. She followed him down an alley where veiled Bedouin women were squatted on mats, their bejeweled fingers dangling over the butter cookie tins they used as tills. She would have liked to encourage these women, and she liked the weavings of red, white, and black stripes. There were camel saddlebags, room dividers, as well as several cushion covers and narrow carpets. She spoke to a woman who said she was from the Bani Khalid tribe, and that she had spun and woven the fleece herself. Sarah asked Ib if one of the weavings might be used as a prayer carpet, but he said no, and they kept walking until they reached the section for Persian carpets. There a medley of voices greeted them.

"Sir, do I have a carpet for you."

"Come in, sir. See my beautiful carpets. No charge for looking."

"The best rugs and cheap. Best price."

"Tomorrow you will buy a carpet. Yes?"

"*Insha'Allah*, God willing," Ib said to each. When they were just a few feet from his favorite dealer, he warned her that she would be looking at lots of carpets, but that she would know when she saw the carpet meant for her. That a carpet should be "meant for her" seemed a curious notion, but one she liked.

Mr. Manoukian, an Armenian with dazzling white teeth, welcomed them to his shop. He pulled out a couple of three-legged stools for them to sit on, clapped his hands and a boy brought in the tea tray. Stacks of carpets lined the walls from floor to ceiling. Mr. Manoukian's assistant, a thin boy with a pimply face, pulled them down, one by one. He unfurled each for their approval, laying it on top of the others they had already been shown. As Ib and Sarah sipped hot black tea, Mr. Manoukian named their provenance: Herat, Bokhara, the Caucasus, and Afghanistan. For most of the carpets, Ib accorded a polite nod, nothing more. Once on seeing an Isfahan with swirling arabesques on a sky blue field, he dropped to his knees to examine it. He did the same when the boy set down a Kirman, a flowering green tree in its center, dripping pink blossoms.

"It's the tree of life. It reminds me of the tree outside my parents' house." He bent forward and traced the outline of the tree with his finger.

"But that tree in Qatif is black; it's heavy and gloomy. It's nothing like this one."

"But it is surviving against the odds. That is what counts," Ib said.

Mr. Manoukian traced his well-manicured hand over the silken fringe.

He had an extraordinarily long nail on his right pinkie. "The tree of life symbolized the eternity of the family," he said pedantically.

"Pretty, but not for me." She shook her head, and the carpet boy pulled down another carpet, a Sarouk, which he laid over the Kirman. Ib folded over a corner to assess the tightness of its weave. When he said the knot count was insufficient, Mr. Manoukian smiled and said that humans must not try to rival the creator. He clicked his fingers at the boy, who dragged a ladder from the corner, leaned it against another stack of carpets, climbed up, and brought down three more carpets, all red Bokharas. Sarah balked at its swastika design, even after Mr. Manoukian explained that the ancient symbol augured good health. Two hours and five cups of tea later, with a mound of carpets in front of them three feet high, she still had not seen the carpet supposedly meant for her.

"I have a special piece. Perhaps you would like to see it?" Mr. Manoukian smiled his stunning smile. He went into a back room, returned with a smallish carpet, bent to the floor, and unrolled it. The carpet's border enclosed pink rosettes around an indigo field with two slim ivory pillars. Suspended in an arc above them was a stylized chandelier. "A Ghiordes," he murmured reverentially. "A prayer carpet. Nineteenth century."

It was exactly as Ib had said. The instant she saw it, she knew it was meant for her. Its antiquity was not why she liked it. It was the design—the single stylized light that shone between the slender pillars. A discount was requested, the price settled. Mr. Manoukian wrapped the rug in brown paper, twisted a cord around either end, and handed it to his assistant to carry to the car. Ib said that it would be his pleasure, and they left the shop with the carpet tucked under his arm. Later that afternoon, they unrolled it in their bedroom, illuminated by the late afternoon sun streaming in the window. She told him how much she liked it, that she had never seen any fabric more beautiful.

"God is beautiful, so we wish to worship him with beauty," he said.

"Maybe. For if there is a God—a kindly one—I want him to know I'm grateful." She paused and gave a hard little laugh. "Although if he doesn't exist, there's no point."

"Sarah." He flushed and looked away.

"I'm sorry. I don't mean to be disrespectful. I want there to be more to life than money, prestige, and things. Something deep. Maybe I'll never get to believe it, but even if I can't, I want it for our child."

"You worry so much. We can be light to each other." He went to the bookcase where he kept the box containing an English version of the Qur'an that he had found for her online. The holy book rested on a green velvet cushion, and he took it out and set it on an x-shaped low wooden stand, which was inlaid with mother-of-pearl. He sat cross-legged on the ground and slowly read aloud the passage that had inspired her carpet. "God is the Light of the heavens and the earth. The parable of His Light is as if there were a Niche, and within it a lamp; the Lamp enclosed in Glass; the glass a brilliant star, lit from a blessed Tree, an Olive neither of the East nor of the West whose Oil is well-nigh luminous though fire scarce touched it. Light upon Light! God doth guide whom He will to His Light."

"Light upon light," she said in a hushed tone. "That's what I want. That's what I need."

CHAPTER 22

A WEEK LATER DURING A LULL IN HER SHIFT, Sarah was reading the *Annals of Emergency Medicine* when her cell phone rang. It was Layla, with what she called, "exciting news too good for the telephone." Sarah coaxed, but she just giggled, saying, "Oh, you are too curious. It is the best news."

She would find out soon enough, Sarah thought as Johnny drove her down Prince Sultan Street toward the school to pick up Layla and Lulu. He was in an excellent mood, for he had finally amassed the sum needed for a down payment on a restaurant in Manila. "You and Mr. Ibrahim must come to visit," he said. "Eliza and I will take you everywhere, especially to the beautiful Pasangjan Falls."

"We might just do that," she said. She was thinking how glad she was that he would be with his children again but that she would miss him and Eliza, when she felt the baby move. She patted her belly and said to it silently, "It's okay, little clinging."

It was time to choose a name. Just yesterday, her mother had called, suggesting Sarah name the baby Patricia, Pat for short, after her English Granny. Sarah said she would like to, but that Arabic had no "p" sound so their child would end up being called "bat." Mom laughed and promised to send a book of baby names. At lunch today, Annie mentioned an Egyptian custom of having a party to welcome the baby, and of lighting seven candles, naming each of them, and then naming the baby after the candle that burned the longest to augur a long life. Sarah liked the idea and decided she would ask Ib about it. Last night, when he had mentioned something about a family name, she imagined whom he had in mind, and she stopped him cold.

Three blocks from the school she heard the blast of a fire alarm. She clapped her hands to her ears as a ladder truck howled past, red light spinning, with its cargo of firefighters in green slickers and yellow helmets. Traffic snarled, resumed, and then stopped again as another fire truck roared past. Her colleagues in the ER would soon be busy treating traumas, burns, asphyxiation, carbon monoxide poisoning, and broken limbs—the works. Traffic came to a standstill on their side of Prince Sultan Street. She leaned forward. "How bad is it?" she asked.

Johnny opened his door and looked out. "We could be here a long time."

She pulled out her cell phone to warn Layla that they would be late picking her up. She let the phone ring twelve times, but there was no answer. Eventually traffic started up again but moved at a crawl. In the distance, she could see a plume of smoke rising. Two blocks from the school, a civil defense officer diverted their car. "There's a fire at Girls' School 13," he shouted and directed them down a side street.

Her heart banged in her chest. She grabbed her cell phone, called the ER charge nurse and ordered ambulances and a burn unit. She would do what she could at the scene, she said, and get back as soon as she could.

"Mrs. Layla. Lulu," Johnny made the sign of the cross. "I know a shortcut." She felt a jolt as he drove the car up onto the sidewalk; he skirted past three cars ahead of them, and turned into a lane behind some rundown apartment buildings. A maid was watering a red geranium in a balcony above; the whine of Arabic music drifted down. Heaps of trash lined the alley, and Sarah closed the window because the hot wind pushed in the stench of rotted garbage. At the end of the lane, Johnny turned back onto Prince Sultan Street, now deserted, and they reached the school parking lot. At first little seemed different: the usual row of yellow school buses lined up along the curb, the usual gang of Eve-teasers clustered around the lamp post, and the dozens of white Toyotas, Hondas, and Fords neatly arranged in the diagonal slots. Johnny nosed the car in between two Hondas, and she jumped out.

"Don't, Dr. Sarah. Don't go!" he shouted after her. "Think of your baby."

She ran, ungainly in her pregnancy as she threaded her way through the parked cars, pausing only when she banged against a car's side mirror, hurting her side. The louts caught sight of her; they hooted and wolf whistled. Overhead a flock of birds rose above the dense smoke. She reached the ranks of school buses parked at the curb, where a woman in a black veil pointed up toward the window at the far left corner of the school building. A single flame drifted upward. "Where's the fire chief? Sarah asked.

"Over there." The woman gestured toward a man in a shiny yellow slicker.

Sarah kept going, barely aware of her surroundings. Fire hoses lay on the pavement, a few in slack coils, others tangled, plump and taut with water. A firefighter with a wrench opened the hydrant. "*Yalla. Yalla*," the Eve-teasers yelled as the firemen aimed the streams of water on the exterior walls. The alarms whined, and the water gushed, arcing in jets, crisscrossing and then streaming down the masonry walls. There was more smoke now, huge billows of it. A bird fell in the blackness. The flames were inside the building, unreachable. She got a whiff of the sickening smell of char, but the real killer was smoke inhalation. She stopped to remove her head scarf and to reposition it to cover her mouth and nose. She craned her neck to see the small, high windows on the third and fourth floors. Iron bars ran up and down the windows.

Two firefighters raised a ladder. Another grabbed an axe, lowered a mask over his face, and attached a breathing apparatus. With steel-toed boots he climbed from rung to rung. At the third floor, he swung his axe. Glass shattered in a thousand glittering splinters and fell onto the sidewalk. Above, the trapped gas spurted out, shining iridescent blue-yellow. The firefighter scrambled back down the ladder. *Coward*, she whimpered. Why would he not go inside to carry out the trapped girls? It made no sense.

She ran on, stopping once again to catch her breath when she reached the fire chief. "I'm a doctor," she said, panting. "The girls? Where are the girls?"

"Still inside," he shouted back. "We'll axe open the doors."

The doors were locked. A wave of nausea gripped her, and she doubled over, about to vomit. Then she saw the firefighter lift his axe and smash the double glass front doors. Three children, clinging to the abaya of an old Bedouin woman, came through. Lulu in pink jeans and a Hello Kitty t-shirt was clutching her Barbie and screaming, "Mama, Mama."

Sarah ran up and took her in her arms. "It's okay. It's okay, my darling. We'll find your mama."

Teenage girls rushed through the doors. They were screaming, faces bare, long hair in wild disarray above their long-sleeved white blouses. A raucous cheer came up from the Eve-teasers, and the girls jerked their arms over their faces. The boys jeered. How dare they! What were they planning? To charge like a crazed pack of rabid dogs and each seize a girl to carry off and rape?

The fire chief shouted at the firefighters holding the high-pressure hoses to turn on the water and to aim for the high windows. Then he turned to the others, shiny in wet slickers. "We're going in. Do not touch your sisters as you lead them to safety."

"*Quf*! Stop!" A voice roared. "Do not enter. *Mamnua*. It is forbidden. It is sin to see their faces. The girls at the gates, send them back for their abayas."

Sarah wheeled around to confront the stern, handsome face of Kabeer, a few steps from her. Two dozen men stood in phalanx behind him, all in shin-length robes. Where had they come from? They spread into two lines and formed a gauntlet, their sticks raised. The shadows of the sticks wavered, making slim diagonals on the pavement. But who was that? She felt sick to her stomach. Surely, it wasn't. She jerked her head downward at Lulu in her arms. A moment later, she turned her gaze back. She was not positive, but it sure looked like Shaheed.

She pressed Lulu's head to her so the child would not see her uncle and with a quick zigzag step rushed away. Behind her, Kabeer bellowed, "Girls with veils and cloaks may leave. Those girls, and those only, must proceed directly to the buses."

She glanced back. Acrid smoke continued to pour from the small high windows. She saw a girl at one of the unbarred windows and heard her cry "Allah" before she leaped. Instants later, she lay crumpled on the pavement. Screaming, everywhere screaming, the girls ran out. Swishing their bamboo canes, the religious police forced them into two lines: those in veils and cloaks they allowed to proceed toward the buses. The others they beat back— incredibly—into the burning school. Horror-struck, Sarah stood transfixed, hugging Lulu close to her breast.

"We're all going to die. Allah help us," a girl screamed.

A woman standing behind Sarah wept.

"Let our little girls go," a man in a red-and-white kaffiyeh cried out as he shoved past Kabeer. "Those girls have done no harm. Let them go." Kabeer raised his stick and rained down blows on the man, who fell to the ground.

Lulu arched her back and tried to wriggle out of Sarah's grasp. "Mama, Mama," she screamed. "I want my Mama!"

"Hush, my darling. She'll be back any minute now."

A plump veiled woman came through the school door and stood there, scanning the crowd. A moment later she cried out, "Lulu, oh my darling, thank God you're safe. Sarah, take her away."

"Mama, Mama," Lulu wailed, her pudgy little arms flailing.

Instead of going to Lulu, Layla dashed down the school steps and headed straight for Kabeer. "Have the girls wait outside, all of them," she cried out in a loud voice. She whirled around, her cloak billowing in the hot wind, and raced back up the steps. At the front door, she took off her cloak and veil and wrapped them around a lumpy girl in a brown and white school uniform. "Hurry, hurry, Nadia, go to the bus. Now! Nadia. Go!" She pushed her toward the steps. Layla turned next to the girls cowering just outside the school doors.

"What's that she's saying?" Sarah yelled, not believing what she had just heard.

"Telling the girls to use their hair for cover," someone said.

"Girls. All of you! Right now! Outside!" Layla commanded. " *Yalla.* Go, girls, go!" Following her in single file, each girl stepped out, features invisible behind the curtain of dark hair that veiled her face. Layla led them to a knobby palm tree about fifty feet from the entrance. "Do not move from this spot," she ordered. Bare-faced, she turned to face Kabeer, who raised his stick. "Don't you dare. I'm going in," she yelled. "To the cloakroom. I'll be right back with the veils and cloaks." She pointed at the Eve-teasers, still clustered under the lamp post, and shouted at the men in the phalanx of *mutawwa'in.* "And you my brothers, don't you dare let any man touch my darling girls. Hair is their cover, as Allah is my witness."

"Don't go, Layla," Sarah screamed, Lulu heavy in her arms.

"Take my darling to safety," Layla cried back. She raced toward the school, took a few awkward steps over a pile of plaster on the steps, and disappeared into the building.

"Listen to me," Sarah screamed. "Smoke rises. Stay close to the floor."

Still awkwardly holding Lulu, she staggered to the fire chief. "Go after her," she screamed. "Quick. Get her a smoke mask. Stop her. Save her."
"No. In the name of Allah," Kabeer shouted. "You must not. The woman is uncovered." He glared at Sarah, burly arms crossed against his chest. Lights flashing and sirens blaring, a half-dozen ambulances careened into the parking lot, followed by the mobile burn unit.

Lulu coughed. Her frizzy hair was singed and the smell of scorch filled Sarah's nostrils. "Mama. I want my Mama!"

"Your Mama is coming soon. I'm going to take you to an auntie." Sarah pushed on, a stitch in her side, toward the mobile burn unit. Lulu kept up a persistent cough until they reached the cool of the burn unit. Once they were inside, Sarah placed a white tissue under Lulu's chin and had her spit. The spittle was black. "Lay still now, Lulu darling," she said in a soothing voice as she placed a mask over the child's face to deliver high-flow oxygen. "We're going for a little ride. Okay?"

Lulu nodded, the whites of her eyes red. The paramedic lifted her onto the wheeled stretcher; Sarah walked alongside holding Lulu's hand, as he pushed it. On their way toward the ambulance, they passed Kabeer and the fire chief.

"For the love of Allah, I beg of you," the fire chief pleaded. "There are still girls inside. Let my men enter for search and rescue."

"Not possible." Kabeer sneered. He crossed his beefy arms on his chest. "We must protect the honor of our girls."

"Yes, but not now. Not when it's a question of life and death. Each second counts. This is no time for religious quibbling."

"Quibbling? How dare you? Life and death, so you say. But what is death compared to religion and honor?"

Sarah gripped the metal bar of the wheeled stretcher to keep herself from jabbing her thumb in Kabeer's crazed eyes. Once inside the ambulance, she sat on the bench and held Lulu's small hand. Layla would be back out any moment, she kept telling herself. Then they were off, speeding through red lights and hurtling over speed bumps.

At the hospital, she performed intubations, administered IV solutions, prescribed Demerol, and set broken bones. Two hours later, a girl was wheeled in, her arms covered in blood. It was Nadia, to whom Layla had given her cloak. She said that she had been in Mrs. Layla's English class on the second floor when she heard the alarm. Everyone knew it was not a drill because they never had drills. She was one of the last ones out of the classroom, and there was smoke everywhere and a crackling sound. Like the others, she had run down the flight of stairs. All the girls were screaming because they knew the front double glass doors were locked. The first girl there had banged away at them with her fists and thrown her whole body at them, but still they would not open. The children from the nursery were there too, sobbing and screaming. Then someone must have smashed the door from outside, and they got out onto the porch, where the *mutawwa'in* allowed those in abayas to leave. She spread wide her bloodied hands. "And Mrs. Layla? How is Mrs. Layla?"

"I don't know," Sarah murmured. "We have to wait to find out."

"Of course. Of course. I wish they'd hurry up. Mrs. Layla is such an excellent teacher."

"I'm sure they'll bring her in soon." As she stitched up the cuts on

Nadia's arms, Sarah imagined the long black silks hanging in the cloakroom limp and phantom-like on the metal hooks, then lifted by the
wind, fluttering up and bursting into orange flame. A dreadful thought
choked her. "Nadia, where is the cloakroom?" she asked.

"On the second floor. Between the chemistry lab and the home economics room."

"Oh, no!" Sarah moaned. The chemicals would explode with the heat,
and their gases poison the air.

More casualties arrived. A few were dead on arrival. Most were
admitted, only a few discharged. The last to be brought in was Layla.
She was unconscious and the dozen cloaks in her arms formed a black
diagonal against her long ivory dress. Her face was a bright cherry-red.
With a trembling hand, Sarah wiped a smudge of ash from her forehead
and checked her nose and mouth for burns and her throat for internal
swelling: none, no heat damage either. It was a simple case of asphyxiation. Sarah took her pulse and blood pressure and ordered blood tests.
She performed a bronchoscopy. The airway was open and stable, so she
placed a high-flow humidified oxygen mask over her face. "Watch over
her," she told the nurse. "Let me know the instant there's any change."

An hour later, she was writing out a prescription when Orla, the Irish
nurse, tapped her on the shoulder and beckoned her into the hall. "Mr.
Al Suleiman's daughter is dead," Orla said faintly. "In Unit B. Someone
needs to pronounce her."

Sarah felt as if she might faint. She grabbed on to the cold metal
frame of a gurney to keep her legs from buckling under her. "Layla
dead? Are you sure?" she asked, her voice shaking.

"Yes. I heard she's your sister-in-law. I'm so sorry."

"That's crazy. She can't be. Can't be." She shook her head and gripped the gurney harder. "No. It can't be."

Annie rushed to her with a glass of water and a couple of pills. "They just told me. Here, take these."

"It can't be. It can't."

"Just take them."

She pushed away Annie's hand, rushed to Unit B and went to the bed. She peered into the dilated eyes and ran her fingers along the neck to feel a pulse. Nothing. Already the body was cool, the skin dry. She unbuttoned the star-shaped buttons on the ivory dress and put her stethoscope under the soft, plump, left breast to listen for a heartbeat and breath sounds. Nothing.

A wave of rage came over her. She would make Shaheed pay. He was revolting, brutal and dark of heart.

Annie came in the cubicle. "Here," she said pressing the pills in Sarah's hand. "You take these. I'll do the death certificate."

Sarah pushed her aside. She went to the nursing station, got the form, and sat down at the desk. She took out her pen, looked at her watch, and wrote the time 4:08 p.m. in the appropriate blank halfway down the page. She signed her name.

Some time later, Ib arrived. Leaden-eyed, she led him to where Layla lay under the harsh glare of the fluorescent lights. With hesitant steps, he walked toward the still figure on the hospital bed. He drew back the white sheet, touched the dark ringlets, and let his hand slide down her soft plump cheek. "Yes, that's her. Our Layla," he uttered in a queer little voice choked with pain. He stooped over the bed, the ends of his red-and-white headdress falling onto the white sheet, and touched his lips to the cold forehead.

"To Allah we belong, and to Him we shall return," he said, his voice suddenly firm. He raised the sheet over the still face.

CHAPTER 23

WITHIN THE HOUR, LAYLA WAS BROUGHT HOME. Malika collapsed, bent over double on the floor; when she eventually sat up, she banged her head against the wall. The dull thuds echoed in the dark hall. "My child. Give me my child." Ib placed Layla in her arms, and she rocked back and forth, Layla's head on her breast, Layla's right foot sticking out of the ivory dress. After her sobs subsided, she kept rocking as she crooned, "My darling, my child, my best beloved."

Tisam tiptoed in from the kitchen, rested a hand on her shoulder, and said gently, "Auntie Malika, it's time."

"No. No. No." She wailed and clutched Layla's body with a wrestler's grip until all at once, her arms went limp.

"Auntie, dearest Auntie." Tisam helped her up. "I will bathe her."

Malika burst into fresh sobs. "No, I will give her the last bath. Oh, my baby."

"Let us go then," Tisam helped her to her feet.

Ibrahim and Ahmed carried Layla into the kitchen and laid her on the white-sheeted table. After the men left, Sarah stooped to kiss Layla's cheek and flinched at the shock of the cold skin on her lips. Malika and Tisam undressed her and removed the bra and panties embroidered with tiny pink hearts; they placed a sheet over her body, still cherry red except for her hennaed palms and soles. Tisam filled a basin, dipped a soft cloth in the warm water, and passed it to Malika, who wound the cloth around her hand and wiped Layla's brow. As Sarah listened to the slosh of water, she remembered the snapshot of Layla as a newborn in the pink plastic tub, her young mother trickling water over the tiny wet head. Now Malika loosened the tangled ringlets; there was the smell of scorch as she washed, combed, and braided them. Tears slipping down her tawny face, three times she washed her daughter's body, lifting the heavy limbs. Sarah tightened her nose against the sharp smell of camphor. After the final washing, Malika placed a small pillow beneath Layla's head. "It is finished," she said, her face contorted with grief. She went over by the sink, squatted on the tile floor, and with closed fist beat her breast.

"Dearest Auntie, don't. Don't weep, my darling. It is forbidden, for God is merciful and will bless her. Now rest while I get the garments for shrouding."

Alone in the room with Malika, Sarah faltered toward her mother-in-law and gently touched her shoulder. Malika jabbed her in the ribs with an elbow. Sarah jerked back her hand and fought the urge to flee, forcing herself to stay out of respect for Layla. Meanwhile, arms lifted in supplication, Malika buttered up God with praise and beseeched him to overlook Layla's shortcomings and to admit her to paradise. Her prayers finished, Malika sat cross-legged facing the wall until Tisam returned with more white sheets and the necessary garments. Together they dressed Layla for burial, perfuming her forehead, nose, hands, knees and feet with attar of rose. Then Malika placed a handkerchief over the shrouded face. She tucked one end of the sheet under Layla's dear head while Tisam secured the other end under her feet. Sarah's throat ached as the scent of rose brought back the memory of Layla perfuming her on her wedding night.

It was time. In accordance with custom, Layla must be buried before the sun set. Shaheed was nowhere to be found, so Malika and Susu sent the neighbors to look for him. Sarah wondered what his mother and wife would do if they knew he was complicit in Layla's death. Let someone else squeal on him, Sarah thought. They would not believe her.

In the living room the family assembled in front of the bier: first the triumvirate of husband, brother, and father; close behind the three children; and the women at the rear. They raised their hands, said, "God is great," and recited the *fatiha*.

"To Allah we belong and to him we return. There is none worthy of worship except Allah," Ahmed said tonelessly.

"May Allah forgive her and have mercy on her. May he send his holy angels to greet her," her father Omar mumbled.

"May Allah forgive her and grant her a high place in paradise," Ib murmured in a low voice, made queer by pain.

Malika said in a hoarse voice, "Let us ask forgiveness for our daughter and pray for her steadfastness, as now she is faced with her accountability."

As the others said their farewells, Sarah stood unmoving. Her throat felt terribly sore and she felt livid.

"*Allah ateek il awfi,* May God give you strength," Tisam whispered, touching Sarah gently on the shoulder. "*Allah ateek il awfi,*" she repeated.

Sarah shook her head. *Allah awfi. Allah awfi.* "Allah awful, Allah awful, Allah awful." The blasphemy pounded her brain.

Shaheed was still nowhere to be found, but the end of the day was less than an hour away and the burial needed to be accomplished. The men placed the bier on the wooden frame, which they hoisted on their shoulders, and left the house. At every corner, more relatives, neighbors and friends joined the procession of the mourners. The women followed, led by Malika. At the edge of the town, they halted for women were forbidden at graveyards. At the path leading there, Malika, standing with arms wide open, led the women in a terrifying ululation.

Feeling faint, Sarah put her hand against the wall of a house and slumped against it. "Sarah?" Tisam linked her arm around her waist. "The baby? Are you all right?"

"I can't...can't breathe."

Tisam tightened her grip. "You grieve like a man, so silently. Do the *zaghareet.*"

"I can't."

"Do it to expel the power of your grief. Do it and you'll feel your own power. Don't wall in your grief and anger. Let it explode."

"It's not me. I just can't. But she didn't suffer long. Not long at all. Just a minute or two. That's what I was trying to tell Malika, but she wouldn't listen."

Tisam made comforting noises, but Sarah could not stand the keening. "I need to get out of here," she said.

Tisam accompanied her, but when they got to the Suleimans, a crowd of dark-cloaked women was already in the salon, and every few minutes one of them would set down her cup of bitter coffee and break into ululation.

"I can't stand it," Sarah whispered.

"Let's go outside," Tisam said. In the courtyard, a bulbul sang in the frangipani tree, and lizards darted in the sunshine. Sarah saw Lulu pull her thumb out of her mouth and ask the twins, "Where's Mama?"

"Our mama is dead," Fawzi said.

"Dead," Farouk repeated.

"I want her. I want my Mama," Lulu whined. "When's she coming home?"

"She's not coming home. Not ever." Tears glittered on Farouk's eyelashes; he turned to Sarah. "Did it hurt?"

"No. It didn't hurt. She just stopped breathing, like a balloon when the air is gone out. See!" Sarah cupped her hands around her mouth, puffed loudly as she widened the circle of her hands, and then breathed softly, gradually letting her hands come together again. "It was asphyxiation, carbon monoxide poisoning. Blood moves in our bodies, but the carbon monoxide kept it from carrying along enough oxygen. Do you understand?" She continued doggedly, knowing that it was gibberish to the children but unable to stop. "Smoke inhalation, that's what it's called."

"Come my darlings." Tisam sat down on the grass, put Lulu in her lap, and drew the twins to either side of her. "Your mother was a martyr. Be proud of her. God will bless her."

Fawzi said, "*Allah Akbar*, God is great."

"*Allah Akbar*," Farouk repeated.

It was already twilight, and Eliza called the children in to eat. Tisam and Sarah went back to the family room, now packed with relatives, neighbors, friends, colleagues, and former students, all perched on the hard-backed chairs that Eliza had lined up against the wall. "*Allah ateek il awfi.* May God give you strength," they repeated as they sipped bitter coffee.

Malika sat hunched over, her eyes red, her body limp, as if crumpled in on itself. "If only I had touched her lips with the water of Zamzam. If only it were me on the bier, me in the grave. Her baby, too? Poor lamb. My Layla was pregnant. Did you know?" She wiped a tear from her cheek with her burly fist.

So that was Layla's "exciting news." Sarah got up, walked unsteadily into the kitchen, and pressed her cheek to the cool enamel of the refrigerator door. Ib had once told her that Azra'il, the angel of death, pulled the soul of the blessed from the body as easily as one pulls a strand of silk from a cocoon. Lifted by the angels, the soul rose to the gates of heaven where Allah would order its name written in the record of those who may enter paradise after judgment day.

She felt an arm around her shoulders. "Are you all right?" Tisam asked. Sarah shook her head. *Allah awfi.* Allah awful. *Allah awfi.* Allah awful. Allah awful, her brain pounded with the mocking refrain.

Tisam rubbed her back. "You need to take care of yourself. Do it for your baby."

Sarah dropped her face in her hands.

"Do not despair." Tisam said that nothing in this world was permanent, for even the seven heavens, the magnificent glorious creation of Allah, the stars and planets, the earth with all its living creatures would come to nihayah, its end. She told of how when the Prophet Muhammad's death was announced, one of his companions had refused to believe it. Then the great disciple, Abu Bakr, persuaded him by saying, "O ye people, if anyone worships Muhammad, Muhammad is dead, but if anyone worships God, God is alive and dies not."

This was Tisam's way of consoling her, but she did not want to listen, especially when Tisam said that Layla's life had been just the length that God intended. "I'm going to lie down," Sarah said.

"That's right, my darling. That's the best thing to do."

On her bed, Sarah curled on her side, drew her knees up her chest, and buried her face in a pillow. Why Layla? Why not Malika, who wished she were dead anyway? Alternatively, if someone were fated to die young—she was thinking crazy like the Saudis—it made more sense for it to be Tisam, who was like Joan of Arc, the martyr type. Or why not herself, for she would never belong here? Why Layla?

A half-hour later, when he returned from the cemetery, Ib came straight to Sarah. She was in the bedroom in front of the mirror tweezing her eyebrows, welcoming each spark of pain. He looked gaunt, and his face was drawn. He had found out that Shaheed had been there at the schoolhouse.

"I cannot believe how much it hurts. Why did he not speak up? Why did he not stop her? Why? The imam says it is a test for us, but what are we to learn? At the graveyard…oh, it was awful. Before the bier was lowered into the grave, Ahmed threw himself on it and screamed, 'little cat, little cat, sweet little cat.' Shaheed was there. How he dared stand there, I do not know—but he and I were in the grave waiting to receive Layla's body. Ahmed lowered her to us, and the imam prayed that God would open a door in the grave through which Layla would smell paradise. And then. Oh, it was awful."

She set down the tweezers, put her arms around him, and held him tight.

"Oh, the horror of it. Ahmed jumped down into the grave. He punched Shaheed in the mouth, several times and Shaheed just stood there, blood dribbling down his beard, as Ahmed cursed him, screaming that he was responsible for her death. I should have stopped Ahmed. We defiled her grave…defiled it."

Sarah swallowed hard, her throat so sore. "Go on."

"We climbed out, and as the gravedigger started to shovel in sand, Shaheed started to defend himself. You know how he talks." Ib mimicked his brother's high raspy voice. "Death before dishonor. Whatever leads to forbidden things must be forbidden. According to him, the Eve-teasers would have dragged the girls off behind the bushes and done unspeakable things."

She felt a fresh wave of outrage as she remembered the chaos of the girls fleeing the schoolhouse and the leering boys. "So to save the girls, they had to destroy them?"

He took in her sarcastic tone, but did not respond to it, saying only that his father shook his fist at Shaheed and cursed him.

"Does your mother know he was there?"

Ib shook his head. "We must not tell her. It would break her heart." He pinned Sarah down with a look. "The *mutawwa'in* are not known for intelligence. Because there were hardly any flames, he claims they did not realize the danger."

"Well, they should have. In the ER, we crack jokes about people 'too stupid to live.' Ones who take crazy risks. But this is criminal. If only you'd been there. You'd have grabbed a mask and gone in after Layla like a flash. You'd have stood up to Kabeer."

Ib took her hand. "I need to ask another favor. On the way home from the graveyard, my father told me of his decision to go into the desert for a period of mourning. He believes it may help him resign himself to this affliction. I am afraid for him—he is so frail."

Fearful of what he might ask, Sarah pulled away her hand.

"I do not want to leave you. Especially not now with the baby." He bent and put his head on her taut belly. "But my father cannot manage alone."

She sighed. "Maybe if you say, you can't go, he'll give up on it."

"You know what he is like. His mind is made up. He will go, one way or the other."

"I need you too."

"Sarah, it might help me."

"How long?"

"Not long. A few days."

He looked so bereft that she could not refuse. "Go with him then, Ib. I'll manage."

"Will you watch over my mother?"

"Now you're really asking too much. She needs you not me."

"It is the only time my father has ever asked me to do something for him."

"Well, go if you have to, but don't ask me to comfort her. I haven't the faintest idea how. Let her get over it the way she does everything else. Let her play with those pearls of hers and sing those sad sailor songs and mope until she feels halfway human."

"Be gentle with her."

"What do you mean?"

"Don't tell her about Shaheed."

"What makes you think I might?"

He gave her a look.

Okay, I promise," she said grumpily. If Malika was too stupid to figure out for herself that Shaheed was a coward and a creep, she wouldn't let on.

Ib and his father left the next morning at dawn.

The day crawled. All afternoon Sarah lay in bed staring up at a crack in the ceiling as Malika's friends keened for Layla. Thirty-one. Young and beautiful, with a husband, the twins, Lulu and a baby on the way, never dreaming her life might be snuffed out. Sarah punched her pillow and pushed her face into it. If she were like the others, she would comfort herself with prayers. But she could not pray, not even that if God were truly in the heavens, he would take care of Layla. She should thank God for blessing her with such a dear friend, but she felt too angry. Why did Layla go back into the school? She was not stupid. Why didn't she stop and think?

In the late afternoon, Sarah took the children to the playground. Ahmed had taken the morning flight back to Riyadh. He would bury his grief in his work. It was typical of him, but it too made her angry. She could not understand such total absence of paternal care. Around six p.m. when it turned dark, she called the children away from the roundabouts and swings. Johnny drove them home, and she fed the children supper and sat with them in front of the television screen. At eight o'clock, she tucked them into bed; she retired about ten. Shadow slunk into the room, leaped onto the bed, and licked her fingers with a rough tongue. As Sarah stroked the sleek fur, she recalled first meeting Shaheed on the family camping trip, and how he'd stood in front of her with a slaughtered lamb slung over his shoulders, blood splattered on his robe. An executioner. Now she felt the hot craving to take revenge— to kill him.

Do no harm. Do no harm. Do no harm—her doctor mantra cautioned. She slipped out of bed, stepped over the jeans she had dropped on the floor and still in her pajamas made her way barefoot down the hall to the kitchen. She made herself a cup of cocoa, drank it, and then sneaked into Layla's room. She switched on the light, opened the closet door, and moved her hand along the silks and satins. She lifted one of the cloaks to her face and sniffed the smell of nicotine. On Layla's bed-side table were a stack of *Vogue* magazines and some tubes of lipstick. She opened one—it was bright red, Layla's favorite. She was about to touch it to her lips when she heard sobbing. It must be poor Susu, stuck with crazy Shaheed. The girl would be lucky if he never returned.

Sarah put down the lipstick on the bureau and left Layla's room. In the hall, the tiles felt sandy against her feet. When she passed the stairs leading up to Shaheed and Susu's room, she cocked her ear but heard nothing. Outside Malika's bedroom, however, she realized who was grieving, and not plaintive sailor songs either but full-throated grief. She stood at the closed door, her palms clammy, and her heart beating fast. She did not have to say a word. All she had to do was to go in and call her Um Ibrahim. How hard was that?

She reached out her hand to knock on the door.

No, better not. She'd botch it.

She let her hand drop and sneaked back to her room.

CHAPTER 24

THREE DAYS LATER, SARAH WAS AWAKENED by the oddest noise. She went to the window and saw particles of sand blasting the glass, pocking it. They were as numerous as snowflakes in a blizzard and as invisible as germs. She listened to the faint *ting ting ting ting* the grains of sand made as they hit the glass. She ran a finger along the windowsill where there lay an inch of sand. A coating of sand lay like a brown sheet on the floor. There was always a fine dusting of sand on all the surfaces of even the best-kept homes here, but nothing like this, and she realized it must be the *shammal,* the hot dry northwesterly wind that every March brought the heat from the great Sahara desert to the cities along the Arabian coast. Johnny had told her about it. Last year, it had stripped the paint off Ahmed's Mercedes, and he had to order a new paint job. Johnny had been amazed by the speed of the onslaught: it had happened in less time than it took his wife Eliza to remove her makeup. Now Sarah wiped her finger on her skirt. She thought of Layla decomposing in a shallow grave, at the mercy of these great winds that could toss up tons of sands and expose her.

Sarah went to the bathroom and stepped on the scales to check her weight. She had already gained twelve pounds in the first twenty weeks, and she was at first relieved not to have put on any more this week although it was probably due to the stress of the fire. She washed her face, vigorously brushed her teeth, and gargled noisily, all of which helped her forget about death. When she went into the kitchen for breakfast, Malika was already dressed at the table, a copy of the morning's *Saudi News Gazette* in her hands. She passed it to Sarah. "Anything about the fire?" She poured her a cup of tea, and Sarah thanked her. With just the two of them in the house, they were formal and cautious with each other, speaking softy and politely.

The lead story on the front page was the *shammal*. She turned the pages, skimming them, but saw nothing of interest until page twelve where in the bottom left-hand corner was a brief from the Saudi Press Agency datelined Khobar and headlined, "Fifteen die in school fire." The article quoted the local head of girls' education as saying that the fire in the four-story masonry structure was "a tragic accident." The facts were covered in two brief paragraphs: the school enrolled 787 girls, aged twelve to seventeen, and seven of them, trapped in upstairs classrooms, had died from asphyxiation. The other eight were trampled in the stampede down the stairway or fell to their death. The school had no sprinkler system, and it was yet to be determined if the smoke detectors had sounded. The cause of the fire was thought to be a lighted cigarette dropped in a trash heap in a corner of the stairwell. Ninety-seven firefighters from Khobar, Dhahran, and Dammam fought the blaze that was extinguished by six p.m. The last sentence read: "A teacher died in an attempt to retrieve cloaks and veils for the girls who in the interest of modesty were for a brief period kept from exiting the building improperly covered."

A teacher? Why the anonymity? Why was Layla Suleiman being treated like some unknown? And what had taken the paper so long to get around to reporting the fire? Sarah glanced up at the masthead with its motto, "Saudi News Good News." There lay the reason. She had not expected investigative journalism, or pictures of the *mutawwa'in* beating the schoolgirls back into the burning schoolhouse—even if there had been a photographer there, the papers never ran pictures of women— but she felt incensed that the paper had not named Layla. It was inhuman not to name her, to act as if Layla had not ever existed.

Malika looked different, sunken and hollowed-out, as if the stuffing had been knocked out of her. She cleared her throat. "Any news?"

Quickly Sarah shook her head. She was afraid that if she mentioned anything at all about the fire, she would blurt out something that would incriminate Shaheed. She could not risk breaking her promise to Ib. She felt enraged about how the paper had paid no attention whatever to Layla's sacrifice. Emotions were tumbling around in her, and she dared not talk anything of consequence.

"No news," she said. "Nothing, just the sandstorm coming, and the usual troubles in Palestine. Tell me about this weather." She did not try to smile. She was too upset for that. However, she could talk about the sandstorm. It was a fine subject.

Malika pushed the teapot aside. "I miss our Layla."

Sarah looked up in surprise. *Our* Layla? Had she heard right?

"And I feel so alone without my men."

"They'll be home soon." She folded the newspaper and set it on the table. She had not before heard this soft voice from Malika.

"And where's that Shaheed when I need him? Where is he, I ask you? I haven't seen him for three days."

That sounded more like her mother-in-law. Zipper your lips, Sarah told herself. Still, she could barely keep herself from screaming that Shaheed was there at the fire and she hoped she never saw his ugly face again. "Prudence...It's a difficult situation..." she could hear Ib's measured tones. She gulped down the rest of her tea, said she was late for work, and hurried out of the kitchen.

At the front door, she got her sandals from the stack on the porch; as she buckled them, she glanced at the sky. Invariably the early morning sky was pale blue with never a puffy cloud. The sun was always present and always the same, pink streaked in the early morning, and then pale the rest of the day until it recovered its pink and gold at sunset. Not today. At 8:04 a.m. by her watch, the entire sky from horizon to horizon was a murky reddish-brown. Violent winds were thrashing the blackened tree in the front yard. The winds had ripped one of its boughs from the gray trunk, leaving the white innards exposed. The ancient tree that had given the house its name, *Bayt Shajra*, House of the Tree, would likely have to be cut down, she was thinking, when abruptly, a man in a thobe stepped out from behind the tree. At first, she could not make out who it was because of the sand particles that clogged the air. She took a few steps toward him and recognized Shaheed. When he recognized her, he looked down at his feet.

"Ashamed to show your face, are you?" She heard the bitterness in her voice.

He took a step toward her and looked slightly to her left. "Sarah?"

She clenched her hands at her sides. "Look at me, for God's sake."

His eyes flickered toward her. "It's about my mother. Please don't tell her."

"Look at me! For once, just look at me."

"I couldn't bear for Mother…" his shrill voice broke.

"Just look at me, damn you!"

His eyes were red and swollen, and he had a cut above his left eyebrow. "I couldn't bear for her to know I was there." His eyes dropped.

"Look me in the eye," she screamed. She stepped closer and smelled his sweat and fear.

"Please don't tell her. I beg of you."

"I haven't. And she can't read, not that the paper would mention it. So your wicked little secret is safe for the time being."

"Praise Allah." Head down, he slunk away.

That Judas. She looked up at the blackened tree. Let him hang himself from it. She would not stop him.

From the carport, Johnny beeped the horn. Without a glance, she walked over, got in the car, and left for work.

A dozen of the most serious cases had been flown to the specialist hospital in Riyadh, but about twenty of the girls were being treated in Khobar. Those with smoke inhalation were all on ventilators. The ophthalmologist assured her that those blinded by the cyanide gas from the chemistry lab would likely recover their sight. The girls in the burn unit were the ones for whom she felt most sorry. They would suffer the most.

She picked up the chart at the foot of a bed. The girl's name was Amina Husseini. She looked like a mummy; most of her body was wrapped in bandages, covering the second and third-degree burns. On the chair beside her bed, a cloak, a pair of blue jeans, and a striped yellow t-shirt were folded neatly. Under the chair, an optimistic parent had placed a pair of sandals, but it would be a long time before Amina could wear them. If ever. Within three to five days, she might suffer renal failure, pneumonia, or infection. And should she escape those, there would be weeks or months of recuperation while the reconstructive surgery was done. She'd be on morphine, lots of it.

Sarah met Annie in the cafeteria for lunch. "You're experiencing one of life's rough spots. You'll get through it," Annie said. "A hundred years from now everyone we know will be dead, anyway." Then she shot her hand to her mouth. "Oh, God, what a crass thing to say. How crappy of me. I'm so sorry."

"Never mind. There's nothing anyone can say that'd be right." She ran her fingers along the warm rim of her coffee cup and thought of how Malika had said "our Layla" at breakfast. Her mother-in-law was suffering too. After Annie left, Sarah dialed Tisam's number and asked her to go comfort Malika. Tisam made excuses. She was busy arranging a meeting of the women at the tell, she said in a voice brimming with excitement. She had already telephoned half the women on her list, and she had thirty more calls to make.

"But this is important."

"I'll see Auntie at the meeting. She can wait till then."

"She needs help right now."

"Poor Auntie. She is easy to soothe. You do it. And don't forget our meeting tomorrow after evening prayers. The sandstorm will be over by then. It's the wind of change. You'll see. Tomorrow here comes spring."

For Sarah it had felt like spring for the past month because of the zinnias and fragrant oleanders, the hibiscus and bright green grass. "The wind of change," Tisam had said. It reminded Sarah of the fashion show on 9/11, and the models with pink and platinum hair, dressed in alluring and original abayas.

"Please come. We need you," Tisam said.

"Maybe. I've got to go now. It's been frantic all day."

Patients continued to come in coughing, wheezing, and complaining of difficulty in breathing. The poor visibility led to several car crashes with the consequent deaths and broken limbs. Added to these were the routine admissions. A distraught couple brought in their week-old baby girl who had been howling for the last five hours. The small fists twitched as Sarah put a stethoscope on the warm chest to listen to the heart and lungs. She felt the little belly and checked the infant's ears and throat. All normal. Colic, nothing worse. She wrote out a prescription and told the parents to call their pediatrician the next morning if their little girl was still crying. The screaming reminded her of the schoolgirls, which made the baby's pain urgent in a way it would not have been a week ago. Then she would have simply said not to worry unless the baby had been crying more than three hours a day, three days a week, for at least three weeks. Tenderly she touched the fontanel under the dark hair and thought of the child Layla had been carrying and of her own little girl. When her shift ended, it was still windy, and her intern Dr. Nabila lent her a double-thickness veil. Eight months ago, she would have refused it. Now she accepted it gratefully; it protected her from the stings of sand gusts as she made her way the parking lot to the car.

"Such a wind," Johnny said as he held open the back door. "It'll strip the paint off the car."

"Worse than a blizzard," she said.

Traffic crawled. She could barely make out the few men on the street. Their red-checked headdresses were drawn up over their noses and pulled down low over their foreheads. At the red light near the Mixed Nuts store, Johnny swerved to avoid a man in a beige thobe. Always there was sand, seeping under doorways, windows and cracks in the walls, but she had never experienced anything like this burning on-slaught. Overhead, the sky was still rust-colored and a smell of furnace lingered in the thick dusty air. The heat intensified.

Once they were on the highway, she asked if Ib and his father had managed to reach town before the shammal hit. Johnny hoped so. As soon as they got home, she went to Malika's room and knocked. No answer, just the faint melody through the door of Malika crooning her mournful sea ballads. She would be fiddling with her little collection of pearls, dusting the sand off them, and soothing herself. Sarah, who had had less than four hours of sleep in the past twenty-four, went to her room where she lay a few minutes listening to the sand battering the window. She must have fallen asleep, for she was awakened by shouts coming from the salon. She got up, walked down the hall to the salon, the sandy tiles gritty on her bare feet, and peeked in.

"You were there," Malika shouted, jabbing her finger in Shaheed's face. "Yes, you. I was at the women's baths today. Everyone, it seems, knew but me. They told me you watched and did nothing. Nothing. We raised you to protect your sister, but what do you do? You betray her. Murderer!"

"*Immi*. Mother, please—"

"By doing nothing, you killed her. Why didn't you stand up to Kabeer? Coward!"

"What could I do? I had my orders. It was her fate to die that day. Oh, do not mourn." His voice turned squeaky with zeal. "She was a martyr, who will enjoy bliss in the garden of God." He reached out his arms. "Mother—"

She beat her fists against his chest. "Our Layla is gone. Layla, Layla," she moaned while he stood there, head bowed, not saying a word. "You dog! You cur!" She slapped his cheek. "For shame. You are no longer my son."

"Allah, have mercy." He ran out of the room, darted past Sarah, not seeming to notice her, and raced up the stairs. Within the hour, he, Susu, and little Saladin had left.

CHAPTER 25

THE NEXT DAY THE SUN EMERGED, shining strong and reflecting the glitter of the sand off the sidewalks and streets. Before the street sweepers could brush it up from the curbs, it permeated the house, coating the tile floors, curving around corners, and settling on mirrors, desks, dressers, and countertops. In the family room Eliza was shaking the brownish-yellow grains from the heavy chocolate-colored curtains while the twins dashed around the drapes yelling, "dust, dust."

Malika scolded and told them to stop their nonsense, and Sarah took them out to the courtyard play. They begged her to whirl them around.

"Me first," yelled Farouk.

"No, me first. Me, me!" Fawzi cried.

"What a thing to ask of a woman in her sixth month," Malika grumbled. It was actually the seventh month, but Sarah was not going to quibble. After a while, she got the twins engrossed in making a fort for their stuffed animals and she was able to leave them and read an article in one of Layla's *Elle* magazines. When she heard Malika shouting, she put it down and went back inside. In the salon, Malika was running a finger along the glass-topped coffee table. "See this streak. That lazy girl! She can't even dust properly. Oh everywhere dust. Layla in her grave.

Ibrahim and my dear Omar not yet home. I may as well be dead."

Sarah offered to deal with Eliza. As she went to look for her, for the first time it occurred to her that maybe Malika did love her husband despite the fact they were so rarely together. She found Eliza in Layla's room vacuuming the pink floral Aubusson carpet. As Eliza pushed the vacuum cleaner, the dust and sand particles rose up, danced, and sparkled in the sunlight that streamed in from the east window before being sucked into darkness forever.

Sarah sent her off to dust the salon. Alone now in the room, she went to the dresser where Layla kept her boar hair brush and tortoise shell comb and dozen tiny perfume bottles. She took the top off one; it held only a dram or so, but the citrusy fragrance reminded her of how Layla had perfumed her on her wedding night and said perfume was the best aphrodisiac. She picked up two tiny brass cymbals and remembered Layla dancing, twisting her hips, and rippling her belly as she sounded these cymbals on her delicate fingers. It seemed incredible that she was in her grave while Kabeer and his henchmen were back roaming the streets with their switches. There had been no investigations, arrests, or trials. There had not even been an official condemnation of the *mutawwa'in*. Those hooligans had so easily gotten away with murder. She grit her teeth, for the injustice of it made her bilious. There should be consequences: swarms of police, the school cordoned off and ringed by yellow police tape, and every man present taken in for questioning. She heard the doorbell ring, and when she went to the salon, Tisam was sitting on the sofa with her arm around Malika.

"*Sorry. Sorry.* I'm sick of the word. Everyone is trying to console me.

'Forgive him,' they say, over and over, and I'm sick of it. I resent it."

"Of course you do. Anyone would," Tisam said.

"It's finished. Finished! It can never be the same. I could not stand to look at him. When I think of Layla...her little tinkle of a laugh..." Malika dabbed her eyes with a tissue.

"He's still your son."

"Don't think you can make me forgive him. I won't change my mind so easily."

"Of course not. No one expects that. But I think it's sad that Susu and little Saladin should suffer too."

Malika snorted. "Don't talk to me about them. Does Shaheed care? Not a bit. Off he goes to Mecca. He's there now, happy and satisfied in his new job."

"Auntie, what happened must never happen again. And it won't. I've got a plan to stop it."

"And what is this plan of yours?"

"Come to the tell this afternoon, and you'll find out. All the women will be there."

"Maybe I will and maybe I won't," Malika said.

"I chose the tell for our meeting because it's your favorite place. Yours and Sarah's. You'll come too, Sarah, won't you?"

When Sarah asked what Tisam was planning, she smiled mysteriously. "Something subversive," she said. "Better than silly political cartoons. You'll see. And the tell is the perfect place to plan it. No men allowed." She grinned, and then she was all business as she glanced at her watch, took her cell phone and a list of names from her tote. She still had a few calls to make.

Following afternoon prayers, the women left Eliza in charge of the
children and set off for the tell. Once they passed the bakery at the edge
of town, the noise of traffic ceased. Parakeets and doves chirped and
cooed as the women made their way down the dirt path alongside the
low mud walls with the bright green crops on the other side. When they
reached the baths surrounded by the tall palms that rose thirty feet high,
Sarah saw that here too, a fresh wind had swept away the dust from the
clumps of periwinkle and lush weeds along the water's edge. She slipped
off her abaya, sat on the bank, and dipped her fingers in the cool water,
letting it fall from her hand to trickle back into the pool.

"Over here," Tisam called. She looked striking in a white dress with
a red shawl draped over her shoulders. She patted the spot beside her
to make room, and Sarah sat cross-legged beside her. "So graceful you
are for a pregnant lady," Tisam said. "You come too, Auntie," she said.
Malika grunted and heaved her heavy bulk down on Tisam's other side.
The grandmothers were the first to arrive, indigo triangles tattooed on
their foreheads. Other women followed in groups of three and four;
Susu came too, accompanied by several cousins. Susu took off her face
veil the moment she sat down, which was not at all like her. Sarah
noticed that Susu's adolescent pimples had disappeared as if pain had
transformed her from girl to woman. The gossip started the moment
Susu arrived: "She left him and returned to her parents…right to do so
…he'll never get her back." Sarah could hear only snippets from where
she sat; fortunately, Susu seemed oblivious to the gossip, or more likely,

she was putting on a brave face. Sarah smiled at her, feeling sorry for the poor girl.

More women drifted in. Tisam held court, greeting each by name. When about fifty were gathered around the edge of the pool, she called them to attention. "Ladies, ladies, quiet please. The subject this afternoon is freedom. Freedom and honor. O, sisters in Islam, last week we buried our daughters and sisters. They were good girls. We mourn them, do we not?" As if on cue, Malika rose unsteadily to her feet, threw back her head and keened, her thick tongue flickering. After her howl subsided, Tisam put an arm around her shoulders. "Listen to the mother of a martyr, dear sisters. If you have tears, weep now, for we shall not see our Layla until we meet in paradise." All the women joined in the loud lament. Sarah too tried to keen the *zaghareet*, but when she opened her mouth, only a whimper came out.

"O, sisters in Islam," Tisam continued. "All of you know me as the daughter of Rahab Shawki. I am a simple girl, as we all are. But we are also daughters of Allah, and that knowledge gives us strength. We are called to avenge our sisters, those sweet martyrs, and we will not be comforted until we do so." She paused, delved into the backpack at her feet, and took out an enlargement of the photo that had served for Layla's identity card. In it, Layla was smiling her sweet gap-toothed smile, dark ringlets tumbling onto her shoulders. "Our sister Layla spoke from her heart, did she not? Her heart and mind were free. Sisters, we trust in Allah's goodness. Allah wants free women to serve him. Shall we be slaves to any man? No! We are slaves only of Allah, who created us— and not from a rib, as the foolish Christians say."

One or two of the women laughed, which angered Sarah. Tisam was playing dirty politics, for Christianity had nothing to do with it.

"Politics—that's for men," a woman with a dowager's hump said. "Look at women in other places. Poor things. Here a woman goes to the front of the line. Our dowry is the highest—"

"Oh yes, my friend, and what does that mean?" a young voice jeered. "It means we'll be spinsters."

"All we can do is pray," said the woman with the hump. "To act is dangerous."

"That may be," Tisam said. "But we who trust in Allah do not fear death, for paradise is our reward. Behold the mother of the martyr." She gave Malika a hand and gently tugged her to her feet. Malika stood in silence, arms thick as tree trunks, face stoical. Her dignified posture spoke of undying resolution, and in this moment, Sarah felt her mother-in-law was altogether admirable.

"The *mutawwa'in* want us to fear them," Tisam said. "So I ask, are you afraid?"

There were a few faint scattered cries of "we are not afraid."

"I couldn't hear. What did you say?" Tisam shouted.

"We are not afraid," more women yelled.

"Louder!" Tisam commanded.

"We are not afraid," Malika roared, and the others began to clap, picking up the chant. "Not afraid. Not afraid."

"Well said, my sisters. No, we are not afraid. But we are incensed, all of us. Those men snuffed out the lives of our darlings. And why? Because of ignorance." She dropped her voice, and the women leaned forward to catch her words. "My sisters, pity the *mutawwa* who murders his sister." She waved her arm in the direction of Susu, who sat with her head bowed as she fiddled with the hem of her veil.

The woman with the hump pointed at Susu, and the furrow between the girl's dark brows deepened as she confronted the rude stares.

The poor girl, Sarah thought. She left her place between Tisam and Malika and went to sit beside Susu.

"The tide is turning, sisters." Tisam held up the newspaper, opened it, and jabbed her finger at an article somewhere toward the back. "See, it is written. No longer will the *mutawwa'in* control our daughters' education. Now they, like our sons, will study under guidelines set by the Ministry of Education. That is victory."

"Victory, victory," they chanted, all but Susu and Sarah, who put her arm around the girl.

"Men in the corridors of power have listened to the cry of our virgin martyrs. They know the *mutawwa'in* have deviated from the straight path. They have not respected the rights accorded to women by the Prophet, peace and blessings be upon him. Sisters, together we will change the system. If we do nothing, our fathers and brothers will assume we accept this life of underlings. We do not. Sisters in Islam, hear me now and hear me well. We will live free but pure, not like the sluts and addicts of America."

That was absurd and Tisam knew it. She was playing dirty politics, and Sarah wanted to wring her slender neck.

"We should do nothing but pray. It is fate," shouted a woman in the back. Susu bobbed her head in agreement.

"To cower and pray? Yes, that is easier." Tisam nodded sagely. "But we can do more. Oh yes. Let love be our weapon. Let us see what love can do. In kindness, let us convince our fathers, our husbands, and our brothers."

"And tomorrow there will be apricots," the woman with the hump scoffed. "It will never happen. Never!" Two or three others laughed derisively.

"What are you talking about?" Tisam cried out. "Of course it can be done. Look at our sisters in the Gulf. In Kuwait, they drive, don't they? In Bahrain, they vote. They don't veil unless they wish, do they? We should have taken the first steps on our march to freedom a long time ago. But it's not too late. Let us seize the day and start now. Now." She clapped her hands leading the chant of "NOW. NOW. NOW," until someone shouted, "Tisam, remember what happened to your mother."

"Sisters who disagree, listen to me. In the protest of 1991, our mothers suffered for their courage, my mother too. But they were few. We are many. We will be five hundred, then five thousand, and then five hundred thousand. Are we not half the country?"

"They'll shut us up in Al Haya Prison."

"But is there a prison in this kingdom big enough to fit all of us?" Tisam mocked. "Sisters, what I propose is honorable. We cannot march in the streets, that is true, but what man dares come here?" She spread her arms wide to take in the emerald pool that nestled under the tell's dark bare slopes. "Here we can plan in safety. For Layla's sake and for that of the schoolgirls, we will change the system to one that pleases Allah." She started the chant:

"Layla! Layla! Beloved of Allah.

Layla! Layla! Beloved of Allah."

Susu sprang to her feet. With eyes squeezed shut, both fists balled and held high in the air, she wailed, "Laaaaay-laaa, Laaaaay-laaa." All at once, her hands fell to her sides, her shoulders crumpled, and she began to weep, a dazed look on her face.

"How she trembles and cries," Tisam said. "Sisters, pity the wife of the *mutawwa*." The women renewed the chant, 'Layla! Layla! Beloved of Allah,' and Tisam called out in English to Sarah for her to join in, but she didn't pay any heed for she was too occupied in trying to comfort Susu.

Abruptly the women started to chant rapturously, "Sa-Rah. Sa-Rah. Sa-Rah."

"No, not me," Sarah shouted. "Layla."

But they kept yelling, "Sa-Rah. Sa-Rah. Sa-Rah," until she felt forced to herself lead them, "Layla! Layla! Beloved of Allah." Susu stood up too, joining in, and Sarah clapped until her hands smarted.

Tisam gestured for the women to sit down. "For decades, our men have been blind to the injustice done us, but now with the stench of char in their nostrils, the sight of the small shrouded bodies in their eyes, the cry of the *zaghareet* ringing in their ears, they too must recognize that change is necessary."

"*Fitna*," someone called out.

"Never. We abhor chaos. And we need our fathers and brothers. That is why we must ask their help. For their sake, we will go— "

"*Shway shway*, little by little," Susu cried. She smiled up at Sarah.

"Little by little, step by step, for as long as it takes," the women repeated.

"What else shall we do?" Susu cried.

A yell was heard: "Shoot the *mutawwa*. Shoot the *mutawwa*."

The women went off in gales of laughter, slapping their knees and sides, all but Susu who had a grim, drawn look on her face.

"Don't worry. It won't come to that," Sarah whispered in her ear.

"I don't like men staring at me," a young voice shouted. "I like my veil. It protects me."

"Dear sisters, those who wish to veil must do so. By all means. Did not our Layla cherish her veil? But it must be the style you yourself—not the *mutawwa'in*—choose. Remember Layla. Remember fashion."

"Fa-shion! Fa-shion!" the women cheered.

"And those who desire not to hide the face that Allah gave them must be free to reveal it. In the holy city of Mecca, we walk unveiled, as the Prophet wished. Why not everywhere? But I warn you…No immodesty! No deranged looks! No sparkly green eye shadow outside the house, no intoxicating scents of jasmine and musk. Remember, we are Muslim women, pure and chaste. Let us save our glamour and allure for our husbands."

That was ironic, coming from gay Tisam, Sarah thought.

As Malika let forth with, "*Allahu Akbar*," the women roared back, "*Allahu Akbar*." Only Susu said it quietly, *Allahu Akbar*, over and over, the exact way she would repeat it when at a loss as to how to comfort Saladin.

Feeling like a hypocrite, Sarah mouthed the mantra, and Susu squeezed her hand.

"What if they threaten us with their sticks?" someone yelled.

"Say, 'your stick is big, my brother. But I fear only Allah. If I die, paradise is my refuge.'"

A mother pushed a plump girl to the center of the women. "My daughter is twelve. She has not yet had her period, yet they took her to Al Hay'ah because she was not veiled."

"For shame."

A girl in blue jeans spoke up. "Once the wind blew off my veil. I was afraid and said nothing to defend myself, and they took me to Al Hay'ah."

"For shame."

"Yes, for shame," Tisam cried. "The imams will taunt us, and they will vilify and revile us. Daughters and sisters, never be ashamed of your fear. Conquer it. Here is what to do. It is easy. When a *mutawwa* threatens you with his stick, keen the *zaghareet*." She threw back her head and ululated, a cry of defiance and triumph. "Can any man do that?"

The women hooted and cackled, and Tisam reached out her hands to them. "Come, my sisters. All of you," she said as all joined hands. "All who hear keening must run toward that sound. When you reach the sister, join her in the *zaghareet*. Seeing so many of us will frighten and confuse the *mutawwa*, and he will flee. And if not…" she looked at each woman in the circle, "and if not…" she repeated slowly, "then break the stick."

"Break the stick. Break the stick. Break the stick."

"Yes. But the one who breaks the stick must not be the sister he harassed, but the one who comes to her rescue. That way they will know we are united. Already they know their time is short. After the death of our sisters, all now can see the system for what it is. Not merciful! Not compassionate! Not Islamic! Sisters, remember this: they have sticks, but we have tongues. Sisters, come, altogether now." Tisam led the women in circumambulating the pool nestled in the shadow of the tell's dark bare slopes. On the third time around, Susu and Sarah linked arms as they cried out, "Layla! Beloved of Allah."

As the call to prayer wafted from a dozen minarets, the women began to leave.

"What can an old woman do?" Malika complained as they walked back. "No one cares whether we veil or not."

"Auntie, never mind," Tisam said, her voice tinged with condescension. "You have already sacrificed so much."

"Poor dear auntie," she whispered to Sarah and Susu when Malika fell a few steps behind. "This brave new world is too much for her."

"She's a real battleaxe," Sarah said. "Maybe she is just what we need."

"I think so too." Susu's eyes glinted like dagger tips at Tisam. "And you must speak respectfully of her."

What had come over the girl? If Shaheed ever persuaded her to return, what would he do? Lock her up in the kitchen? How it would all end, Sarah could not guess.

CHAPTER 26

IB AND HIS FATHER would soon be returning, perhaps tomorrow. When she got home from work, Sarah started packing; she was going home at last—home to Firdaus. She took armloads of her clothes from the closet and piled them on the bed. Her sandals and shoes she stuck in the bottom of her blue suitcase. As she folded pants, skirts, and dresses, she realized how in the past two weeks, her belly had ballooned so that some of her clothes no longer fit. She had outgrown her two favorite dresses, one with a print of sunflowers and the other a navy shift with white polka dots. She took them down the hall to Layla's room to add to the box of clothes that Malika was donating to the poor. How the woman had wailed yesterday as she slipped Layla's fashionable dresses off their pink hangers and filled the empty cartons. Sarah looked through the boxes that had not yet been taped shut. She fingered the ivory-colored teacher dresses, the dress of gold lamé that Layla had worn to the party at the American Consulate, the designer jeans, patent leather heels, the Hello Kitty t-shirts, the lacy, silken underwear, and the collection of cloaks, both those that Shaheed approved and the sheer, flirty ones with pretty satin or lace edging, the ones that Layla yearned to wear.

Feeling mournful, Sarah went back to her room. On her bedside table lay the volume of Rumi, which she had not yet packed. She blew the film of sand off the dust jacket and leafed through the poems. Don't grieve, was Rumi's advice, for all would be well. Well, what did he know? She stuffed the book in her suitcase.

She wanted to visit the tell one last time before leaving, but Layla's students were coming to pay condolences in a couple of hours: more tears; more bitter coffee. She would have to hurry if she were to get back before they arrived. She went to the hall closet and grabbed the first cloak she saw. It must belong to poor Susu; the fabric was thick muslin, a dull, ugly black that Layla would never wear. Sarah considered going back to her room to get one of her own, but she was in too much of a hurry, she didn't want to run into Malika, and in any case, she would be unrecognizable in Susu's ugly veil. She tossed it over her shoulders. It fell only to her shins, which left her white jeans sticking out.

The front door squeaked on its hinges as she closed it behind her. Some hundred yards down the alley, she reached the bakery. She stopped to wipe the sweat from her forehead; she noticed a construction lot with an enormous hole for the foundation and beside it a great pile of crushed stone. Annie once told her a rumor about how a woman was stoned—she was buried to her waist, and after a judge threw the ritual first stone, a dump truck tipped its load of stones, and that was the end of her. In Qatif on that picnic with Ib last July, when they had been necking in the tent and had heard the shepherd yelling after his lone errant sheep, Sarah had been terrified he would catch them, but she had not known the full horror of the possible if unlikely consequences.

Not far from the building lot rose a yellow tower crane, like a yellow cross against the dark blue sky; it too had not been there last week. Another reinforced steel and concrete high-rise building would be going up soon, with its inevitable accompaniment of thick clouds of dust, and the jackhammer's ear-splitting din. Ib had once made a feeble joke that the crane was the national bird of the kingdom. How the Saudis so patiently put up with the stress and hassle of the constant construction she could not fathom. They never complained, stoical in their quest for the veneer of modernity. Technology, they craved, yet they were blind and deaf to the blessings of liberty. It depressed her. Last week at the tell, when Tisam had given that inspirational speech, she had felt certain hope that with the deaths of Layla and the schoolgirls, a change had been set in motion and there was no stopping it. Now, she doubted anything would change; people were buried in their accustomed ways. With these dismal thoughts in mind, she walked on past the bakery and took the trail leading to the women's baths.

On either side of her, low walls enclosed plantings of alfalfa, squash, and the long, thin cucumbers of early spring. She kicked off her sandals and pressed her toes into the damp sand. An electric-blue lizard flashed before her, and in the spiky leaves above, a songbird puffed out its cheeks, a flash of yellow under its tail feathers. When she rounded the bend, the tell rose before her, dark as a negative of Mount Fuji. As she walked toward the bank, she stubbed her toe against a potsherd lying on the ground. She swore under her breath, picked it up, and traced the thin black zigzag that decorated one edge of the rust-colored clay. As she put it in her jeans pocket, she wondered who had made it and how long ago.

At the water's edge, she folded Susu's abaya into a neat square, and placed it near a hibiscus bush. She sat down, drew up her legs, hooked her arms around them, and thought about Tisam's pea-brained strategy of scaring off the Eve-teasers and faith cops alike by doing the *zaghareet*. Or was it so crazy? Annie once told her that Ataturk had cleverly rid Turkey of the veil by passing a decree allowing only prostitutes to wear it. The veil was to hide the harlot's shame. And of course, no man would want his sister or wife to wear it if this would cause others to doubt her chastity. What Westerner could have dreamed up that scheme? Tisam's insistence that Muslim women were accountable only to God sounded strange too—but appealing. It meant men had no power. If only God counted, then you were free.

Sarah pulled off her jeans, and noticed the maternity panel was stretched. It would not be much longer now. She laid the jeans beside Susu's cloak. Then she plunged in the cool water, swam to the middle of the pool and duck-dived, pushing herself deeper, deeper still, until far below she glimpsed the gray crenellated walls of that ancient city where women had let men see their smiles. When she could not hold her breath a second longer and felt she was about to burst, she kicked and surfaced. She floated for a while, and then swam alternating between the crawl and the breaststroke until she felt tired.

She swam back to the shoreline, clambered up the bank, and sat gazing up at the tell. For forty centuries, it had grown, inch by imperceptible inch as each civilization rose on the remains of its predecessor, only to disintegrate and be replaced in its turn. Those dark slopes hid the

bones of the dead—may they rest in peace. And all that time women
had bathed unmolested in this pool. In tall clay jugs, they carried home
its pure water, to drink and cook with, and to wash the infants and the
dead. Images of Layla flooded upon her: Layla dancing, a red rose in her
black ringlets; Layla doing a cannonball; Layla giggling with Lulu; Layla
letting fly the falcon perched on her wrist.

Sarah got up and plucked a hibiscus from the bush. She leaned over
the bank, placed the red flower on the water, and watched it float away.
Let all women who come here be healed: that was her wish, her prayer.
Soon twilight would fall, pink softening the emerald green of the pool.
It was time to go. As she pulled up her jeans, she felt the potsherd in
her pocket. She would keep it as a souvenir of this day, she thought as
she had tossed on Susu's abaya. A sudden craving to see the second pool
took hold of her. She hurried down the narrow path under the canopy
of trees. A branch lashed her cheek, and she slowed her pace, now carefully picking her steps. Some minutes later, as she neared the pool she
heard what sounded like someone sobbing.

Perhaps she could help. With a light, purposeful step, she walked faster, pushing aside the branches that barred her way. Yes, most certainly
someone was in pain. In the clearing, a heavyset woman squatted on
a boulder, her back toward Sarah. The woman was rocking back and
forth, and her black scarf bulged from the abundance of hair. Her dress
stuck out under her cloak; Sarah recognized the dress the moment she
saw the print of gold tiger-stripes on dark brown.

Malika.

Her heart pounding, Sarah darted behind a bush. Her mind raced, trying to figure out what to do. Any moment now, the evening call to prayer would sound, and Malika would stop her loud lamentations and head home. Sarah turned, about to flee when she heard the piteous moan, "Allah, Allah, Allah."

Free, Sarah thought, she was free. No, she would not run away from that suffering. It would be an act of will. Layla, she would do it for Layla. She drew Susu's ugly cloak tight around her shoulders. She bit her lip. Go ahead, just do it, she commanded herself. She pushed herself, one deliberate step after another. She took the fearful last step and she was there—at Malika's feet.

"Susu. Darling Susu! You've come back." Malika opened wide her arms.

Sarah crept into them. Her heart hammering in her chest, she clung for dear life.

"Susu?"

Poor blind Malika. Sarah clung to her hidden in the dark muslin that smelled of sour breast milk and sandalwood. From deep inside her, words of hope and trust burbled up into clear speech. "Um Ibrahim, Mother of Ibrahim, *Allah ateek il awfi*. God give you strength." She clasped Malika's gnarled hands and kissed them. As Sarah felt the powerful arms curve and tighten around her, a bolt of joy surged through her. Arm in arm, they walked toward town, neither of them uttering a word until they reached the end of the path. Then Malika said, "I've been thinking, my daughter, all afternoon I've been thinking that I may have that cataract operation, after all. Do you think that is advisable?"

"An excellent idea, Um Ibrahim." She squeezed Malika's hand.

"Oh, of course. Of course, it is," Malika said, as though she had always thought so. "My husband will be so pleased."

As they approached the bakery, Malika remembered they were all out of bread. As her mother-in-law padded into the store, Sarah was thinking of how gratified Ib would be about this reconciliation when abruptly she felt herself jostled and a sudden breeze, cool on her nape. She cried out and touched the back of her neck. Who had snatched her head scarf? She wheeled around and saw a teenager dash away waving it like a flag. Abruptly, a black-bearded man advanced on her. With his short thobe he looked like Kabeer, but he was not. He raised his stick. "Yalla. You come," he commanded.

"Who the hell are you?" she wanted to scream, but she stood frozen and mute. His stick pricking the small of her back, he prodded her toward a black paddy wagon, where another *mutawwa* was unlatching the back door.

What was it Tisam had said? Sarah inhaled a deep breath, threw back her head, opened her mouth wide, and stiffened her tongue. From deep within her erupted the primal cry of power and defiance.

The man guffawed. "Ha! *Amrikiya* craz-ee woman."

"Um Ibrahim," she yelled to Malika who was leaving the bakery, her pink plastic bag filled with flatbread, her face veiled in black. "Um Ibrahim."

Malika growled. She advanced on the brute, grabbed the stick, snapped it in two pieces over her knee, and flung them against the wall. "*Yalla*! Go!" she screamed. "How dare you offend my daughter? My daughter!" She puffed her cheeks, leaned back her head, and let forth a most bloodcurdling *zaghareet*.

Would there be an answering cry? Sarah looked wildly around. No one was on the street except for a wrinkled, white-haired crone bent double with age and so withered that her menfolk allowed her to go unveiled. She tottered forward, stooped, and picked up one of the small stones from the great heap next to the bakery. She swung her arm back and flung the stone at the *mutawwa*. It missed him by a yard.

"Grandmother," he sneered, "you throw stones at me?" He shoved her, knocking her into the gutter.

Sarah felt the potsherd in her pocket. She reached in, pulled it out, clenched her fist around it, and squinted her eyes to take aim.

"Do no harm," the physician's mantra came to her, as swift and involuntary as a reflex, and instantly, she dropped the stone. She uttered a cry, at a loss for what to do, when inspiration hit. "Do the *zaghareet*," she cried.

Lying in the gutter, the crone ululated, and within a few minutes, other women appeared from the shadows. They shook their fists and in a black clot they advanced on the *mutawwa*. "*Yalla! Yalla!* Get away from here!" Some of the women ran to the heap of gravel by the cinder blocks next to the bakery. A stone was thrown, and then another. A heavyset woman grunted as she hauled up one of the cinderblocks. She staggered with it the few feet toward the man, and heaved it at him, grunting again.

He screamed. The sleeve of his left arm was splattered with blood above the elbow. Another rock veered in a high arc but fell a foot away. One more stone struck his left leg, and he grabbed on to it with his good arm. More women rushed at him. Jeering, stones clenched in their fists, they surrounded him. "*Yalla!* Go!" they screamed. "Son of a terrorist whore."

Limping, he staggered away. He had gone a few dozen yards when a stone struck him between the shoulder blades, and he stumbled to the ground. The women, their faces ugly with hate, fell upon him.

"Stop! Do no harm," Sarah cried. Running up clumsily to them, she dashed the stones from their hands. "We have tongues. Let's use them. All together now."

"Sarah, beloved of Allah," Malika cried as the women threw back their heads, and ululated in joyous solidarity.

CHAPTER 27

LATE THAT AFTERNOON, a delegation of Layla's students arrived. In the family room, myrrh was smoking in the incense burner, its bitter perfume reminding everyone of the precious friend and teacher they had lost. At first Sawson, Samia, Jasmine, and Iffat did not want to remove their veils. Malika insisted and when they did take them off, Sarah noted the blisters on their cheeks and how their hair was frizzled or cut short where the fire had singed it. Eliza served bitter coffee, and as the girls sipped it, in soft murmurs they praised Layla as "the best of teachers." Sawson recited Abdun Ghanim's "Love's Lament," and when she reached the line, "Our sufferings had vanished/ if but our hearts were stone," she sniffled so badly she had to stop and take a tissue from her bag.

These girls were Layla's stars, the ones who made up for the dreary hours of drill. For a while, they talked about her: how she made learning fun with debates, jazz chants, and spelling bees; how she always smelled so fragrant; how she would stay late after school to wait with a girl whose ride hadn't come; how she gave out chocolates for prizes; how she never made fun of slow learners; and how she was kindly to a girl whose cat died. As she listened to these tributes and realized how

much her daughter had been respected and loved, Malika rubbed her
eyes with the back of her hand. The girls reminisced about their last
class. Layla had assigned essays on *Pride and Prejudice*, and the propriety
of Mr. Bennett accepting the cad who had seduced his daughter. She
had died before the essays were due, but these girls were determined to
finish the assignment as a tribute to her. Now they were discussing Mr.
Bennett's quandary.

"My father won't even give me to a tradesman," said Samia, a stu-
dious-looking girl with gold-rimmed glasses. "How could he give her
to her seducer? His family would lose honor. What do you think, Dr.
Sarah?"

"I don't know. I've never read Jane Austen."

"You will love her. She's not like Shakespeare—oh, he is too hard."
Samia pronounced the name, "Shakes-beer."

"Don't say that. I like him." Jasmine recited in a hoarse voice: "The
quality of mercy is not strained/It falleth as the gentle rain from heav-
en…" She broke off, coughing. "I have a sore throat…the fire…" she
apologized.

Sarah expressed the desire that she too had been required to memo-
rize poetry. Malika, half-blind and illiterate, knew poems and stories by
heart for they had been passed down to her in the oral tradition. It was
she who had taught Ib both the story of the murderer of the ninety-
nine, and the poet who was dissatisfied in heaven. She had a prodigious
memory.

"We learn by heart. Little by little, a line at a time," Jasmine said. "So,
it's easy. That was Mrs. Layla's way."

After Eliza cleared away the coffee cups, the girls chatted about Aisha, whose fiancé dumped her when he learned that her face would be permanently scarred. It was despicable, but also understandable, they agreed. As they discussed Aisha's plight, Sarah thought of the challenges of bringing up a daughter here. She thought of the baby bracelet she had bought yesterday and hoped Ib would like it. Just then, she felt a kick and cupped her hand on her belly.

"The baby?" Malika came and sat beside her and touched her on the arm.

"Yes, it moved." Shyly, she took Malika's hand and placed it so she could feel the kicks.

"Praise Allah," Malika said, her face wreathed in a smile.

Samia pointed to Malika and giggled. "The woman who broke the stick." The girls began to chant, "Break the stick. Break the stick."

"How did you find out about that?" Sarah asked.

"Oh, the grapevine." Samia casually tossed her frizzled hair.

Sawson had a presentation to make and called for quiet. In her hands she held a large album covered in black velvet. She opened it and inside it was inscribed in silver ink, "To the mother of the martyr." As she gave Malika the tribute book, the girls applauded.

"Thank you. Sarah will read me these kind words later," Malika said in a voice heavy with emotion. She passed the book to Sarah, who leafed through it. Most of the tributes came from local students, but there were also heartfelt messages from Jeddah and Taif in the west, and Riyadh and Dirriyah in the heartland. As she handed the book back to Malika, it occurred to Sarah how her mother-in-law seemed gentler now, neither hiding her illiteracy nor humiliated by it.

At six o'clock, Malika lumbered to the television set in the corner of the room and switched it on to Channel 2 for the evening news. Sarah had hoped for an official government condemnation of the *mutawwa'in* at the scene of the schoolhouse fire, but apart from the shift of women's education to the Ministry of Education, nothing had changed. On the screen, the Saudi flag fluttered, green for peace and Islam. There was the usual fanfare for station identification, but at the anchor's desk, instead of the usual man in thobe and red-checked headdress, tonight there was a woman. A black scarf hid her hair, but her face was unveiled, a stunning face with piercing jade-green eyes. The students gasped, their mouths falling open. For a moment, Sarah stared blankly at the screen.

"Saudi Arabian Evening News with Reem al Hadawi," the young woman said in a matter-of-fact voice as if she had uttered those plain words ten thousand times before.

"Allah," the girls cried out. A hush came over the salon. Malika rose to her feet, spread her arms wide as if in benediction, and cried out, "*Al-hamdulillah*, praise God, who comes to the aid of the needy."

"Praise God," the girls shouted, jumping to their feet.

"Shh, listen." Sarah shushed them for she expected a momentous announcement would follow—that women could drive or everyone could vote. There was nothing of the sort, and she felt disappointed, cheated even.

"Reem is so professional," Sawson said. "You see, Dr. Sarah, everything is changing."

Everyone agreed except for Iffat, who argued cynically that men would do anything to see a woman, and since the other Gulf channels used women newscasters, the kingdom had yielded to pressure from Saudi advertisers.

"But how must Reem's husband feel, to know that strangers will see his wife every night?" Jasmine asked. "He will think they lust after her. He will beat her."

"Girl, you listen to me," Malika declared in a husky voice, "If he does, she will show her bruises, and he will be punished. No longer are we to be silenced."

The next day, as Johnny drove Sarah back from her shift at the hospital, he told her that Ahmed had asked him and Eliza to stay on another year for the sake of the children. Ahmed had even arranged to bring the children and Eliza's mother to the kingdom and had found housing for them. "A good man, that Ahmed," Johnny said. "The restaurant in Manila can wait a few years more. We'll be together now with the children. That's what counts."

When she arrived home, Ib's duffel bag was in the hallway. Sarah ran into the family room with her arms outstretched. "Ib, at last!"

"Your wife is a marvel," Malika said serenely as Sarah hugged him. "Pregnant and yet swift as a gazelle."

"Sarah?" Ib turned to her, a perplexed look on his face.

"Later. I'll tell you later," Sarah murmured. She went to the sofa where her father-in-law was and shook his hand. He looked immensely fatigued, but he smiled at her and thanked her for keeping his wife company.

"We were just talking about Tisam," Malika said. "She doesn't take her responsibilities as an aunt seriously. She tells Ahmed she'll watch the children, but what does she do? Dumps them on me, and off she goes. And that Ahmed, even now he cares more about his work than his own flesh and blood. The twins are wetting their beds, and look at Lulu, how she wanders about with her thumb in her mouth. I can't think what to do."

"Do nothing. Nothing at all. Just wait. God is merciful. But if we have just a spark of affection left for Shaheed—" Ib pressed his thumb and forefinger together. "Just the smallest—"

"Don't you tell me I should forgive him."

"Only you know whether you can. Maybe it is impossible, Mother, but if you can, then do it. Please, do it if you can."

"I can't," Malika said firmly.

Omar passed her a fresh tissue. "Don't upset yourself, *habibi*. Whatever we do, it has to be a family decision, you, me, Sarah, Ibrahim, all of us."

At the mention of her name, Sarah's eyes widened. It was the first time she had felt so included.

"Let him stay in Mecca." Malika's voice was strident. "Let him be happy there."

"But he never went to Mecca. He is here in Qatif, staying at a cheap cheap hotel while Susu and the baby are with her parents. She refuses to return. Mother, he wanders around like a lost sheep."

"It serves him right."

Ib took her hand. "Shaheed cannot—"

"I can't bear to hear his name."

"But if you saw his face—so pained—you would feel sorry for him. He is so ashamed. That is why he left."

"Not at all," Malika snapped. "I told him to leave our house forever, and off he went for his fancy new job in Mecca."

"Mother, he is not in Mecca. After the fire, the government froze all those jobs. He said that just to save face."

"Well, let him find something else."

"But that is not what's tormenting him. It is shame. 'Mother will never forgive me,' he repeats. He feels so guilty."

"And me? Am I not suffering?" Malika wailed and dropped her face into her hands.

"Think of Layla. Think of what she would want." He lowered his voice so Sarah could barely hear, but she thought Ib told her to remember the story his mother had taught him of the murderer of ninety-nine and the City of Kindness.

"I could kill him," Malika burst out.

Ib put an arm around her shoulder, and she pushed it off. "It is too hard. I cannot."

There was a commotion and the children stormed into the room. Fawzi screamed that Farouk had hit him, while Farouk yelled that it was a mistake and that Fawzi had started the fight. "Quiet! Your grandfather is very tired," Ib said and he took them back outside. Meanwhile Lulu crawled up on Sarah's lap.

"It's naptime. Come along, my darling." As Malika picked her up and started to take her out of the room, Lulu arched her back and struggled.

She screamed, her face beet red. "I want my mama. I want my mama."
She lurched out of Malika's arms, and ran to Sarah, who carried her,
howling and kicking, down the hallway to her bedroom. Sarah sat down
beside her on the cot and offered to tell her the story of Goldilocks.
Lulu, her thick eyelashes wet, lay rubbing the satin edging of her pink
blankie. When the story was finished, Sarah tucked her in. After Lulu
fell asleep, she tiptoed out of the room and went down the hall into her
and Ib's bedroom. She took the pink pouch from the dresser and went
outside to find Ib. He was in the courtyard watching the twins play
leapfrog; she led him off to the far bench under the frangipani tree.

"At last…alone." Ib hugged her, then eased back and held her at arm's
length. "My mother and you? What happened?"

"I…we…a lot…It was at the tell. All the acrimony is…" she stammered, searching for words, "well, it's all gone, just melted. I really did
love Layla so much. We were both grieving, and that changed everything."

He took her hand, and nuzzled it. "Strange as it seems, something
happened to me, too. When I left, I was ready to kill Shaheed, but in
that immensity of sand, especially at night with the stars…" His voice
trailed off. "It helped my father and me to go to him today."

"But he's your brother. You've always loved him. It can't be the same
for me. You shouldn't expect it."

She had expected that he would commiserate, but he did not. Instead,
he told her how he and his father had witnessed Kabeer's chastisement
that morning. They had seen him, his hands gripping the irons bars of
a portable cage; the guards had had to drag him out, their arms under

his armpits. The flogger, a Qur'an clamped between his chest and upper arm, stood at his back, and whipped him thirty-three strokes. Kabeer screamed at each one. A coward, he had stuffed towels under his t-shirt to cushion the blows that rained down on him, from his shoulders to his buttocks.

"Will Shaheed get whipped too?"

"No, he was just following orders. But he feels disgraced and shamed."

"Will the flogging be reported?"

"I doubt it."

With every fiber of her being, she knew that such corporal punishment was barbaric, yet she was glad of it. "Kabeer had it coming to him," she said.

"Yes. But now, we need to heal as a family. I have been racking my brain trying to think of a solution. Perhaps if Mother were to allow Shaheed to accompany her on the pilgrimage?"

"She'll never agree to it. She can't stand the sight of him."

"If we were to encourage her, she might be willing. It is worth a try."

"But they've each already gone on Hajj. There's no need to go again." Sarah frowned, and crossed and uncrossed her legs. She did not want Shaheed to get off the hook. Let him squirm. He needed to be taught a lesson.

"Darling, Shaheed needs to go." Ib reached into his thobe pocket and pulled out his string of prayer beads.

"I don't see why. The requirement is to go once in a lifetime. He's done it. So has she. We should wash our hands of it."

"The reward of pilgrimage is forgiveness for sins." Ib looked up at her, a pleading expression on his face.

"Then, let him go by himself." She looked at the amber beads that dangled from his slim olive fingers. He clicked them softly one against the other; the sound of it irritated her.

"Mother needs to forgive him. Otherwise she will not have a moment's peace."

Sarah sighed and shrugged her shoulders. Ib sat there, fiddling with his beads, his head bowed. The silence was unbroken except for the rhythmic *click, click, click,* of the beads. She noticed a few white streaks in his hair, and it shocked her. He looked ruined. "Oh, I've missed you so, so much," she blurted out, not wanting to add to his grief. "And you're right. Your mother has been so unhappy. I don't want that. Not anymore."

He squeezed her hand. "Here, with memories of Layla all around her, Mother cannot possibly forgive him. As one of two million souls chanting in that sea of faith and hardship, she may. Please help me convince her."

Sarah picked up a blossom from the grass. She pulled off each of the yellow-edged, still-fragrant petals and watched them flutter down. As she wiped the sticky, milky juice off her fingers, she thought that now she actually did have influence with her mother-in-law. She stared off at the twins, now kicking a soccer ball at the far end of the lawn, and felt cross with their father, who still had not arrived. Ahmed simply was not devoted to them while, for all his faults, Shaheed was.

"I can't forgive him." Sarah said, unable to mention him by name. She took a deep breath. "But maybe I can speak to your mother." Her own mother had called last week, and when she and Ib went inside, she mentioned that her parents might visit when the baby was born. "Our house is their house," Malika said politely.

Sarah smiled, wondering how the two formidable mothers would deal with each other. "I haven't been a very good daughter, you see, Um Ibrahim, so that is why I feel so lucky that she's coming."

"Not luck, my girl," Malika said in her raspy voice. "It is a law of nature. Have you not heard?" She curved both stout arms in a generous circle. "When Allah created mercy, he spread one of its hundred parts among all mothers on earth so they should be able to love their young."

"At times it can be difficult to love one's child," Sarah said obliquely.

"Perhaps, but soon you too will know this love." Her voice softened, and she touched Sarah's belly.

"About Allah's mercy, Um Ibrahim. You say he gave one of the hundred parts of mercy to be shared among women? Only one? Is that enough?" she asked guilelessly. "I am sure more is needed. It can be so difficult to forgive."

A long silence ensued, punctuated by the *click, click, click* of Ib's beads.

Malika shrugged. "Then take solace in the fact that Allah saved ninety-nine parts for himself. Remember always that he is to judge us on resurrection day, but that we are loved and will be forgiven."

"Mother, you are wise," Ib smiled. His shoulders drooped as the tension had left them. It was as if, Sarah thought, he were now sure that eventually Shaheed would be accepted. She walked out to the garden. Right now, Malika needed her son beside her, and she wanted to leave the two of them alone for a while. It was pleasant now, in the cool of late afternoon, and she was occupied in her thoughts. "Home," she thought as she gazed at the blackened tree in the front yard. Where was home? Could it be anywhere, even here? She looked back toward the house. For too long she had been marking time here. But now everything had changed. She felt in her pocket for the satin bag that held the baby's identity bracelet, and a great intensity filled her. She would live here, if necessary even die here.

"Sarah?" It was Ibrahim.

She smiled and went to him.

"Mother sent me to find you. She's worried you may feel lonely." They sat on the bench holding hands as the shadow of the tree lengthened on the stubby grass.

"I want you to know," she spoke slowly, choosing her words with care. "My home is here, here with our work, your parents, Layla's children and our baby." She touched the pink satin of the soft pouch to her lips and placed it in his hand.

He took out the diminutive bracelet. "How warm it feels," he murmured, the gold bracelet shining as he dangled it in the dying sunlight. Set between seed pearls on the thin nameplate, engraved in calligraphy, was the name *Layla*.

ACKNOWLEDGMENTS

I am deeply grateful to my sister Caroline Grant, my first reader, for her enthusiasm, her curiosity, and her support. As I was getting going, my daughter-in-law Jamie Backstrom read the manuscript with sensitivity and care. Later, so did wise friends Anne Fuhrman, Marilyn Klaus, Rosemarye Levine, Cindy Mollander, Elizabeth Schultz, and Deborah Singmaster. Their insights have made this a better book.

Special thanks to the sponsors of the *Langston Hughes Creative Writing Award* program for their encouragement of new and emerging writers in Lawrence, Kansas, my hometown and that of the admirable poet.

I'd like to thank my writing group, *The Sin Eaters*, for their good company, wise counsel, and treats.

To Terry Smith, who helped me finish off the book, my heartfelt thanks for her warm heart and keen eyes. And to my husband Bob Fraga, my appreciation and love for rooting me on.

Although I did time—mostly happily!— in Saudi Arabia for nine years, I was not there in 2001-2002. I owe a great debt to the reporters and editors of *Arab News*, from whose work I learned about the kingdom during those difficult years.

LaVergne, TN USA
29 March 2011
221990LV00002B/12/P